THE UPSIDE-DOWN KINGDOM

THE UPSIDE-DOWN KINGDOM

Donald B. Kraybill

Introduction by
John F. Alexander

HERALD PRESS
Scottdale, Pennsylvania
Kitchener, Ontario

Library of Congress Cataloging in Publication Data
Kraybill, Donald B.
The Upside-Down Kingdom.

Includes bibliographical references and index.
1. Kingdom of God. 2. Christian life—1460-
I. Title.
BT94.K7 248'.4 78-9435
ISBN 0-8361-1860-X

THE UPSIDE-DOWN KINGDOM

Published simultaneously in Canada by Herald Press, Kitchener, Ont. N2G 4M5
Library of Congress Catalog Card Number: 78-9435
International Standard Book Number: 0-8361-1860-X
Printed in the United States of America
Design: Alice B. Shetler

10 9 8 7 6 5 4 3 2

To those
"who have turned the world upside down . . .
acting against the decrees of Caesar,
saying that there is
another king,
Jesus"
(Acts 17:6, 7).

CONTENTS

AUTHOR'S PREFACE

This book is a study of the kingdom of God in the synoptic Gospels. As such, it is not a novel work since many other books also deal with this topic. Two aspects of my Anabaptist theological heritage accent the uniqueness of this particular treatment of the kingdom of God.

First of all, I am a theological layman. Having been taught that one should not let theology solely up to the theologians, I have written as one layman sharing with other untrained theologians. I have completed graduate degrees in sociology and tend to read the Scriptures through the lenses of that academic discipline. Such an endeavor is quite precarious because as one wanders back and forth between the disciplines of theology and sociology, one is bound to insult the guardians of both traditions. Theologians and biblical scholars may not be pleased to have an untrained layman dabbling in their field. And I'm sure that most sociologists would be quite disturbed to learn that one of their clan is reading the New Testament through their cherished sociological glasses, which are not supposed to focus on "spiritual" things. The combination of a radical reformation heritage and sociological training yields a perspective which may even seem somewhat irreverant to the sentimental layman. For others I hope this approach will be both stimulating and provocative.

In the second place I have taken the New Testament and Jesus in particular quite seriously. I have limited the study primarily to the synoptic gospels since they provide us with the sharpest portrait of the life and teachings of Jesus. It will soon become obvious to the reader that I believe Jesus has a lot to say to us moderns. His life and words are a relevant authority for those who confess Him as Lord today. We will discover some difficult and hard sayings of Jesus in this study. His words and insights bring a note of judgment on our affluence, war-making, status-seeking, and religious exclusivism. I do not pretend to "live out" all that I have written. In fact, I see many brothers and sisters who are doing a much better job of following Jesus than I am. Nevertheless, I have tried to describe the message of Jesus accurately even when it brings judgment to my own door. I have tried to practice the Upside-Down Kingdom perspective in publishing the book by limiting my royalties as author to the amount of expense incurred in preparing the book.

There is always a tendency for Christians to want a few explicit rules to follow in their spiritual sojourn. I have attempted to deal with the biblical material in a fresh way, but those who are looking for new rules will be disappointed. I have given many hints and I think the book will raise a multitude of questions, but I firmly believe the answers must be formulated in the context of small groups of God's children. I hope the Upside-Down Kingdom perspective will in a small way provoke stimulating discussions which will enable God's people more accurately to discern His will for their lives.

Numerous persons have provided helpful counsel throughout the writing process. The following individuals gave constructive feedback to an early draft of the manuscript: Don Blosser (Chapters 5-6), Charles De Santo, J. Elvin Kraybill, Paul G. Landis, Beverly Lord, Willard Swartley, Eugene Witmer, and John Howard Yoder. I am grateful for the way they graciously shared their time and ideas. Joanna Johnson scrounged in the library for historical and cultural references. The members of our house fellowship—Gerald Bender, Zelah Bender, Ken Brubaker, Pam Brubaker, Stanley Godshall, Susan Godshall, Fran Kraybill, Ann Miller, and Park Miller—read a rough copy of the manuscript and gave invaluable advice. I cherish their love, care, and encouragement. Four typists—Jane Garber, Jean Moyer, Virginia Roland, and Gladys Singer—competently converted my hand-scratching into good copy.

Don Kraybill
December 1977

INTRODUCTION

Jesus is very popular. Most everyone thinks He's one of the great moral teachers of all times. It's okay to criticize Marx or Adam Smith, Roosevelt or Barry Goldwater. But hardly anyone ever criticizes Jesus.

Or obeys Him. In fact, we go to great lengths claiming He didn't teach what He clearly did. We have to, of course. To admit He taught what He did would require us either to change (repent) or to criticize Him. And neither of those is acceptable. So we obfuscate.

The problem is that Jesus was an extremist, and we are moderates. His evaluation of our way of life was that it is upside down. According to Jesus, we don't need a face-lift; what we need is to be torn down and completely rebuilt. Born again, He called it. He wanted us turned right side up.

But from our perspective, we need only moderate change. Oh, we aren't perfect. We all have our failings. Some of them are even serious. But basically our way of life is only tilted a little to one side. A tune-up will do the job: be kinder to those we're closest to, give another $50 a month to relief, work for blacks to move into our neighborhood.

It would never occur to us that Jesus called us to more than kindness; He called us to be servant/slaves, to polish the shoes of those around us. To give $50 a month more to relief is quite a bit, but Jesus called many of us (maybe you) to sell everything. And maybe instead of working for middle-class blacks to move into our neighborhoods, we should move into a ghetto. He wanted us to stop being upside down.

But that is extreme. So we prefer Aristotle. Oh, we don't say that, but we live it. The golden mean is much more practical than the golden rule. Jesus told us to treat others the way we'd like to be treated. But that is taxing. So we prefer Aristotle: be moderate in all things, virtue lies between the extremes. None of this talk about repentance and rebirth, about being upside-down.

But we have to pay lip service to Jesus. One way to do this is to focus on the generalities of Jesus' teaching and ignore the details. The heart of His teaching is love. To most of us that means we should have a soft, warm feeling toward others. And that is a good start, but it is not nearly extreme enough for Jesus.

He got specific and told us what He meant by love. And here Don Kraybill's *Upside-Down Kingdom* will be especially helpful. He gets down to the details. Jesus actually called us to be helpful to our enemies, to be good friends with bums and prostitutes (try it sometime), to exchange pursuit of status for slavery, to change our whole approach to money. Kraybill explains Jesus' teaching on these subjects carefully and accurately. If we hear and follow, our lives will begin to be right side up at last.

But that will be costly for us. So we may try to find ways around what Jesus taught. The standard line is that Jesus didn't mean what He said. His teaching was hyperbolic and picturesque. To interpret it literally is naive.

Take, for example, Jesus' teaching that we should turn the other cheek (Matthew 5:39). To William Neil that is so extreme it isn't common sense: "Putting up with a slap in the face is obviously not the same as risking a blow from a blackjack by a burglar. In that case self-defense would be common sense. . . . A slap in the face is merely a picturesque way of describing a personal insult, and, in this event, turning the other cheek means refusing to return the insults" (*The Difficult Sayings of Jesus,* Eerdmans).

Or take these verses. "If any one would sue you and take your coat, let him have your cloak as well; and if any one forces you to go one mile, go with him two miles. Give to him who begs from you, and do not refuse him who would borrow from you" (Matthew 5:40-42).

These *are* difficult sayings, and they violate all my instincts. Does Jesus mean that when I'm walking downtown I should give money to all the beggars who ask me? Wouldn't they just go get drunk? Wouldn't I be broke in no time flat? And am I obliged to loan out my record of Oistrakh playing Beethoven's violin concerto when I'd probably get it back scratched? Or how about my paintbrushes? I'm a pretty good house painter, and so I have some pretty expensive brushes. Nearly every time I loan one out it comes back hard as a brick.

As Neil puts it, "We can see . . . that Jesus does not mean His hearers to take Him literally." For if a man gave his cloak as well as his coat, that "would of course leave the man naked except for his loincloth!" And going a second mile is "obviously the last thing a conscript would dream of doing." And as for loaning to all comers, "to obey this literally would encourage spongers and reward the thriftless and shiftless at the expense of those who work for a living. Jesus is obviously not encouraging indiscriminate charity, which is demoralizing." All Jesus is trying to say, says Neil, is that we should be generous and respond to harshness with kindness.

I find myself sympathetic with this point of view. What Jesus is saying is perfectly foolish if taken literally, and what Neil is saying is perfectly reasonable. I can expand Neil's case much more easily than Jesus'. And yet. . . .

Neil makes me nervous. His heavy use of words like *obviously* and *of course* and his appeal to common sense make me wonder. Such things are generally a sign that those using them cannot defend their case and are therefore falling back on what we all agree on—on common sense.

At the risk of being simplistic, I suggest we must choose between Jesus and common sense. What is common sense except the wisdom of this world? What reason is there to suppose that this world knows how we should act? It has after all made quite a mess of itself.

Besides, Jesus was obviously lacking in common sense, and He was always doing things which He *of course* shouldn't have done. Yet something in Jesus' life speaks to us so deeply that millions have felt He must be God Himself. And isn't it exactly what Neil is explaining away which speaks so deeply? If all that is required is common sense, then why do we need Jesus? We could get everything Jesus taught out of common sources like *Time* magazine.

I suggest that Jesus came to tell us things that are not obvious and that He offered a worldview that is quite contrary to the worldview of our culture. He called us to repent (to turn completely around) and be born again.

That is, He called us to a whole new life—a life so radically different that we can only dimly imagine its rough outline. To move into this exciting, upside-down world that Jesus brought requires continued openness to basic change, as the Spirit and the Word lead us. But if we measure everything by common sense, we are trapped in the old creation.

Perhaps I am only saying that what seems obvious to Neil doesn't seem obvious to me. Perhaps it's only that he's a moderate and I'm an extremist. But I think there's more to it than that.

For one thing, Jesus' life was extreme. It was impractical and foolish. For example, He had nowhere to lay His head. He gave away everything except the clothes He wore.

For another, He so challenged the accepted wisdom (the common sense) of His day that the rulers killed Him. You don't kill someone for saying, "Be kind to the kind, and be generous."

And finally if Jesus did literally mean what He said, what more could he have done to tell us that? How could He have lived more extremely, less moderately than He did? What could He have said that we couldn't have found some way around?

All this is not to say that I know what Jesus meant. It's not at all clear to me that I should lend out my Oistrakh or my paintbrushes, but I do know that Jesus means our lives are to be changed in drastic ways. It's a direction not a conclusion. From cover to cover *The Upside-Down Kingdom* points in that direction in very concrete, practical ways. And the direction is that we are to forever stretch to grow up into the fullness of Christ, not to forever settle more comfortably into the present world order. So an alarm should go off inside us every time we find ourselves saying, "Jesus couldn't mean that, it's too impractical and costly."

But what about all those beggars downtown? One of the chief objection to giving them money is that if we did, we would soon be broke. But that is a very peculiar objection—maybe our being broke is exactly what Jesus had in mind. The reason we find being broke so unthinkable is because our culture finds it unthinkable, not because it's unchristian. After all Jesus was Himself completely broke, and He told the rich young ruler to get that way. Maybe our trouble is simply that we are too conformed to this world to believe Jesus could mean what He said.

Another problem is that if we give beggars money, they just drink it up. But we could take them to McDonald's or establish a soup kitchen like the Catholic Workers have or like Pacific Garden Mission.

But those things take time. If every time I went downtown I took all the beggars to McDonald's, I'd never get all my busywork done. Or is that exactly what God wants?

How about my paintbrushes that I want cleaned properly? Well, I could talk to borrowers very honestly and spell out in detail what they cost and how to clean them. If they then want to take responsibility for them it would probably be okay. The hang-up is that in our culture such openness is not normal. So we scarcely know how to assert ourselves to that extent.

But what if someone tries to rob me? Should I just let it happen? Dorothy Samuels in *Safe Passage on City Streets* tells about a robbery. Two girls were accosted by a guy who put a knife to the throat of one of them and demanded money. But they had no money. Instead of fighting or trying to trick him, they told him to trust them and they would take him back to their apartment to get some money for him. Naturally he couldn't believe what they were saying to him, but in the end he went along. When they got there all they had was a $10 bill, which they gave to him. He was so astonished he didn't know what to do. At first he said he didn't need all that—only $5. But since they had no change, he finally took it and ran.

Now I don't imagine the young man straightened out. Probably their act did no good. But at least it was a sign of the kingdom—to him and to the girls. And no one was hurt. If they had been smarter, one of the girls would probably have got her throat cut. The wisdom of this world is not nearly as wise as we think it is.

My point is this: the unthinkable, impractical things Jesus commands are not half as unthinkable as we suppose. We just need to decide where we get our standards—from Jesus or our culture. If from Jesus, we will have to change in very extreme ways and it may seem costly.

However, my all too limited experience of such things is that once I let go, following Jesus is tremendously liberating.

What I need is to break out of common sense and start living the life of the Upside-Down Kingdom. At first it sounds like bad news, but, combined with forgiveness for our endless failure, it is the good news. If we launch out into that life, we'll be astonished at how good it is. We'll be "like a tree planted by streams of water, that yields its fruit in its season, and its leaf does not wither (Psalm 1:3).

John F. Alexander, Editor
The Other Side

1
DOWN IS UP

Mountainous Plains

The voice of one crying in the wilderness:
Prepare the way of the Lord,
  make his paths straight.
Every valley shall be filled,
  and every mountain and hill shall be brought low,
  and the crooked shall be made straight,
  and the rough ways shall be made smooth;
  and all flesh shall see the salvation of God.—Luke 3:4-6.

John the Baptist shouted these words of Isaiah the prophet as a red carpet for the advent of Jesus. These dramatic words paint a picture of a revolutionary new kingdom. Will Jesus inaugurate a bulldozing operation to level mountains and fill valleys? Does He intend to set up a planing mill for rough lumber? The Baptist uses four images to describe the coming kingdom: filled valleys, leveled mountains, straightened curves, and smoothed bumps. He reminds us that radical shake-ups and change accompany the kingdom. Each image undergoes a thorough transformation from its previous state. The old ways are altered so abruptly that they won't even be recognized. The message is clear: the shape and form of the new kingdom contrasts sharply with the old social order. In the pangs of pain which must certainly infuse the new breaking in, all flesh will see the salvation of God. John's announcement is a warning that this new order will be an Upside-Down Kingdom in sharp relief against the prevailing social landscape.

Mary's song of exaltation—the Magnificat—sung at the home of Zechariah and Mary, leaves no question about the details to which John vaguely alluded. Mary expects the Messiah's arrival to initiate an Upside-Down Kingdom filled with surprises for all.

> For he who is mighty has done great things for me, and holy is his name.
> And his mercy is on those who fear him from generation to generation.
> He has shown strength with his arm,
> he has scattered *the proud* in the imagination of their hearts,
> he has put down *the mighty* from their thrones,
> and exalted those of *low degree;*
> he has filled *the hungry* with good things,
> and *the rich* he has sent empty away.
> Luke 1:49-53, emphasis added.

Five types of people are in for the shock of their lives. In this gospel according to Mary, the positions at the top of the social pyramid occupied by the proud, the rich, and the mighty are shattered. Instead of enjoying the privilege of their prestigious seats, they are scattered, put down, and sent away empty. The road to change is a two-way street. The poor and hungry at the bottom of the social hill are elevated to the top. They are exalted and filled with good things. Mary sings words of hope and judgment. Hope for those of low estate as she described herself in the beginning of the Magnificat (Luke 1:48). Judgment for the ones at the top who have trampled over those on the bottom rungs.

These frightening words of good and bad news flesh out the details of John's prediction of abrupt change. Mary expects the advent of the kingdom heralded by the Messiah to upset drastically the patterns of social structure. As a poor Galilean peasant girl, Mary anticipated the messianic reign to turn her social world upside down. The rich, mighty, and proud in Jerusalem would be sent away. The poor of the earth around Galilee would be exalted and honored. Her longing and hope provides us with a key which fits the lock holding the secrets of the Upside-Down Kingdom.

Inverted Kingdom

Scholars generally agree that the central theme in the ministry and teaching of Jesus is the kingdom of God, or as Matthew calls it, the kingdom of heaven.[1] The phrase "kingdom of God" was a unique and distinctive phrase on the lips of Jesus which set Him apart from His contemporaries. In the synoptic gospels it is the single phrase which ties together Jesus' message in its entirety. The three words "kingdom of God" form the one and only concept which permeates all of Jesus' ministry giving it unusual coherence and clarity.[2] Extracting this concept from Jesus' life and teaching would be like blasting away the foundation of a skyscraper.

Debates on exactly what Jesus meant by the kingdom have continued down through the centuries until the present. On the pages that follow we'll test the thesis that the kingdom of God is an inverted or upside-down way of life in contrast to the usual or prevailing social order. When a thing is inverted it is turned upside down or inside out.

To sharpen the issue we can think of two ladders side by side—one representing the kingdom of God and the other standing for the typical kingdoms of this world. An inverted or inverse relationship between the two ladders means that something at the top of one ladder is at the bottom of the other ladder. An object highly valued on the one ladder is on the bottom rung of the value system of the other. An inverted relationship appears in the refrain of a song from my Sunday school days. In it the rain and flood move in opposite directions:

> The rains came down, and the flood came up,
> The rains came down, and the flood came up.

The gospels suggest that the kingdom of God is inverted or upside down when compared with the conventionally accepted values, norms, and relationships of ancient Palestinian society and of modern culture today. This does not mean that the kingdom is geographically or socially isolated from the center of society. This is not a plea for social avoidance or withdrawal. Neither does this perspective assume a church-world split with the social territory neatly staked off into two separate plots of ungodly and holy ground. Kingdom action doesn't take place outside of the societal ball park. It's a different game played in the middle of the old ball park. Kingdom players follow different rules and listen to a different coach. Patterns of social organization which are routinely taken for granted in modern culture are questioned by kingdom values. Kingdom ways of living do not mesh smoothly with the dominant society. In fact they may sometimes appear foolish. The kingdom way often elicits responses of surprise and astonishment from the secular audience.

The kingdom of God is not only upside down, it's also normative and relevant to our situation today.[3] In other words, the secrets of the kingdom speak to the issues and dilemmas of our day. Their meaning can be translated into our modern context and they carry an authority which suggests how we "ought" to order our lives today. This doesn't mean that we will find definite answers in the Scripture for every ethical question that we can ever think of. The gospels will obviously not provide solutions for every modern ethical dilemma. But the gospels do raise the right questions. They prod us to inquire about the meaning and purpose of our lives.

Relational Kingdom

Before considering the biblical text we must clarify what the kingdom of God is all about. In a real sense the term defies definition since it is pregnant with many meanings. This in fact is the secret of its genius. It stimulates our imagination again and again. Biblical scholars generally agree that the term "kingdom of God" indicates the dynamic rule or reign of God. The kingdom of God occurs when persons are ruled by God. The German scholar Jeremias points out that the reign of God always stands for the government, authority, and power of the King. It does not refer to a territory in a spatial sense. Nor does it have an abstract or static meaning. The kingdom does not stand still on a particular piece of ground—it is always in the process of being achieved.[4] The kingdom points us not to the place of God but to the act of God. It is His ruling activity. The kingdom is present whenever women and men submit themselves to God's reign in their life.

Some discussions about the kingdom conclude that the kingdom occurs when God rules in the hearts of people. This position suggests that the kingdom is primarily an inward experience of the mind, something which each person thinks about. The definition of a term like kingdom by its very nature implies a collective order which transcends the ideas and thoughts of any one person. A kingdom in a literal sense implies that a king rules over a group of people. It suggests that there are social standards and policies for the conduct of collective life in that kingdom. Agreements spell out the obligations which the citizens have with each other and their king. The rule of the king has corporate implications for the relationships among his subjects.

The sociological distinction between an *aggregate* and a

collectivity helps to clarify the kingdom idea. An aggregate consists of a number of persons who are together in time and space but who do not influence or affect each other. Persons waiting for the "Walk" light at an intersection are an example of an aggregate. They stand together at the same place and same time, but they are generally not talking and interacting with each other. In contrast, a meeting of the executive committee of a parent-teachers' association is a collectivity because members are interdependent. They influence each other, formulate common goals, and agree on accepted ways of reaching their goals. A collectivity does not necessarily have to be together in the same time and space. A kingdom could not operate as a collectivity if it merely consisted of people in the same place and same time all thinking in their individual hearts about their king. The idea of kingdom suggests a collective interdependence based on the policies established by the king.

Some people imply that the kingdom of God is an aggregate. I think it is more appropriate to conceptualize the kingdom of God as a collectivity—a group of persons whose *hearts* and *relationships* are in subordination to the reign of God. The kingdom is manifest when God rules in the hearts and social relationships of His people. The kingdom is not present through a series of hot lines from the King to each individual subject. The reign of God infuses the network of wires which link all of the citizens together. The King's unique character is expressed in His special manner of ruling. The unique identity of His kingdom emerges from the special shape and form of the common policies and practices which tie His citizens together.

But what does that really mean? How do we discover what God's reign looks like? What is the shape of His policies? How do we translate the lofty idea of the reign of God into practical human terms? The answer is found in the incarnation. God unveiled Himself in Jesus of Nazareth. He disclosed His identity in Jesus. We can discover the shape and form of His kingdom by carefully studying the life and teachings of Jesus. God spoke with clear diction in a language we all understood when He sent Jesus as His Word. The kingdom of God is the one concept which weaves together all of Jesus' teaching and ministry. Parables are frequently introduced as examples of the kingdom. The Sermon on the Mount and Plain include numerous references to the kingdom. The Lord's Prayer welcomes the advent of the kingdom. His answers to questions are often couched in kingdom language.

The clues for interpreting the kingdom go beyond His specific kingdom words. The activity and behavior of Jesus also provide data which inform us about the nature of the kingdom. He did not speak and act in a social vacuum. His behavior, as well as the content of His words, had particular meanings in the social setting of His culture. Reconstructing those meanings adds to our understanding of the kingdom. Thus, we are informed about the nature and way of the kingdom by both the word and behavior of Jesus of Nazareth. He provides us with the most concrete example and expression of God's rule. His words and behavior must be our starting point in grasping the way of the kingdom.

A Right-Side-Up Kingdom

If Jesus inaugurated the kingdom of God, then perhaps it would be more fitting to call it the Right-Side-Up Kingdom instead of the Upside-Down Kingdom. Indeed, if we agree that the kingdom portrays God's blueprint for the way men ought to live, then certainly we ought to tag it the Right-Side-Up Kingdom. Although the kingdom of God is not literally upside down, the inverted image is helpful because it reminds us of three things:

1. *Social life has a vertical dimension.* We often hear remarks about a vertical relationship with God and a hori-

zontal relationship with our fellowmen. This carries with it the false assumption that the social order is level with lines connecting all the "fellowmen" together on a flat plane. In reality social life is not a flat plane but has a rugged topography. In social geography there are also mountains, valleys, ruts, and plains. Individuals and groups vary a great deal in the amount of power and control they exercise. The chairman of a committee wields much more power than the average committee member. Lawyers have more influence than grocery store clerks. Jews, as an ethnic group, have much greater influence in American political affairs than Chicanos. Some people are on much higher social mountains than others in terms of their influence, prestige, and power. The term "upside down" keeps the reality of this vertical ranking of persons in front of us.

2. *We forget to ask why.* The "upside-down" handle also encourages us to question the way things are. Children quickly learn to take their societies' values for granted. Cereal is the "right" breakfast food. Socialization—the learning of the ways of our culture—is very persuasive and thorough in shaping the assumptions by which we live. We take our way of life for granted. We tend to think that the way things are is the way they ought to be. Having cereal for breakfast day after day infuses it with a sense of rightness. We internalize the values and norms paraded on the screen and billboard as "just the way life is." If our economic structure sets the minimum wage at $3.10 per hour, we accept that as a fair and moral wage without a second thought. If someone trespasses on our property, we prosecute without any qualms, because, after all, "that's what the law provides for." We demand an 8 percent commission because "that's just the way it is."

The values, beliefs, and norms of our society become so deeply ingrained within our thought processes that it's difficult to conceive of acting in a different way. The way of Jesus often appears upside down or backwards in contrast to the prevailing value system which our minds have absorbed so thoroughly. If it does anything, the kingdom of God shatters most of the assumptions which govern our social life. As kingdom citizens we don't assume that things are right just because "that's the way they are."

3. *The kingdom is full of surprises.* Again and again in parables, sermons, and acts Jesus startles us. Things are not like they are supposed to be. The stories don't end as we expected. The Good Guys turn out to be the Bad Guys. The ones we expected to receive a reward get spanked. Things are reversed. Paradox, irony, and surprise permeate the life of Jesus. The least are the greatest. The immoral receive forgiveness and blessing. Adults become like children. The religious miss the heavenly banquet. The pious receive curses. Things are just not like we think they should be. We are baffled, perplexed, and most of all surprised. We are caught off guard. We step back in amazement. We aren't sure if we should laugh or cry. The kingdom surprises us again and again by turning our world upside down.

Detours Around the Kingdom

Constructing a footbridge between the pressing questions of today and the biblical record is precarious. Centuries of water lie between the cliffs jutting from each shoreline. Detour signs on both sides barricade and deter easy passage. Before attempting to construct a bridge between yesterday and today, we must stop to consider four detour signs. These cautions which have been raised by some people often dilute the kingdom message and make it irrelevant for today.

Sign One: Jesus Is Culturally Bound

The first sign warns us that erecting a bridge between the first and twentieth centuries is foolish because the cultural landscape on the two sides of the water is so radically different. Jesus lived in a small town in a rural area which never heard of industrialization, technocracy, nuclear holocaust, neutron bombs, urbanization, and multinational corporations. According to this detour sign, the kingdom He announced was only fitting for His kind of social milieu where everyone in the small village was known on a first-name basis. In such an uncomplicated web of intimate social relations, it was at least possible to talk about loving enemies and forgiving neighbors. His plan for social order sounded feasible for gentle shepherds and serene peasants. Since His teaching and ministry is culturally bound to such a different era, it is impossible to transport it across our footbridge to the twentieth century.

Thus, according to this caution, we can study the Scripture to learn about biblical ethics and we can describe the "oughts" for living in New Testament times; but we can't drag them across the bridge and consider them normative for today. On this side, the fine print of the detour sign tells us to construct Christian ethics from scratch and stand them on their own feet of common sense since the biblical experience is so ancient and culturally removed.

Now I agree that it is irresponsible to jump directly from an isolated Scripture text to the modern era, since the particular passage may carry a special cultural meaning which does not speak to our present time. If, however, we can identify the meaning of the biblical text within its own cultural setting, then it's reasonable to transport the meaning across the bridge leading to today. It is essential to understand the values, norms, and intergroup relations of the ancient social situation before the meaning of a text can be fully understood. Once we have extracted the meaning within its own cultural context, we can then haul it across the span that connects us with yesterday.

Although the external cultural expressions are strikingly different between Galilean peasant society and post-industrial society, the same fundamental issues persist on both sides of the chasm: the distribution and use of power, nationalism, the emergence of social hierarchies, racism, economic oppression in intergroup relations, violence, and arrogant individualism. In short, evil and sin infuse the values and social structures of both yesterday and today. As we unlock the secret meanings of the gospels within their cultural setting, those meanings relevantly engage the basic issues of our time.

The ancient cultural setting of the gospels is not a liability or handicap when we take the time to interpret the biblical materials in their cultural context. In fact, that's the very moment that they become powerfully relevant as we perceive the parallel between the issues of the first and twentieth century. Contrary to typical thinking, the relevance of Jesus would decrease if His life and ministry were supracultural. The fact that they are grounded in a particular cultural milieu is the key to their relevance if we will take the time to hear them in their setting. Culture, rather than hiding or antiquating the message of the kingdom, clarifies it.

Certainly the arrival of complex organizations, nuclear technology, and modern science places us in a very different world. But the human tendency toward sinful arrogance and the abuse of power continues today as much as ever. The tools and instruments in a technocracy are different but the logic and motivation remain the same. The consequences of evil are more devastating than ever with sophisticated technology in the form of nuclear weapons.

Sign Two: Jesus Goofed on the Timing

The second detour sign informs us that Jesus was mistaken about the timing of the kingdom's arrival. Since He goofed in thinking that the kingdom was going to arrive in His own lifetime, we certainly can't take it very seriously today, let alone talk about its relevance for how we ought to live. The issue of the kingdom's timing, one of the stickiest problems in synoptic studies, has provoked heated debate in the scholarly community during the last century.[5]

In 1906 Albert Schweitzer wrote *The Quest of the Historical Jesus* where he argued that the Gospels show that Jesus actually expected the end of time and the consummation of the kingdom during His own lifetime. For instance in Matthew 10:23, when the Twelve are sent out, Jesus tells them: "I say to you, you will not have gone through all the towns of Israel, before the Son of man comes." In Luke 9:27, after discussing the disciple's cross, Jesus says, "But I tell you truly, there are some standing here who will not taste death before they see the kingdom of God." With these and other passages Schweitzer argued that Jesus Himself only understood the kingdom as a later event which was to come in the very near future. Thus, if Jesus held this view that the world was about to end, His ethical teaching could only be intended for the short interim between His life and the imminent arrival of the kingdom. So, according to Schweitzer, Jesus' teachings were intended only for this short "interim" and they don't make any sense for long-term and enduring social relationships.[6]

A British theologian, C. H. Dodd thinks that Jesus was aware that the kingdom was present in His own ministry on earth. References such as Luke 10:9, "The kingdom of God has come near to you," and Luke 11:20, "The kingdom of God has come upon you," were used to support his view which insisted that the kingdom was already manifest in the life and ministry of Jesus. Dodd's interpretation stressed the presence of the kingdom in the incarnation and in the growth of the church and gave little attention to its future climax.

Another position on the question of timing is the dispensational view which relegates the kingdom primarily to a future and literal millennial reign on the earth at the second return of Christ. According to this view, Israel rejected the offer of the kingdom at the first appearance of Christ, and now it will be realized in a future embodiment on earth. The futuristic bent of this position dilutes any serious interest in applying the teachings of Jesus to our lives today.

More recently, scholars see the kingdom of God in the teaching of Jesus as integrating both *present* and *future*. George Ladd says, "There is a growing consensus in New Testament scholarship that the kingdom of God is in some sense both present and future."[7] Ladd finds four meanings of the kingdom in the gospels: (1) an abstract meaning of the reign or rule of God, (2) a future apocalyptic order into which the righteous will enter, (3) the presence of the kingdom already among men, and (4) a realm which persons are entering now.[8]

This understanding of the kingdom paves the way for Norman Perrin's very helpful clarification that the term kingdom of God should be understood as a general symbol rather than a specific symbol.[9] Symbols refer us to something else. The written word "dog" is a symbol. As you read the symbol "dog" it refers you to a certain kind of animal. A specific symbol is one that has only one referent—it can only remind us of one thing. A black female cocker spaniel puppy points us to one very specific kind of dog. In contrast a general symbol can have multiple meanings and numerous referents. "Animal," for example, can point to many different kinds of organisms. If we think of the kingdom of God as a specific symbol, it can refer us to only one meaning. If it only indicates one event, then we are forced to ask whether or not that event has occurred—yes or no. Such a specific symbol can be exhausted by a single concrete act in history.

Viewing the kingdom as a general symbol, we realize that it leads us to many referents which hold multiple meanings. Then instead of asking questions about time, we probe what the kingdom evokes or represents. For what does it stand? Toward what does it point us? Furthermore, as Perrin reminds us, a general symbol is not invalidated simply because a specific event doesn't take place. We obviously don't participate in a symbol but we can respond to the meanings which the symbol signals—the experience of accepting the rule of God as King.

In this study we embrace the kingdom with its variety of meanings, its hope in the Old Testament, its inauguration in the ministry of Jesus, its dynamic at Pentecost, its endurance in the lives of believers mediated throughout the centuries by the Holy Spirit, and its final consummation in the future. Signs of it burst forth as persons submit their will to the way of God. As George Ladd describes it in the title of a book, the kingdom is *The Presence of the Future* among us already.

Our assumption throughout this book is that the kingdom of God is here today as the Spirit of God rules among His people. The members of the kingdom even now are those who obey the Lord of the kingdom. Those who follow in the way of Jesus are already part of the kingdom movement. This doesn't mean that by an evolutionary process of osmosis the kingdom will eventually infiltrate national and international social structures. The kingdom is better understood as light, salt, and a narrow way which will always run counter to the dominant social order.

Sign Three: Ponder the Spiritual Meaning

Surprisingly this third detour sign prevents many persons from trucking practical ethical instruction across the bridge between ancient Palestine and today. Certain words in a language take on sacred and holy meanings. In our minds we sort words into holy and profane boxes. It's also natural to contrast opposite words with each other: hot versus cold, big versus small, and the like. In religious circles the term "spiritual" stands at the top of the sacred ladder and is frequently contrasted with "social" which must be near the bottom. Spiritual realities, the logic goes, come from God and are holy. Social things, on the other hand, originate from men. Social realities are suspect and far from the heart of God. It is assumed that spiritual things are much better than social things. In fact social things have little spiritual value. Have you ever heard persons say that they hope a certain church function doesn't become just a social event—implying that it would no longer have spiritual meaning. This unfortunate dichotomy between spiritual and social (notice how I unconsciously ordered them) often detours us around kingdom ethics.

On the one hand spiritual things refer to great metaphysical truths. They include our belief of salvation, peace, and assurance. They may also refer to the mysterious working of God's Spirit in our lives. On the other hand, social things point us to earthly and mundane concerns: housing, fellowship, salary, recreation. In particular, they point to our humanity—our social needs for approval, love, creativity, and satisfying relationships. This false segregation of the spiritual and that which is social results in a warped reading of the Scripture which allows us to seek the spiritual truth at the expense of the social. We marvel at the atonement of Jesus and forget that He also demonstrated a new way of living.

Any gospel which is not social is not gospel. God so loved the world that. . . . He didn't just sit in His great theological rocking chair stroking His white beard and glory in His love for the world. He did something about it. He became social in the form of His Son. He lived, interacted, and behaved in a real social environment, disclosing God's social way. In the incarnation the spiritual "word" became a social "event." To say it another way, the social event was itself a word which communicated to men. Word and deed are inseparably cemented into one in the incarnation. In these last days God has spoken to us not in Greek or English but with a Son—through a social event (Hebrews 1:2). The genius of the incarnation is that the spiritual and social worlds intersect in the person of Jesus Christ. To separate them is to deny the incarnation. The spiritual Word was fleshed out among men. The two—social and spiritual—are inextricably woven together in the gospel account. It is unfortunate that the term "social gospel" has acquired a negative meaning which blinds many of us to the true nature of God's sojourn among men.

An example of the perpetuation of this dichotomy shows up in the summary of a recent study of Jesus. The author concludes that the ethical standards of Jesus are really minor when compared to His call for repentance which "is a purely religious ethical act, i.e., is in and of itself an act involving only oneself and God and neutral regarding other human beings and the world."[10] The underlying assumption here is that repentance is a spiritual phenomena with no social implications. One also wonders why Jesus is relevant for repentance if He's not relevant for ethics. Such a cleavage represents a gross misunderstanding of the gospel. We do not have two gospels—one spiritual and one social, one concerned with salvation and another concerned with hunger. We have a single integrated gospel, the gospel of the kingdom.

I once heard a pastor spiritualize the story of Zacchaeus. After telling the story he reminded the congregation that Jesus can take us out of the spiritual trees that we get ourselves into. If we are ever treed, we can be freed by Jesus who calls us down. A more realistic reading of the text sees a rich exploiter who meets Jesus, repents, and immediately corrects the economic injustice he caused. The spiritual experience and the social retribution are one story—inseparable—a story which Jesus describes as a visit by salvation.

To flesh out the social implications of the gospel does not mean that spiritual insights are second rate or neglected, rather it asserts that spiritual insights always have social ramifications. The integration of social and spiritual into a whole is not a humanistic way of doing theology from below. It affirms an incarnation that moved beyond the holy of holies in the Jerusalem temple to the social realities of Palestinian society. Spiritualizing the biblical texts lifts them out of human experience and consequently makes them difficult to transport across the bridge. When the full social meaning of a text is explored, its relevant cargo can be shuttled across the chasm to the social realities on our side.

Sign Four: Only Change Your Character

The next barricading sign tells us that the kingdom makes a difference only in our personal character. To put it another way, the teaching of Jesus is relevant for character-building and personal ethics but not for social ethics.

Typical of many discussions, George Ladd concludes that the primary desire of Jesus is for righteous character. Conduct should be a manifestation of such righteous character but "it is of course true that there is little explicit teaching on social ethics in the gospels."[11]

The distinction between personal and social ethics sounds like a nice classification at first but it's very problematic on second thought. It suggests that decisions and actions which are personal do not have social implications or consequences. Furthermore, it also assumes that the individual operates in a social vacuum detached from ongoing social processes. Jesus, according to this view, was concerned with the private matters of the inner life which are sealed off from public exposure: attitudes, motives, feelings, emotions, personality traits, integrity, and the like. Hence, the ethic of Jesus is construed to be relevant only for inner feelings and actions which have no impact on other persons. He only touches our emotional outlook, determining whether we have an optimistic or pessimistic view of life, a sense of hope, and inner peace.

The problem with such a personal/social breakdown is the difficulty of isolating any behavior which is not social. As a sociologist I can think of very few actions which are purely "personal." Perhaps scratching one's leg would pass the test. But even this creates problems. The proper way to scratch a leg is learned in a social context. Cultural norms determine the time and method of scratching. Social meaning is attached to the propriety of scratching—woe to the president who scratches his leg during a press conference! The difficulty in conceptualizing a personal ethic is that even ideas, values, and character traits have a social origin. They don't just drop out of the sky. They are learned in some kind of social context: discussions with friends, reading a book, listening to tapes, or observing parents behave for fifteen years. This doesn't mean that the individual contributes no originality or creativity. Nor does it mean that individuals are culturally programmed social robots. Our minds become the crucible where various social influences are processed and mixed together. Each person blends these social influences together in his or her own beautiful and unique way.

Not only do inner feelings and motives have a social origin, they virtually all have social ramifications. A feeling of despair affects how a person interacts with others. The attitudes which Jesus pinpointed interestingly were social attitudes—feelings directed toward other persons. Hating someone in your heart is equivalent to murder, lustful motivations are like committing adultery. Inner feelings and emotions aren't sealed off within our private personal castle. They emerge out of social experiences and direct themselves toward others. It is impossible to think of so-called character traits such as love or integrity outside of a social context. Discussions of integrity, honesty, and meekness have no meaning for an individual stranded on an isolated island. If Jesus were only concerned about proper personal attitudes, He could have spent all of His time in the wilderness lecturing on the virtues of inner harmony.

The fact that ideas and feelings have social origins and consequences does not eradicate the role of the Holy Spirit.

God created us as social beings and His Spirit uses others to minister to our needs and directs us to needy others. Second, the fact that internal feelings and thoughts are social products with social implications doesn't mean that the inner life is not important—just the opposite. Its role takes on much greater significance when we understand its connectedness with others. Thoughts do influence our behavior. Jesus stressed the need for a pure internal righteousness in contrast to Pharisaic hypocrisy, but he also understood that the inner life has social manifestations.

Thus, it should be clear by now that our contention is that kingdom social ethics taught and lived by Jesus can be transported over the bridge which links the first and twentieth century. Although many laymen easily make the jump over the chasm, our proposal resists the current of much recent thought which encourages Jesus to return to His own time since "He does not provide a valid ethic for today."[12] At the same time it pushes forward the concern lamented by other scholars that recent studies of social ethics have made little use of the concept of the kingdom of God.[13]

We do not expect to find a full-blown system of formalized ethics specifying moral axioms and prescriptions for every conceivable situation. Nor do we espouse a sentimentalist mentality of simply "walking in His footsteps." The gospels, however, we believe, do provide us with episodes, stories, and pictures loaded with insights about "the good" and "the right" which apply to our modern situation. These pictures of the good and right found in the kingdom are not merely impossible possibilities which serve as romanticized ideals far removed from daily living. They intersect at ground level with the knotty problems of human existence today.

Questions for Discussion

1. What do John the Baptist's and Mary's prophesies re-

garding the kingdom tell us about the nature of the kingdom?

2. In addition to the ladder and ball game, what other images would appropriately symbolize the Upside-Down Kingdom?

3. What difference does it make to view the kingdom of God as an aggregate or collectivity?

4. What other detour signs prevent us from applying biblical ethics today?

5. Which detours provide the easiest justification for disregarding biblical teaching?

6. List some other examples of "spiritualizing" the meaning of the gospel.

2
MOUNTAIN POLITICS

The Three-Legged Temptation

The synoptic writers report that Jesus was presented with three forms of a Right-Side-Up Kingdom before launching His Upside-Down Kingdom. The authors agree that the temptation was a forty-day ordeal. The number "forty" represents trial and oppression in Hebrew history. The flood lasted forty days and nights, and the wilderness wandering continued for forty years. Moses was up on the mountain forty days and nights. Goliath taunted the Israelites for forty days. Mark gives no information about the meaning of the test, but Matthew and Luke, both in Chapter 4, concur that Jesus evaluated three aspects of another kingdom symbolized by the mountain, the temple, and the bread. These three distinct, yet interrelated, options formed the legs of a stool which would have seated Jesus as a bona fide political Messiah.

The three temptation episodes point to a Right-Side-Up Kingdom which reflected the three prominent social institutions of Jesus' day: political (mountain), religious (temple), and economic (bread).[1] Social institutions do not necessarily refer to people *per se* or to organizations. They are the established patterns of social behavior which organize the life of a particular segment of society. Economic institutions consist of the intermeshing web of numerous social rules which govern financial activity by specifying rates of interest and the rights of creditors and debtors. These conventional practices for conducting economic relationships are usually taken for granted by the members of a social system. They make financial behavior predictable and orderly. Social institutions are deeply ingrained in the culture of a society and in the minds of its participants which makes them very difficult to change. A similar social institution or complex of social norms organizes the educational sphere, family life, recreational activity, and the religious behavior of a society.

The triad of temptations posed real social detours to the true messianic mission. Together the three-part temptation fulfilled Jewish hopes for a Messiah who would shuck off oppressing nations, feed the poor, and bask in miraculous approval from above. Luke's word that the devil departed from Jesus "until an opportune time" suggests that these tempting shortcuts for the suffering Messiah didn't evaporate after forty days in the wilderness; they plagued Jesus right up to the end of His ministry. When Peter rebukes Jesus for talking about suffering, Jesus emphatically declares, "Get behind me, Satan!" (Mark 8:33). Such emotionally loaded words can only mean that the conventional way of violent political force continued to be a viable option in the mind of Jesus. In the midst of a squabble over power Jesus tells the disciples that they are the ones who have continued with Him in His trials (Luke 22:28). It is clear that throughout His ministry Jesus was faced with conventional political strategies which would have deterred Him from the upside-down way. To grasp the nature of the Upside-Down Kingdom, it is necessary to understand the mountain, the temple, and the bread alternatives. Only as we clearly perceive what Jesus rejected can we know what He affirmed. In this chapter and in the next two, the three aspects of the temptation will serve as foci to review the sociopolitical context in which Jesus lived. Each chapter will deal with one part of the tempter's offer. We will begin with the political temptation and then review the religious and economic dimensions in the following chapters.

Jesus the Great

According to Matthew (4:8) the political temptation was presented from the vantage point of a very high mountain. Luke (4:6) reports that the temptation was for all the "authority and glory" of the kingdoms of the world. This was Jesus' chance to be a new Alexander the Great, an opportunity to wield all the political power of the great Mediterranean world with its accompanying splendor and glory. Once again Israel would be supreme—a light and power to all the nations. God's vengeance would roll out across the other empires of the Middle East. The pivot of world authority and influence would shift from Rome to Jerusalem. Caesar could no longer tax and insult Jews, for now Caesar himself would be Jewish. For Jesus, the mountain temptation represented the possibility of worldwide political power—not merely coercive force but also the glory and acclaim of sitting on the world's highest peak of power. This very right-side-up way contrasted starkly with the humble servant role. Why was this a temptation? Why should Jesus care about the Roman occupation? Why should this be a tantalizing lure?

A short historical detour is necessary to understand the political hopes of Jews living during Jesus' time.[2] The Old Testament ends with the Hebrew community under the control of the Persians who had kindly allowed them to return to their homeland in 538 BC after fifty years in Babylonian captivity. A peaceful coexistence with the Persians permitted the rebuilding of the temple under Zerubbabel. The situation changed rapidly with the jump to fame of a young Greek. Alexander the Great conquered the Persians in 334 BC and by 332 BC all of Palestine had fallen under his control as he rampaged on into Egypt. He hoped to usher in a worldwide civilization unified by the Greek way of life known as Hellenization. For the first time Greek traders and the Greek language made themselves at home in Palestine. A fever killed Alexander the Great at the age of 32, and his empire fell into the squabbling hands of his generals. Palestine turned into a buffer zone and was shuttled back and forth between the jealous generals at least five times in less than ten years. One of the generals, Ptolemy, governor of Egypt, and his successors, finally managed to control Palestine for over 100 years. He is reported to have entered Jerusalem on a Sabbath day under the guise of pretending to offer a sacrifice, only to capture many Jews and export them to Egypt as colonists.[3]

The Madman

In 198 BC Syria captured the Jewish kingdom from the Egyptians. A few years later in 175 BC the Syrian King Antiochus IV came to power and created havoc for the Jews. He was nicknamed the "madman" although he called himself "the illustrious." He promptly set up policies strictly forcing Greek culture on the Jewish people. Aspects of Greek life and culture found their way to Jerusalem. A gymnasium was constructed as a center for athletic training and social contact. Young Jews were ashamed of their circumcision which couldn't be disguised in the nude athletic contests held in the gym. Many underwent operations so they would appear uncircumcised. Young Jewish males also wore Greek clothing and, in particular, a fashionable broad-rimmed hat which the god Hermes was pictured wearing. The Jewish writer of 2 Maccabees 4:14 laments that Jewish priests had deserted their sacred responsibilities to watch the sporting events such as wrestling, discus throwing, and horse racing. The Greek language became prominent in Jerusalem. Although the Hebrews resisted Hellenization, they might have endured it if the madman's tactics had stopped there.

Twice the Syrian madman plundered the Jewish treasury to support his war activity. He carried the precious furnishings of the temple—the altar of incense, the seven-branched lampstand, and the table of the shewbread—off to Antioch in Syria. Eduard Lohse describes the madman's policies:

> The walls of Jerusalem were torn down and a fortress was built on the hill of the ancient city of David. The Jews were forbidden, on pain of death, to keep the sabbath and to circumcise their children. The king's inspectors traveled throughout the country in order to supervise the fulfillment of these decrees. In Jerusalem a pagan altar was erected on the site of the altar of burnt offering, and sacrifices were offered there to the supreme god, the Olympian Zeus in 167 B.C.[4]

During the reign of the madman, two successive Jewish high priests bribed him for their positions by paying large sums of money. Carrying a copy of Holy Scripture meant death. Sacrifice to Yahweh was stopped by the erection of the altar to Zeus. Ten days after the altar's completion a pig was sacrificed on it—a horror to Jewish ritual purity. The temple sanctuary was smeared with blood and soldiers committed the grossest indecencies in the sacred temple courts.

In addition there was economic oppression. Morton S. Enslin reports the Syrian madman's greed for taxes included "taxes on the salt mined at the Dead Sea; taxes amounting to a third of the grain harvested, to a half of the all too scanty fruits; poll taxes, crown taxes, temple taxes, to say nothing of the sovereign right to seize cattle and stores in the name of military conscription—all this fomented unrest."[5] If Jewish culture, worship, and identity was going to survive, Jews would need to fight.

The Hammers

Although the high priests and many of the people

welcomed Greek culture, a small group of traditional Jews resented the foreign influence. This conservative element, known as the Hasideans (meaning pious) protested the Jewish embrace of Greek culture, but they did not revolt against the policies of the madman. Revolt came in the countryside. An old priest named Mattathias and his five sons lived in a small village about twenty miles northwest of Jerusalem. When one of the king's inspectors came to the village to force the Jews to offer pagan sacrifices, Mattathias refused and killed another Jew who was ready to offer a pagan sacrifice on the altar. He also killed the king's inspector. The father and five sons fled to caves in the Judean hillside where they were joined by the pious Hasideans who were finally willing to resort to violence to rid the land of the Syrians. From their wilderness base they carried small resistance campaigns into villages to destroy pagan altars and punish apostate Jews.

On one occasion some rebels refused to retaliate against Syrian troops because of their respect for the Sabbath. The enemy attacked and massacred them. Full-scale resistance and offensive attacks began. Mattathias soon died and his son Judas the Maccabean (which means "the Hammerer" in Hebrew) organized a successful military campaign against the Syrians. Eventually the Maccabeans regained control of the temple area in Jerusalem. In 164 BC, three years after the temple had been defiled by swine's blood, it was rededicated. A feast of dedication known as Hanukkah is still celebrated by Jews today in remembrance of this event.

Although the temple was returned to Jewish supervision, the fortress in Jerusalem, manned by the Syrians, remained intact. After the temple was restored, the pious Hasideans withdrew their support of the revolt since they were not interested in political freedom. This group eventually served as the womb for the Pharisee movement. Another group soon to emerge was the Sadducees who insisted on political independence, a goal finally achieved under Simon, one of Mattathias' five sons, in 142 BC. He soon declared himself priest, military leader, and spokesman for the people. This began an eighty-year period of political independence under the control of the so-called Hasmonean family. During this time the same person often ruled as king and high priest. Coins were minted, and the Jewish state conquered Moab, Samaria, and Edom.

Conflict between the Pharisees and Sadducees forced them to take sides between ruling factions within the Hasmonean family. A military stalemate between two brothers brought the Romans into the picture in 63 BC. Pompey, the Roman general, besieged Jerusalem for three months. Finally on a Sabbath day the last area of resistance, the temple, was taken and over 12,000 Jews were massacred. Pompey entered the holy of holies, reserved exclusively for the high priest once a year, and to his amazement found it empty. His profane act insulted the faithful Jews who interpreted it as the judgment of God descending on His guilty people.

So after almost 100 years of national political autonomy, the Jewish state was once again under the thumb of a foreign power. From now on it would be a tributary of the large Roman Empire. Thus in the 500 years of its political history before the birth of Jesus, it was batted back and forth in a game of political Ping-Pong between the great powers of the Middle East: Babylon, Persia, Greece, Egypt, Syria, and now finally Rome. Although Rome would continue to dominate Palestinian politics, the fire of freedom ignited by Judas the Hammerer could not be extinguished. It rekindled again and again until Rome finally stamped it out in AD 135.

Great Herod

After Pompey secured Palestine for Rome, the high priesthood was controlled by Jewish leaders but the occupant of the throne had to appease Roman desires. After some stormy years of instability, Herod went to Rome and was declared "king" by the Roman senate. Even with the help of Roman military power, it took him three years until he was able to subdue his Palestinian citizens and gain complete control of Jerusalem in 37 BC. He continued to rule until 4 BC and was on the throne when Christ was born about 5 BC. It is this Herod who approached the wise men and who later killed the male children in Bethlehem because of the threat of a new king.

Under Herod the Great the territory of Palestine almost doubled, resulting in an area larger than that controlled by David and Solomon. He artfully maintained a delicate balance between Roman power and Jewish nationalism. He could keep his crown only as long as he pleased Rome. He didn't have to pay taxes to Rome but was required to send troops in time of war. He could maintain his own army as long as it didn't pose a threat of secession from the empire. Above all he was to maintain peace and administer the territory efficiently.

The outstanding mark of Herod's 33-year reign was a lavish building program. Although he didn't force Hellenization on the Jews like the madman, Herod's architecture followed the Roman patterns. Temples, gymnasiums, cloisters, aqueducts, and amphitheaters were constructed on an enormous scale. He built several new cities, including Caesarea on the Mediterranean coast with an artificial harbor. A number of fortresses and palaces were built throughout the countryside. Huge construction projects, including pagan temples, were also carried out in Gentile lands of Sidon, Tyre, Nicopolis, Sparta, and Athens to name just a few.

Herod came from Gentile ancestry and was never completely trusted by the Jewish leaders. To gain their confidence he initiated a complete renovation of the sacred temple in

Jerusalem in 20 BC—the eighteenth year of his reign. The Jews were suspicious that he would tear down the existing temple built by Zerubbabel and never replace it. To demonstrate his sincerity he provided a thousand wagons, hired ten thousand workmen, and trained 1,000 priests as masons and carpenters so that the holy shrine would not be defiled by unconsecrated feet during the reconstruction. The old temple area was enlarged to twice its size and the resulting magnificent structure was Herod's pride and glory.

But Jewish/Roman tension continued. Out of courtesy to Rome Herod placed a golden eagle, the empire's royal symbol, over the great east gate of the city. Some forty pious Jews were so insulted that they tore the eagle down in defiance. Herod retaliated by burning them all alive. The magnificent temple built by Herod was in operation during the life of Jesus and was later destroyed by Romans in AD 70, only seven years after it was finally completed.

Herod's insatiable ambition made him both ruthless and sympathetic to Jewish concerns. He had to maintain Jewish stability to receive Rome's continuing smile, but he dared not allow threats from potential successors or uncontrollable Jewish nationalism. His building projects required heavy taxes and revenue, although he did distribute free corn once during a famine and reduced taxes during hard times. Some of the taxes went to the new temple which received Jewish approval, but others irritated Jewish leaders since they subsidized lavish and pagan temples in faraway places. Jeremias reminds us that under Herod the Great the taxes "were ruthlessly exacted, and he was always thinking out fresh ways of subsidizing his vast expenditures."[6] The people certainly felt the oppressive tax burden including gifts to Herod and his friends as well as that exacted by the tax collectors. There was bitter popular outcry because of the way he squandered the common wealth which had been sucked from the lifeblood of the people.

During his reign Jewish worship and ritual practices proceeded with relative freedom. In his later years, the Pharisees refused to sign an oath of loyalty to the king and Roman emperor and were punished. Although the kingdom had grown, Herod was not popular with the people. Much suspicion centered around his vicious treatment of his family. His several wives—ten in all—lived in his palace. Over the years he killed two of them plus at least three sons, a brother-in-law, and one of his wives' grandfathers. The Roman emperor is reported to have remarked, "Better is it to be Herod's pig than son."[7]

When he was about to die he knew that the people would rejoice, so he ordered leading Jews to be shut up in the Jericho arena and executed upon his death. He wanted to be certain that there would be mourning at his death, even though it was not for his death.[8] Fortunately, the prisoners were freed after his death in 4 BC.

The Roman Connection

Herod's will divided his kingdom into three parts allotted to his three remaining sons. His son, Herod Antipas, was to rule over the district of Galilee west of the lake including Jesus' hometown of Nazareth. The two Herods are frequently confused. Herod the Great was ruling at the time of Jesus' birth but died shortly afterward in 4 BC. Herod Antipas, son of Herod the Great, was the contemporary of Jesus. Herod Antipas sliced off the head of John the Baptist and was appropriately called a fox by Jesus (Luke 13:32). Since Jesus was from Galilee, Pilate referred him to Herod Antipas who happened to be in Jerusalem during the trial of Jesus. Herod Antipas, after ruling for 42 years, was banished in exile to Gaul by the Roman emperor.

A second son of Herod the Great, Phillip, was responsible to rule over the territory north and northeast of the lake of Galilee. He reigned peaceably over this turf for 37 years and is not featured in the gospel accounts since it was primarily a Gentile area. The third portion of Herod's kingdom, Judea and Samaria, was governed by his son Archelaus using Jerusalem as the center. Joseph, returning from Egypt with the baby Jesus, was afraid to go to Judea when he heard that Archelaus had succeeded his father, and so he settled instead in Nazareth located in Herod Antipas' territory (Matthew 2:22).

The three brothers—Herod Antipas, Phillip, and Archelaus—were required to meet the Roman emperor to confirm their father's will and legitimate their power. But Archelaus had trouble on his hands even before he could leave Jerusalem for the emperor's blessing. He removed the Jewish high priest and appointed a new one. During the Passover feast disturbances broke out. Archelaus promptly killed three thousand rioters, sent the rest of the pilgrims home, and left himself for Rome. The Roman officer who was to temporarily administer the southern part of Herod's kingdom until Archelaus was confirmed, robbed the temple treasury openly during Pentecost.

Fervent Jewish patriots could take no more—insurrection spread with leaders emerging simultaneously throughout the country. The whole land erupted with bloody disorders after Herod's death in 4 BC. A former slave of Herod's, named Simon, led a band of guerrillas which destroyed the Herodian palaces. In Judea a former shepherd named Athronges and his four brothers led a violent resistance movement against Archelaus for a number of years.[9] Judas the Galilean, whose father Hezekiah had been killed by Herod the Great for patriotic activities, was the brightest of the flaming revolutionaries. Judas led the revolt from the town of Sepphoris, an hour's walk northeast from Nazareth in Galilee. He plundered Herod's arsenal at Sepphoris. Since Archelaus was still in Rome, the Syrian governor in the north also under Rome's jurisdiction intervened. Sepphoris was burned to the ground, and its population sold into slavery. The Syrian governor continued south and killed two thousand of the rebel leaders, leaving the people in the countryside sullen and angry. This exploding turmoil indicates that the fuse on the politico-religious bomb in Palestine was burning rapidly near the end of Herod's reign.

Little is known about the short reign of Archelaus, 4 BC-AD 6. He apparently antagonized Jewish sensitivites, especially by marrying a woman who was divorced from her second husband. The Jewish indignation and hatred was so strong that both the Jews and the Samaritans sent a delegation to Rome pleading for the removal of Archelaus. Surprisingly, the Emperor Augustus agreed and sent Archelaus into exile in AD 6 during the childhood of Jesus.

This brought a significant change in the political organization of Judea. Now instead of being ruled by a quasi-Jewish king, it became a Roman province governed by a Roman procurator (sometimes called a prefect or governor) responsible directly to the Roman emperor. The Roman Empire had two different types of provinces:

(1) The more important and wealthy areas received a governor of senatorial rank called a *legate*. The Syrian legate, Quirinius, controlled Syria to the north of Palestine with a standing army of several legions, each consisting of up to 6,000 foot soldiers.

(2) Minor provinces like Judea, which required a few troops to keep order, received a governor called a *procurator* who was from a lower Roman social class than the legates.

The procurator was directly responsible to Caesar and had full military, judicial, and financial authority. Judea had only auxiliary troops recruited from the Gentile population of the country since the Jews were exempt from military service. The procurator had five cohorts of 600 men each under his command and garrisons were maintained throughout the country. A cohort of 300-500 soldiers was permanently stationed in Jerusalem in the Fort Antonia overlooking the temple area to prevent riots. The procurator lived in Caesarea on the Mediterranean coast but went to Jerusalem with additional support troops during Jewish festivals to make sure that the thousands of pilgrims didn't create a disturbance.

Dagger Men

When the first Roman procurator was sent to Judea in AD 6 to replace Archelaus, the Syrian legate, Quirinius, was sent to Jerusalem to take a census of the population for tax purposes. This first action under the new Roman connection met with strong resistance by stubborn Jewish nationalists who wanted a free homeland. The switch from the puppet King Archelaus to a direct Roman connection was dynamite in an already tense situation. The intensely nationalistic Zealots feared the body counting and felt that since the land belonged to God, all taxes also belonged to Him. Land and head taxes were viewed as a new form of bondage and idolatry.

Even though Galilee was not included in the census of AD 6, since it was under Herod Antipas' jurisdiction, Judas of Galilee continued the bloody rebellion. Slicing the Palestinian pie into three pieces had not destroyed the solidarity of Jewish nationalism. The zealous revolutionaries had their bases in caves throughout the Judean desert. They recruited followers from the oppressed rural peasants. After surprise attacks they would retreat into their cave hideouts in the desert. Often the Jewish peasants in settlements bore the brunt of the Roman revenge.[10]

The Zealots, so called because of their zeal for the law, didn't hesitate to use violence to free their homeland from oppressive Roman rule. Although their roots went back to the Maccabees in the second century BC, the Roman census conducted for tax purposes in AD 6 inflamed their indignation. In light of God's kingship the zealots declared that it was outright blasphemous to refer to the emperor as "king" and "lord." As far as they were concerned, this was a direct violation of the first commandment which prohibited the worship of other gods. Paying taxes to the emperor was considered idolatry and apostasy. The Zealots would not so much as even touch a coin which had the emperor's image imprinted on it. A subgroup of the Zealots known as "cut-throats" and "dagger men" were assassins who eagerly slit the throats of Romans, Jewish tax collectors, and other Jews who collaborated with the Romans. These dagger men were particularly active during the three annual pilgrim festivals in Jerusalem when the population of Jerusalem swelled to five times its normal size.

The slit and run tactics of the Zealot liberation front effectively maintained a climate of fear and unrest all over Palestine. In the Zealot mind, spilling the blood of a pagan or a Jew who cooperated with pagans was as honorable as bringing a special sacrifice to the temple altar in Jerusalem. Judas the Galilean and other Zealot leaders kept tightening the screws of violence on the Romans throughout the first century AD until the explosion of widespread revolution in AD 66. Religious zeal consumed and sustained the Zealots in their passion to rid Palestine of the Romans and set up an independent Jewish state. As one scholar has pointed out, "Of all the peoples within the Roman empire, none so persistently and steadfastly resisted, both politically and spiritually, the Roman occupation rule as did the Jews."[11]

Thus, as Jesus began His adult ministry, Palestine was in a state of boiling revolution. It was divided into three parts. Philip, Herod the Great's son, still ruled the region northeast of the Sea of Galilee as a quasi Jewish king. Herod Antipas, another son, ruled the Galilee area in similar fashion. The Roman procurator directed the Judean affairs in the south from his office on the seacoast port of Caesarea.

Pontius Pilate

Pontius Pilate, appointed in AD 26 was the fifth Roman procurator of Judea. Compared to the Jewish leaders, Pilate appears open and fair toward Jesus in the gospel accounts of the trial. But there is another side to Pilate. His administration was also characterized by brutal excesses which offended the Jewish religious sensibilities. Shortly after he had arrived, Pilate ordered troops to go from Caesarea to Jerusalem. They entered the city under cover of night with banners bearing the picture of the Emperor Tiberius. In the morning the idolatrous banners were discovered. Incensed Jews flocked to Caesarea demanding that the images, violating the second commandment, be removed. On the sixth day of the demonstration Pilate directed the mob into the Caesarea race course, surrounded them with soldiers, and threatened to kill them if they didn't return home peaceably. When he realized that they were willing to die, he ordered the offending banners withdrawn.

On another occasion Pilate dedicated some shields containing the inscription of the Emperor Tiberius in Herod's palace which served as Pilate's Jerusalem residence. Again this insulted the Jewish fathers who wanted Jerusalem consecrated exclusively to the worship of Yahweh. The Jewish citizens eventually protested to the Roman emperor who instructed Pilate to move the shields to the temple of Augustus in Caesarea. This is typical of the ways in which Pilate aggravated the Jewish temper.

Even the one positive contribution of his governorship ended in a clash. Pilate began the construction of an aqueduct to bring water to Jerusalem from 25 miles away. This would directly benefit the temple which needed huge quantities of water daily to purify the continual sacrifice of large animals. Pilate thought the temple treasury should pay for the cost since it would be an obvious beneficiary. The temple authorities protested this secular use of money which was dedicated to God. Pilate insisted and crowds of angry Jews gathered to protest the sacrilege. They were physically dispelled by Pilate's troops. Luke 13:1 may refer to such an occasion when Pilate mingled the blood of Galileans with their sacrifices.

Pilate's career ended in AD 36 when his troops squashed a group of Samaritans who had assembled on their holy mountain, Mt. Gerizim, to follow a self-acclaimed Samaritan messiah. After the Samaritan incident Pilate was recalled to Rome and lost his procuratorship. Philo of Alexandria described the conduct of Pilate's office as marked by "corruption, violence, degradations, ill treatment, offenses, numerous illegal executions and incessant, unbearable cruelty."[12]

Suicide at Masada

Roman and Jewish relations continued to deteriorate in the years between AD 36 and AD 66. Jewish freedom fighters who lived in caves in the country would frequently attack Romans and Jewish aristocrats who cooperated with the Roman occupation. The crisis came to a head in AD 66 when the procurator, Florus, stole seventeen talents from the temple treasury. Indignant Jews walked around Jerusalem begging for money for "poor Florus." Enraged, Florus allowed his soldiers to plunder the city. The daily animal sacrifice made on behalf of the Roman emperor's welfare was stopped by the temple priests. Insurgent Jewish rebels occupied the temple area forcing the governor to retreat to Caesarea.

Zealots under the leadership of Menahem, a son of Judas of Galilee, captured the Roman Fort Masada at the top of a well-protected peak near the Dead Sea. The Romans responded in AD 67 by conquering Galilee. Zealots from Masada and Galilee converged on Jerusalem for a final stand against the brutal Roman forces. During the Passover season in AD 70 the Roman General Titus, with an army of 24,000 men, launched an attack on Jerusalem. The Zealots were crushed by the Roman power. Before fire destroyed the temple, Titus grabbed the seven-branched candlestick and the table of shewbread to take as trophies back to Rome. A few of the Zealot rebels held out in the Masada fortress by the Dead Sea until AD 73. When the Romans finally gained access to the top of this mountainous summit, only one old woman was alive—the zealous patriots preferred suicide rather than defeat at the hands of the Romans. The utter destruction of Jerusalem by the Romans in AD 70 changed the course of both Jewish and Christian history.

During the period from 40 BC to AD 73 the Jewish historian Josephus mentions at least five Jewish military messiahs who led insurrections against the Roman occupation. Luke reports that Barabbas, released in exchange for Jesus, was in prison for starting an insurrection in the city (Luke 23:19). The flame of Jewish nationalism wasn't about to be extinguished by the Masada defeat. In AD 132, sixty years later, in response to Hadrian's edict forbidding circumcision, it burst forth again under the leadership of Bar Kochba who set up an independent Jewish state with a force of 200,000 men for three years. A whole Roman legion of 5, 000-6,000 soldiers was lost before Bar Kochba was cut down. The Romans smashed 1,000 villages, executed 500,000 people, and sent thousands away as slaves.

Although the Jews were usually permitted to perform their prescribed sacrificial rituals during the Roman occupation, there were underlying irritants. Since the time of Herod the Great the high priests were appointed and disposed of by the political head of state which meant that the high priest was really a Roman puppet. Furthermore, the eight-piece uniform worn by the high priest which symbolized the essence of Jewish faith was guarded by the Roman soldiers in the Fortress Antonia to prevent possible uprisings. It was given to the high priest only on festival days. Finally a daily sacrifice was offered in the temple to Yahweh on behalf of the Roman emperor.

And so we find Jesus facing the devil in the midst of this bloody revolutionary climate. The Palestine of Jesus' childhood was not serene. Only as we understand that it was filled with revolutionary fervor and military atrocities can we grasp the reality of His political temptation. The possibility of a political kingship was not an idle offer; it was the goal of the Zealot insurrectionists who were based in Galilee a few miles from Jesus' hometown.

The Low Mountain

The temptation Jesus rejected was not merely to join the ranks of Judas the Galilean. Although the Zealot bandits considered themselves the enemies of the Romans, both the Zealots and Romans used the same methodology of violence to force their will on others. If Judas the Galilean or Bar Kochba had been successful, they would have perpetuated and defended their new Jewish state with the same militant strategy of force used by the Romans. It was not only the temptation to unshackle the Roman control that Jesus struggled with, it was also a lure to endorse the accepted mode of governing by coercion and force.

This was the social institution which Jesus was rejecting high on the mountain. He was saying an emphatic "no" to the complex of social norms which assume that it is right and proper to govern others by brute force. According to the prevailing rules of the political power game played by both Romans and Zealots, death, violence, and bloodshed were legitimate tactics. Jesus rejected this right-side-up institution of coercive political power because He intended to demonstrate a new power—a new manner of ruling. He refused to play the game by the old rules, for He was about to show an upside-down way of governance.

Mountain Politics

The mountain symbolically represents this new version of divine power.[13] It was on the mountain that God met His people through Moses (Exodus 24). At the peak of the mountain God's people become energized with a new kind of power. On a mountain Jesus characterizes His new power as merciful, meek, pure in heart, and peaceful (Matthew 5). The disciples received their call on the mountain (Luke 6:12, 13).

After feeding the five thousand Jesus returned to the mountain for prayer and rejuvenation (Mark 6:46). The second divine confirmation that "this is my beloved son" came from the cloud at the top of a high mountain (Mark 9:2). From the Mount of Olives situated across the Kidron Valley from the Holy Mountain Jesus began His kingly descent into Jerusalem on a donkey (Matthew 21:1). A few days later in the same Mount of Olives He was arrested because He didn't resist capture (Luke 22:39). After the resurrection the disciples met Him on a mountain in Galilee where they had been directed by Him (Matthew 28:16). And on the Mount called Olivet the risen Jesus told His followers that they "shall receive power when the Holy Spirit has come upon you" (Acts 1:8, 12).

The mountain symbolizes the strength of divine power and the nearness of God. Jesus redefined the meaning of power when He refused to engage in the conventional use of force. It is hard to toss the lure of force aside. Matthew and Mark both report three occasions when Jesus spoke about suffering and dying as the new messianic form of power. Each time the disciples showed their lack of understanding by arguing over how much power and authority they would have in the kingdom. In all three cases, Jesus responded by teaching them about suffering discipleship. He made it clear that the heroes of the Upside-Down Kingdom are not warrior kings clothed in armor and surrounded by chariots. The heroes of this kingdom are children and servants. These lowly ones point out the way of this unusual kingdom. They operate not by the power of might and force but by the sustaining power of the Holy Spirit which flows from the Mountain of God.

Was Jesus a Cutthroat?

Because of the increased consciousness of international repression and revolution during the last two decades, Jesus has sometimes been portrayed as a modern Ho Chi Minh.[14] Jesus, it is said, was in fact a leader of the vicious Zealot movement. He espoused the bloody tactics of the Hebrew dagger men in order to expel the Romans. The proponents of the "Jesus was a Zealot" argument contend that Jesus actually was a violent revolutionary. They think that the Gospels, written approximately forty years after His death, glossed over His violence with sweet peace talk so that the early Christians wouldn't appear as a political threat to the Romans.[15] In other words the Gospel writers are said to have covered up the violent aspects of Jesus's life and presented Him as a peace loving shepherd. A number of reasons are given for placing Jesus with the Zealots.[16] He instructed the disciples to sell their clothing and buy swords at the Last Supper (Luke 22:35-38). He drove money changers out of the temple with a whip (John 2:15). The Romans who considered Him a political seditionist and agitator, crucified Him as "king of the Jews" (Luke 23:38). Barabbas, a known Zealot who had led a political insurrection, was apparently considered less dangerous than Jesus and was released instead of Jesus (Luke 23:25). In His own words Jesus said that He came to bring a sword—not peace (Matthew 10:34). Like the Zealots Jesus proclaimed the nearness of the kingdom of God. He spoke critically of kings who ruled over people (Mark 10:42) and even called Herod a fox (Luke 13:32). At least one of His followers, Simon the Zealot, had definite Zealot affiliations (Luke 6:15). These facets of Jesus's ministry are often used to place him with the Zealots.

In the Gospel accounts we find that Jesus was indeed a revolutionary—of sorts. He was a revolutionary in the sense that He defied the power of the prevailing religious, political, and economic institutions, but He was not a revolutionary in the sense of a violent anarchist. He was a revolutionary when He stated that the law of love supersedes the controls of human institutions.

I will not refute the allegation that Jesus was a Zealot point by point.[17] A few general observations set Jesus clearly apart from the Zealots. The Zealot's understanding of the kingdom stressed the need for man to help God usher in the kingdom. In contrast, Jesus told His followers, "Fear not, little flock, for it is your Father's good pleasure to give you the kingdom" (Luke 12:32). Although Jesus, like the Zealots, leveled a strong social criticism against the rich, it always was in the context of Mammon's threat to supplant God and His worship. The teaching on wealth would have also threatened Roman interests and should have been deleted by Gospel writers if they were merely attempting to placate Roman officials. Just because Jesus may have appeared to Pilate as a political revolutionary does not mean that He acted that way for one moment.

Purging the temple cannot be taken as a mandate for violence. Jesus was certainly dramatic and forceful. If a major riot had occurred, the 600 Roman soldiers on constant alert in Fort Antonia overlooking the temple area would have quickly intervened. The temple act was a prophetic condemnation of the profiteering money changers and the exclusion of the Gentiles from the fore court of the temple. The prophetic Word—not action—stood at the center of the temple purge. The one bit of ear-cutting resistance at the time of Jesus' "capture" in Gethsemane he severely rebuked. If the disciples had been heavily armed, a major clash would have developed. Had the disciples been perceived as a violent threat, they certainly would have been captured and crucified with Jesus instead of being allowed to flee into the darkness. The disciples of violent revolutionaries are normally also apprehended if their leader is captured.

Perhaps most convincing of Jesus' break with the Zealots is the fact that He warmly fellowshiped with tax collectors and publicans. The tax collectors were hated by the Zealots. They were patriotic traitors who made the system of Roman domination work. They were Jews who encouraged the Roman oppression of their fellowmen. Zealots wouldn't hesitate one moment to kill tax collectors. The fact that Jesus frequently initiated intimate fellowship with tax collectors infuriated Zealots. Jesus taught that the radical call of kingdom membership would weaken the coercive tug of other human institutions. The radical demands of following Him will bring division and conflict. It was this sword that He brought—the sword which the persecutors use against the church—not the sword of His followers. Jesus' message of joyous detachment from the pressures of human institutions stood in sharp contrast to the manipulative tactics of the Zealot subversives.

The final evidence that Jesus was not in the Zealot party comes from His teaching and His life. As we have already seen, He rejected the explicit political temptation on the mountain. In unambiguous language He instructs us to love enemies, do good to haters, bless cursers, and forgive up to 490 times. We are instructed to aspire to service instead of ruling. He demonstrates the way of love in parables where enemies help enemies. The paramount teaching is His own example before the cross. Under the agony of violence He refused to retaliate. With nails searing His flesh He refused to curse—but asked forgiveness for "they know not what they do."

We are forced to conclude that Jesus was a revolutionary in violating Sabbath laws, criticizing wealthy hoarders, eating with sinners, and agitating the masses. His message of the kingdom's break-in undercut the power and underscored the temporary character of the other social institutions. Consequently the Romans considered Him a threat to their false political tranquillity. The right-wing Sadducees hated His condemnation of their rich temple operation. The progressive Pharisees decried His irreverence of their laws. And the Zealot liberation front couldn't stand His talk about suffering. When Jesus foretold His suffering, Peter said, "No, Lord, not you." Jesus quickly shoved the temptation aside with, "Get behind me, Satan."

Of all three aspects of the temptation, the Zealot option of cutthroat violence was the most difficult one to shove aside because in so many ways He agreed with their diagnosis of the oppressive social situation. But to endorse and use violence would have negated His entire platform of suffering love. Jesus is a revolutionary who goes to the root of the problem—the evil in human hearts. He calls for repentance. He pleads for love regardless of social protocol. He announces that only God should be worshiped. He admits before Pilate that He is Lord of this new kingdom. Under His lordship aggressive love replaces violence as the dominant mode of action.

There is not a simple answer to the question, was Jesus a revolutionary. On the one hand, yes—He did threaten the status quo. He did rock the cozy boats of Sadducees, Romans, Pharisees, and Zealots alike. In many ways He probably appeared quite similar to the other social insurrectionists of His day. But on the other hand there is a definitive no. If He was a revolutionary, He was an upside-down one who had exchanged His dagger for words and acts of love. Love became the new Torah, the absolute norm in his Upside-Down Kingdom.

Questions for Discussion

1. Do you think the temptations were "real" temptations

in the sense that Jesus had the freedom to accept or reject them?

2. In your mind what was the most significant aspect of Jewish political history before Christ was born?

3. What modern situations call to mind the revolutionary situation in Palestine at the time of Jesus?

4. What nationalistic movements today are comparable to the Zealots?

5. Why were the disciples so slow to understand Jesus' approach to the use of force?

6. What does it mean to say that Jesus was a revolutionary?

7. What temptations to assume power do we face today?

3
TEMPLE PIETY

A Heavenly Parachute

Ruling the world by force from the Jerusalem mountaintop wasn't the only lure. There was religion itself to contend with. The devil's next trick invited Jesus to embrace institutionalized Jewish religion. This was a massive and complex social system infused with do's, don'ts, pilgrimages, and sacrifices. It was a huge octopus which encompassed all of life in Palestinian culture from civil law to national festivals.

The upside-down way was most certainly headed for a direct showdown with the religious heavyweights who operated the sacred institutions of Hebrew ritual in the name of God. Religious fervor runs deep and strong. Religious authorities would rage with anger as the way of Jesus cut through their cherished assumptions and practices. Their teeth would grind with hatred at the blasphemous suggestion that God was in their midst upsetting tables in their holy temple. The temple shrine was the apex of their entire religious system. A miraculous appearance—as a sudden bolt out of heaven—would certainly convince even the most skeptical Sadducee or Pharisee. Why not ask God to accredit or certify His mission from the very beginning? This would circumvent all the harassment from the religious leaders. A divine legitimation within the sacred boundaries of the temple territory would guarantee the fervent support of the temple priestly hierarchy. The masses and crowds would quickly follow if the scribes and wise men unconditionally embraced the newcomer. The temple imagery invited immediate and miraculous intervention within the prescribed religious system as a public seal of the Messiah's authority.

Twenty-Six Acres of Piety

The temple in Jerusalem was the focal point of Jewish religious life for the 500,000 Jews living in Palestine and also for the 3 ½ million Jews scattered throughout the Roman empire. There was one Jewish altar where the high priest performed the sacrificial rites of atonement each year for the entire Jewish community. There was one and only one holy of holies where the high priest entered the presence of God annually. Regardless of where the arteries of Jewish religion flowed, they all pulsated with the heartthrob of the Jerusalem temple in the holy city of David. It is most natural for the cunning devil to take Jesus to the temple for temptation.

Moderns attempting to visualize the temple tend to think of a contemporary church building with the capacity to seat 200-300 persons. A modern shopping center covering many acres might be a better representation. The temple area covered over twenty-six acres and was surrounded by magnificent marble colonades. The temple building itself was 150 feet square and sixty feet high. Gold and silver covered much of the structure including the roof and the furnishings. From the distant countryside it appeared as a snowcapped peak on the holy mountain. There was so much gold in the temple that after its destruction and plunder in AD 70 the province of Syria was glutted with gold reducing its value by half.[1]

A Hebrew proverb exclaimed, "He who has not seen the holy place in its detailed construction has never seen a splendid building in his life."[2] Even the disciples of Jesus were impressed when they remarked with awe, "Look, Teacher, what wonderful stones and what wonderful buildings!" (Mark 13:1). Approximately 18,000 workmen lost their jobs when the temple reconstruction begun by Herod in 20 BC was finally completed in AD 62.

About 18,000 priests and Levites divided into twenty-four groups called "courses" were involved in running the temple.[3] These lay priests and Levites lived in the countryside of Galilee and Judea and came to the temple for a one-week tour of duty twice a year. They also came during the three annual festivals attended by Jewish pilgrims from all over the world. In addition to the regular priests in the temple area there were money changers who sold pilgrims "pure" money for their tithes and livestock dealers who sold animals for sacrifice. A bureaucratic elite of chief priests administered the total operation. When the temple veil was purified, 300 priests were needed to dip it in a tank of water. Two hundred Levites were needed each evening to close the temple doors. The temple treasury, functioning as a huge national bank, contained the tithes and offerings required of Jews throughout the world and held title to a considerable amount of property. The temple was no small business. It was an elaborate operation which generated the major source of revenue for the city of Jerusalem.

Devout Jews, even from beyond Palestine, came to the temple three times a year to celebrate festivities centering around the temple. In the spring the Feast of Passover celebrated the deliverance from Egypt. About fifty days later the Feast of Pentecost was observed to give thanks for the first fruits of the harvest. In the fall the Feast of Tabernacles included a solemn march around the altar to thank God for the completed harvest. In addition to the pilgrim feasts, the great Day of Atonement was celebrated in the autumn when the high priest sacrificed a goat for his own sins and sent another one into the desert for the sins of the people.[4] During these pilgrim festivals, Jerusalem's normal population of about 25,000 exploded upwards to 180,000 people.[5]

The temple stood as a monumental reminder that the Jews as God's elect people, had direct access to Him through their sacrificial ritual. Each morning and each afternoon the "continual" burnt offering in the form of an unblemished lamb was sacrificed on behalf of the whole community of Israel. An offering of incense mixed with spices also burned daily. After the major communal sacrifice, private sacrifices were offered by devout Jews. The priests were involved in various duties including removing ashes from the altar, preparing firewood, killing the lamb, sprinkling blood on the altar, cleaning the lampstand, and preparing the meal and drink offering.[6]

According to Jeremias, the temple was the most important building of all in Jerusalem. It was the home of Jewish worship and symbolized the presence of God on earth. Persons came to pray because here their prayers went directly to the ear of God. Here the Nazarite on completion of his vows and the Gentile convert offered their sacrifices. The wife suspected of adultery was brought to judgment here. To the temple the people brought their first fruits and the mothers presented offerings for their purification at the birth of each child. From all over the world Jews sent their temple tax and three times a year the whole world of Jewry flooded here for festivities.[7]

The temple represented more than nice symbolism: it was also the seat of Jewish power and influence. Here resided the high priest, priest of all priests and the 70-member Sanhedrin, the final and ultimate Jewish authority in religious, political, and civil matters.

Sanitized Piety

The high priest was the most important member of the

priesthood and of the nation itself. He was clothed in a splendid eight-part outfit, each piece thought to have atoning power for specific types of sins. The high priest was the only person with the unique privilege of entering the holy of holies on the Day of Atonement each year. He also officiated at the sacrifices on the Sabbath and during the pilgrim festivals. Even his death had atoning power, since slayers who had fled to a city of refuge because of accidentally killing someone could return home upon the high priest's death.

He was subject to extremely strict laws of ceremonial purity. He could not touch a corpse or enter a house of mourning. Since a high priest was once contaminated by an "Arab's spittle" on the evening before the Day of Atonement, the high priest was required to undergo a seven-day purification period secluded in a special room. No one was to see him naked or when he was shaving or taking a bath. The purity of his pedigree had to be immaculate with direct ties back to the family of Aaron. Strict marital rules permitted him to marry only a twelve-year-old virgin who was the daughter of a priest, Levite, or Israelite of pure descent. Many priests married the daughters of other priests.

The high priest's role was not merely pompous and ceremonial. The locus of considerable power rested on his lap since he also was the president of the seventy member Jerusalem Sanhedrin. This great council had complete judicial and administrative authority in religious and civil matters. Its judgment on religious issues was respected far beyond the borders of Judea. It was a self-perpetuating body made up of chief priests, scribes (usually from the Pharisee party), and noble lay persons. Although lower courts met in various districts of Judea, the Sanhedrin was the supreme Jewish authority. The power of the high priest grew considerably under the Roman procurators after AD 6 since he was the key spokesman for the Jewish people, not only in ceremonial matters but also in political negotiations with the

Romans. This religious and political clout was wielded by only a few wealthy uppercrust families in Jerusalem. Sixteen of the eighteen high priests between AD 6 and 67 came from five of the prominent families.[8]

Under the powerful high priest and Sanhedrin flowed an extensive hierarchy and pecking order of other subordinate religious officials. The captain of the temple was responsible for the conduct of worship and the management of the temple staff. He ranked next to the high priest in prestige since he often assisted the high priest in performing his solemn duties. On the next rung were twenty-four priests who directed the twenty-four groups of approximately 7,200 ordinary priests, living throughout the countryside who participated in temple ritual at least five times a year. Next there were 156 priests who served as the daily managers of the group of priests assigned to temple duty for that particular day.

The temple's administrative affairs were the responsibility of seven permanent overseers. Next in line came three treasurers who managed the temple treasury by collecting tax, purchasing sacrificial materials, and supervising the sale of animals to pilgrims. They also maintained the ninety-three gold and silver vessels needed for the daily ritual and managed the land and property owned by the temple. Next in rank were the ordinary priests, approximately 7,200 in number (like Zechariah in Luke 1:5) who lived in the countryside but who came at least five times a year to perform their sacred duties.

At the bottom of the ladder came the Levites numbering almost 10,000. They also lived in the surrounding villages but were responsible for temple work when their weekly shift was on duty. The Levites were inferior to the priests but still enjoyed a prestige distinction. Singers and musicians formed the upper level of the Levite crust, while the rest were involved in the dirty work of the temple: gatekeeping, police duty, and sweeping the open parts of the temple area.[9]

Temple Piety

The political, social, and religious affairs of all Judea and international Judism were oriented toward the great temple in Jerusalem. Synagogues in each village throughout the countryside faced the holy temple. The temple's influence permeated the hinterland through the network of 18,000 priests and Levites whose social and religious status was tied into the temple operation. The frequent pilgrimages and trips for sacrifice cemented even the ordinary Jewish peasant into the temple's mystique. It was to the peak of this huge sacred operation that the devil led Jesus for testing.

Laying Down the Law

At the heart of the temple operation and at the core of all Jewish religion lay the Torah.[10] Usually known as the "law," it is more accurately translated the "doctrine" or "religious teaching." In the most particular sense it referred to the five books of Moses—the Pentateuch. Gradually, however, students of the Torah built up an excessive tradition of interpretation or commentary on the Torah. This "fence around the Torah" translated the Torah into daily life. So in a general sense the Torah meant not only the five books of Moses but also the meticulous oral commentary which grew up around it.

The Torah, it was believed, contained the absolute and unquestionable will of God. Obedience to it was a test of a person's obedience to God. A cult of worship developed around the Torah even to the extent of personifying it as the "well beloved daughter of God." It was said that Yahweh devoted His leisure hours to the study of the Torah—even reading it aloud on the Sabbath. It was regarded as the unalterable rule and absolute standard for all aspects of religious life—the only source of God's truth. Continual reading and discussion of the Torah was the most sacred religious activity. In the commentary of tradition which had grown up around the Torah, the pious Jew could discover whether or not it was lawful to eat an egg laid on the Sabbath. One could learn whether water poured from a clean bucket into an unclean one also contaminated the clean one from which it had been poured. The ritual of sacrifice in the Jerusalem temple and the worship in each village synagogue rested solidly on the highly esteemed and revered Torah.

As we have seen, the priests and Levites provided the expertise and manpower for the operation of the temple. In the case of the Torah, the scribes explained its secret meanings.[11] The jungle of traditions which had grown up around the Torah could only be unraveled by a carefully trained scribe—also known as a "doctor of the law." Scribes were also reverently called "rabbi," "teacher," "master," and "father." The role of the scribes emerged, along with the synagogue, probably in the period of Babylonian exile. They wore a special robe which was a long mantle reaching to their feet and etched with a fringe. Because of the scribes' esteemed status, people would rise respectfully as these men of wisdom passed by on the street. The highest seats of honor in the synagogue were reserved for the scribes, since they had precedent in honor even over the aged and parents.

Knowledge of the Torah and its traditions gave the scribes their power and high status among the people. Often in their early teens young men would prepare for a scribal career by taking a regular course of study for several years. The young student would follow an older rabbi for years until he had mastered the fine points of the Torah and its commentary. When he had reached the prescribed age of possibly 40, the student was ordained as a full-fledged member of the company of scribes with the full rights of an ordained scholar. After ordination he was able to make his own decisions on issues of religious legislation, ceremonial purity, and criminal and civil proceedings. Only these ordained scholars could transmit and create the traditions of the Torah.

In addition to the high priests and noble families, the

scribe was the only other type of person who could have membership in the powerful Sanhedrin. Young Jews from all over the world streamed to Jerusalem at the time of Jesus to sit at the feet of teachers whose influence was felt throughout the whole international Jewish community. Jerusalem was the intellectual center of Judaism's theological knowledge. Jeremias summarizes their status by saying, "The scribes were venerated, like the prophets of old, with unbounded respect and reverential awe as bearers and teachers of sacred esoteric knowledge; their words had sovereign authority."[12]

Party Politics

So far in our exploration of institutionalized Jewish religion we've identified the formal roles of the religious structure: priests, Levites, and scribes. We have also looked briefly at the temple, Sanhedrin, and synagogue. In addition to these formalized jobs and organizations, there were two major religious political parties—the Sadducees and the Pharisees. These two opposing parties developed during the Maccabean era in the second century before Christ. They had both religious and social differences. The crucial religious watershed between them was their understanding of the Torah. The Sadducees accepted only the written Torah—the five books of Moses—as authority. They refused to accept the oral commentary on the Torah which the Pharisees developed. They were staunch defenders of the true Torah without any commentary or practical application. In addition the Sadducees denied the resurrection, personal immortality, and the future life. They also rejected belief in demons and angels. In sum the Sadducees represented the conservative religious element of Judaism. They were the defenders of the true faith of Israel handed down by Moses.

Socially the Sadducees lived primarily in Jerusalem and were members of the wealthy aristocracy. Many of the chief priests and leaders of the noble families were members of the

Sadducean party. They were closely involved with the operation of the temple and held dominating influence in the Sanhedrin. In short, they controlled the wealthy Jerusalem upperclass—both in religious and social affairs. This meant that they supported both the political and religious establishment in Jerusalem. They were warm toward Roman political control as long as sacrifices to Yahweh could be made on the temple altar and they retained their privileged status. Thus the Sadducees were the conservatives of their day in religious, political, and social spheres.

In contrast, the Pharisaic party represented the progressive wing of Judaism.[13] They were not violently radical like the Zealots, but as the liberals of their day they insisted on applying the Torah to practical everyday issues. The Pharisees, or "separated ones," were the primary developers of the oral tradition or commentary which applied the Torah to almost any hypothetical situation a devout Jew might face. While the Torah itself laid down rules of purity for the officiating priests alone, the Pharisees attempted to make these rules binding for the everyday life of the priests and for the common people in general. By encouraging even the average citizen to follow the priestly details of purity, they hoped to build all the people of Israel into a holy priesthood.

The Pharisees are often confused with the scribes. While it is true that the leaders and influential members of the Pharisees were usually scribes, most of their members came from an assortment of pious common people. Many of the scribes were not members of the Pharisee party. In contrast to the Jerusalem based Sadducees, the Pharisees operated throughout the rural countryside actively promoting their doctrine in local synagogues. They were the champions of the common people in opposition to the rich Sadducean elite.

Although they gained the support of people from all walks of life, they numbered only about 6,000 since they insisted on extremely strict rules for ceremonial purity and tithing. Before joining, prospective members had to go through a year of probation to prove they were able to observe the meticulous laws of purity. The Pharisees bucked the ruling establishment in Jerusalem and they also disdained common people who were careless and indifferent to ceremonial purity and tithing. They were strict on legalism but were open and receptive to new applications of doctrine—ever seeking to bend the Torah relevantly for new situations.

Messianic Wishes

At the birth of Jesus, messianic hopes were alive in the minds of Palestinian villagers. The expectation of a Messiah who would usher in the peaceable reign of the kingdom of God were intensifying during the century before the birth of Christ. Although many variations of the hope persisted, the predominant vision was for a new ruler, one anointed by God who would reestablish the Davidic throne and the glories of the former empire. *The Psalms of Solomon,* written the century before Christ, picture the Messiah as one who will overthrow the Gentiles who have rudely intruded in God's holy place. He will also chase out the corrupt priests who have perverted the worship of Yahweh. The scattered tribes will be reassembled in the promised land, and days of unparalleled blessedness will blossom. Jerusalem, the holy city of God's presence, will be supreme internationally, "a place to be seen in all the earth."[14] The vision of the messianic reign is reiterated to Mary by the Angel Gabriel in Luke 1:32, 33:

> He will be great, and will be called the Son of the Most High;
> and the Lord God will give to him the throne of his father David,
> and he will reign over the house of Jacob for ever;
> and of his kingdom there will be no end.

A similar refrain comes from the mouth of Zechariah, the father of John the Baptist, as recorded in Luke 1:68-72:

Blessed be the Lord God of Israel,
for he has visited and redeemed his people,
and has raised up a horn of salvation for us
in the house of his servant David,
as he spoke by the mouth of his holy prophets from of old,
that we should be saved from our enemies,
and from the hand of all who hate us;
to perform the mercy promised to our fathers.

There was uncertainty on exactly how the presence of the Messiah would be manifest. Some thought He would come out of the skies riding on a cloud, while others expected Him to be born of man but suddenly be revealed in a decisive disclosure. Jerusalem, home of the great temple, was also the classroom for study and debate of messianic texts like these.

The temptation account doesn't specify the exact detail of the temple jump; possibly it was over the edge of the temple wall falling hundreds of feet into the Kidron Valley below. Or perhaps the temptation was to descend into the court at the entrance of the temple. Regardless of the mode of divine parachuting, the meaning of the temptation was a plea to legitimate miraculously beyond any reasonable doubt the fact of the Messiah's arrival. It was to take place at the center of Jewish religious life where things were done properly in accordance with the exact letter of the law. The scribes, Sanhedrin, high priest, and other religious heavyweights would serve as sacred witnesses to certify the authenticity of the Messiah's arrival.

This would save all the bitter confrontations and hassles with the religious establishment. The powerful aristocracy controlling Jerusalem politics would accept such a miraculous feat with welcome arms. There would be no need for wandering among the poor people of the land around Galilee. This trick done with strict and proper religious protocol would guarantee the approval of the total religious establishment.

Upside-Down Messiah

Although the thought of receiving the blessing of the mammoth Jewish religious establishment must have been tantalizing to Jesus, He chose to reject this right-side-up form of religion. This temptation continued to make its appeal right up to the crucifixion, for as the guards were arresting Him in Gethsemane, Jesus reminded the ear-cutting disciple that He could call down more than 72,000 angels to His defense. Rather than succumbing to institutionalized Jewish religion, Jesus uprooted its very foundations. He deliberately told parables which insinuated harsh judgment on the Jewish leaders. He intentionally violated some sacred Sabbath laws. And in what the religious leaders considered an act of profanity, he chased out the temple merchants and called the holy shrine a den of robbers. He did not completely overturn established religion. He taught in the synagogue and in the temple. He told cured lepers to show themselves to the priest according to tradition. He directed Peter to catch a fish to pay the temple tax. But he directly confronted institutionalized religion wherever and whenever it became idolatrous or oppressive in burdening the faithful.

Jesus with His upside-down style of religion was not about to bless the oppressive religious structures which ranked men according to pious deeds. He replaced the machinery of formalized religion with compassion and love. Jesus Himself would become the new high priest. His Holy Spirit moved the sacred holy of holies out of the temple and into the mind of each person. No longer would men worship the Father in a holy temple or from a sacred mountain but from now on they would approach Him in spirit and in truth (John 4:23). Jesus' own prophesy of the temple's destruction and prediction of raising it up again in three days (His resurrection) became data for accusing Him at His trial (John 2:19, Mark 14:58). The upside-down way meant that from now on the Holy Spirit would live in each believer's temple—no longer constrained to an elaborate building and ritual procedure structured by man. In His own words He tells us, "Something greater than the temple is here" (Matthew 12:6).

Jesus Himself would be the final sacrifice—the unblemished lamb of God slain not only for the sins of the Jewish community, but for the sins of the whole world. Jesus held the secrets of the new Torah—the law of love which superseded the legalistic details of the first five books. The new law of love overlooked the picayune details of ceremonial cleansing, washing, and sacrificing. Jesus affirmed upside-down religion when He told a scribe he was close to the kingdom of God when he realized that love for God, self, and neighbor was much more important than all the burnt offerings and sacrifices (Mark 12:34). In Jesus we have upside-down religion—no building, program, or hierarchical clergy but a final sacrifice, a definitive offering, a new temple in each believer's heart, and a supreme Torah of love.

Jesus rejected the opportunity for elaborate display. In fact He prefered the messianic secret. He was very slow to disclose His identity throughout His ministry. He spoke in riddles and parables. He forbid the miraculously cured to speak. This was no arrogant horn-blowing Messiah. The Pharisees didn't find a magician who performed special signs. His life itself was the sign. Care for the lost, compassion for the poor, and love for all were the messianic signs. The heroes of upside-down religion were not the scribes, chief priests, Pharisees, or Sadducees—not the religious influentials of the day. Surprisingly the new heroes were repentant sinners, publicans, tax collectors, and harlots—the throwaways of institutionalized religion.

Questions for Discussion

1. How does the picture of the temple in this chapter compare with your previous knowledge of the temple?

2. What are some parallels between institutionalized religion in Judaism and institutionalized religion now?

3. Do we have any "oral law" today which serves as a commentary on the Scripture?

4. Why was Jesus so cautious about his messianic identity?

5. If you had been Mary or Zechariah, what kind of Messiah would you have expected?

6. In what ways are we tempted to engage in elaborate religious display?

4
WILDERNESS BREAD

Welfare King

The temptation to turn stones into bread is often taken as a personal temptation to Jesus to squelch His private hunger. Although this interpretation may hold a grain of meaning, its full essence lies in a grasp of the economic condition of the masses in Palestine. Bread symbolizes the heart of economic life. It's the universal cornerstone of many diets as it reappears on tables meal after meal week after week. Not only in the temptation but also in the Lord's prayer—"give us this day our daily bread"—it stands for the basic economic necessities of life. In His personal hunger Jesus was empathizing with the thousands of poor peasants whose entire existence was organized around hunger pangs. His convulsing stomach made it urgent to do something for the others who suffered likewise.

The temptation however is not to gobble down boulders of bread to relieve a forty-day fast.[1] The thought of bread in the wilderness reminds Jesus of God's limitless manna freely distributed during the forty-year walk through the desert. Memories of hometown Nazareth also come to mind. Poor peasant farmers are pushed off their land by ruthless creditors. He sees visions of masses suffering under a system of double taxation. The lepers, blind, and poverty stricken, removed from productivity and trampled on by religious and social practices cry out for help. Why not miraculously feed the masses and throw a divine banquet for His followers? Freely disbursing food would solidify a broad base of social support in Galilee.

Even the religious authorities were afraid of the power of the masses. The nighttime arrest of Jesus was prompted by the fear of the crowds. Jesus Himself perceived that the mob spirit of a well-fed crowd could seize Him and make Him King by force (John 6:15). Bread was the quickest way to the heart of the crowd. The power of the crowd was no figment of the imagination. Mark peppers His gospel account with many references to the crowd and multitude from all over the countryside—numbering in the thousands—following Jesus wherever they could. Luke 12:1 says that the surging multitude was packed together so tightly that they trampled each other down. Neither Pilate nor the high priest could defuse the contagious solidarity of mob action.

The temptation was more than illegitimate abuse of crowd power. It pretended to reduce the incarnate God to a welfare king. The enticing thoughts came one after another: "Alleviate their poverty without suffering." "Let the religious authorities continue in their idolatry." "Don't preach the judgment of God on the den of robbers—just distribute bread to the hungry." "Avoid the causes of economic injustice in the temple system and Roman occupation—just provide bread for the poor Galilean peasants and let the rest of the world go by." This devilish sidetrack represented the tendency to reduce man to a mere physical organism devoid of spirit and soul—a mere bread-eating animal without ideas and emotions created in the image of God. This bread temptation in the wilderness focused squarely on the economic structures of Palestine that created and perpetuated hungry masses.

Plush Aristocrats

We have seen the spectacular beauty of Jerusalem as Judaism's highest religious peak. It also towered above the rest of the country in social and economic prestige. An elite aristocracy called Jerusalem their home.[2] This included the chief priests of the temple hierarchy, wealthy landowners, merchants, tax collectors, and the Sadducean Party. Men of wealth who could live off of the rent from their estates, skilled artists, clever traders, and poets all migrated toward the metropolis which housed the temple. Jerusalem wasn't merely the foremost of Judean cities; there actually were no second- or third-rate ones.

Extravagance oozed from the affluent elite. They wrapped gold bindings around the palm branches which they carried to festive temple ceremonies. They brought their offering of first fruits in golden vessels on Pentecost. A city ordinance prohibited them from covering their phylacteries with gold. Two men are reported to have wagered the equivalent of more than a year's salary on being able to anger one of the leading rabbis.

Many of the rich in Jerusalem derived their wealth from vast estates in the country. These were worked by slaves and hired men or rented to tenants. One of Herod's chancellors owned an entire village. It was said that another person had inherited 1,000 villages, 1,000 ships, and so many slaves that they didn't know their master. According to the sages a man of wealth was one who had a hundred vineyards, a hundred fields, and a hundred slaves to work them. Some of the special artists working in the temple received the equivalent of three hundred dollars a day. At the same time unskilled workers in Jerusalem received their food and about 25 cents for a day's work.

The wife of one high priest had the distance from her house to the temple carpeted so she could walk without injuring her barefeet on the Day of Atonement when everyone was required to go barefoot. An uppity-up snobbishness permeated the culture of Jerusalem's elite. They would not sign a document as a witness unless they were sure the other witnesses were also well-to-do. They would only accept a dinner invitation if they were assured that the other guests were of high social status. Their arrogance kept them from mingling with the masses of common people except to employ them as slaves and hired men.

The rich class gave large dowries when their daughters married. One such dowry exceeded a million gold denari. (A single denarius was the equivalent of a day's wage.) The exorbitant status of Jerusalem in contrast to the countryside also emerged in "mixed" marriages. A small town man who took a Jerusalem bride was required to give his weight in gold as a betrothal gift. If the bride was from the country she also brought her weight in gold to her Jerusalem groom. Joseph of Arimathea described in the Scriptures (Matthew 27:57) as a rich man was undoubtedly part of this rich upper crust. Jerusalem also had a sizable middle class of retail traders and craftsmen as well as a poor segment.

Scum of the Earth

Over 90 percent of the population did not have prestigious social connections or financial means. These masses were known as the "people of the land." At one time this designation meant simply the common people, but later it specifically referred to those who were careless and nonchalant in their observance of the laws of Moses. The Pharisees avoided contact with them and refused to eat with them. They were looked down on with contempt, so much so that according to rabbinical law they could not appear as a witness in court nor be appointed as the guardian of an orphan. The Pharisees would not marry them and considered their women as unclean vermin. In the final analysis the term "people of the land" was used primarily to distinguish between the urban and rural population.

Galilee, sixty miles to the north of Jerusalem, was the main center for these "scum of the earth" people. Galilee was the richest in resources and the most densely populated area of Palestine. Before the reign of Herod the Great, many Gentiles purchased land there. But in the last half of the century before Christ it was resettled by Jewish immigrants so that by the birth of Christ the predominant population was Jewish. Herod Antipas, the ruling king of the area, built the city of Tiberias along the Sea of Galilee as his capital. He minted coins without his image on them to placate the Jewish population. The region, however, still carried its former stigma since it continued to be known as "Galilee of the Gentiles."

The Galilean population of about 350,000 included a large number of slaves and about 100,000 Jews who had accepted the Greek way of life embraced by Herod Antipas. The people of this area had little education and were ignorant of the fine points of the law, although they did have a synagogue in each village. They were so overwhelmed with the burden of making a living that they had little time to worry about the minute details of ritual purity. Although the following description by a Pharisee must be taken with a grain of salt, it does show the bitter resentment which the Pharisees held toward these unorthodox people of the land.

> A Jew must not marry the daughter of the people of the land for they are unclean animals and their women forbidden reptiles. And with respect to their daughters the scriptures write, "cursed be he that lieth with any manner of beast" (Deuteronomy 27:21). . . . Said R. Eleazar: one may butcher a people of the land on a Day of Atonement that happens to fall on a Sabbath (when any kind of work such as butchering constitutes a violation of a double prohibition). His disciples said to him, master, say "slaughter" (instead of the vile word butcher). But he replied "slaughtering requires a benediction, butchering does not require a benediction."[3]

Although gross exaggerations, they communicate the hatred of the religious aristocracy toward the common people of Galilee. The feeling was mutual, for it was also said that the people of the land hate the Jewish scholars more than the heathen hate Israel. Another rabbi, who once had been a member of the people of the land himself, said, "When I was a people of the land, I used to say, 'I wish I had one of those scholars, and I would bite him like an ass.' " His disciples said, "You mean like a dog." He replied, "An ass's bite breaks the bone; a dog's does not."[4] Among these provincial, backward, and naive people of Galilee a fierce streak of Jewish nationalism bubbled out in the insurrection led by Judas the Galilean. This revolutionary fervor was directed not only at the occupying Romans but also at the rich Jerusalem aristocracy which accommodated and courted them. Nazareth, a village in the heart of the people-of-the-land country, was hometown for Jesus.

Although Galilee was a rich and fertile farming area with a major fish exporting enterprise along the Lake of Galilee, the masses of the people ironically lived in dismal poverty. The majority were forced to get along with one set of clothing. There was a saying that "the daughters of Israel were comely but poverty makes them repulsive." Oppresive economic factors created the political turmoil and restlessness in first-century Galilee. The social ferment resulted not merely from irritating Roman rule or irrational nationalism but from the increasingly harsh economic grind.[5] Taxes had been high during the era of Herod the Great but most of them were at least funneled into the magnificent temple at Jerusalem and were consecrated to God. Even so, at Herod's death a delegation of Jews to Rome complained to the emperor that he derived much of his wealth by confiscating land and goods. It is estimated that Herod the Great may have privately owned one half to two thirds of his kingdom.[6]

Much of Galilee was divided into large estates owned by

wealthy merchants and Sadducees living in Jerusalem and by Gentile landowners who lived outside of Palestine. The parables of Jesus also attest to this condition with their numerous references to absentee landowners who placed a steward in charge of their property to supervise the work of day laborers. Peasant farmers also owned small plots of land. But they were gradually losing the ownership of their plots because of their debts. The small farmers were forced to mortgage their property to pay their taxes which often amounted to half of their harvest. Tax collectors and estate owners took possession of the land of peasants who continued to accumulate outstanding debts. Often the peasant family would end up trapped on the plot, working as day laborers for the wealthy and absent landholders. André Trocmé describes the situation: "Within a few decades, small and middle-sized plots of land had disappeared, whereas the properties owned by the temple and the imperial crown grew beyond proportion. . . . Driven to misery, many peasants abandoned their land and joined bands of robbers that survived by pillage and lived in caves in the mountains."[7]

God's IRS

At the core of the poverty was a system of double taxation which was overbearing to the poor peasant. First, two dozen or so different types of Jewish tithes and offerings were required of the devout Jew. On top of this religious system were the numerous taxes which the Romans extracted. Although it is difficult to calculate the exact proportion of taxes, most scholars agree that forty to seventy percent of the peasant's annual income eventually fell into the hands of various kinds of tax collectors and creditors.

The religious taxes were prescribed by Jewish law. First was the half shekel temple tax which Jewish males over the age of twenty were required to pay each year. The equivalent of two denarii, or about a two days' wages, this tax was due at the beginning of the Passover month each spring. A few weeks before the beginning of the month, tax collectors armed with power to collect went into the regional districts to gather the tax from persons who would not be pilgrimaging to Jerusalem for the Passover. In Matthew 17:24 we find the account of these collectors asking Peter for the tax. A few days before the Passover the collectors would return to Jerusalem.

This tax, used for the operation and maintenance of the temple, could only be paid in the form of a Tyrian silver coin because it contained a higher quality silver than most coins. Since the Roman denarius was the widely used currency, money changers exchanged the Tyrian silver for the common denarius, often at considerable profit.

The farmer also gave an offering of the firstfruits of his crop as a sign of gratitude for the coming harvest. Then there was a tithe of the harvest itself and a tithe of the herd which were to be used to support the Levites. In the time of Jesus, the priests in Jerusalem would take the tithe—sometimes by force—preventing it from ever reaching the Levites. There was also a second tithe for the poor. There may have even been an additional tithe for the poor every third year. Farmers were also required to leave gleanings on the field for the poor. On top of this was the sabbatical year practice of leaving the land fallow every seventh year "involving the loss of at least a year-and-a-half of agricultural produce in every seven-year cycle—a crushing burden, indeed, upon a people which was unable in any year to save a substantial part of the crop."[8]

The Pharisees at the time of Jesus were tithing the herbs from their gardens—a practice which Jesus called inconsistent in light of their negligence of justice and mercy (Matthew 23:23). In addition, there were many personal contributions such as peace and sin offerings and offerings for the dedication of a child.

The Roman IRS

After the religious taxes came the crushing Roman tribute. The efficient Roman bureaucracy collected taxes on men, houses, animals, sales, imports, and exports. First a land tax took about one-fourth of the crop. Then a poll or per capita tax was levied on each male over the age of fourteen and on each female over the age of twelve.[9] The land and poll taxes were gathered by tax collectors appointed by the Roman government from the ranks of well-to-do families. They had to guarantee the receipt of taxes from their own resources. Police accompanied the tax collectors and were sometimes guilty of abuses.

In addition to the Roman land and personal tax, there were numerous tariffs and tolls such as import duties, bridge and road tolls, and market fees. The collectors of these tolls, known as publicans, worked for "tax farmers" who had successfully offered the highest bid for the toll income of a certain district over a period of time. The publicans, especially, exploited the public's ignorance of the toll fees and were regarded as utter deceivers.[10] The market in Jerusalem, which had been farmed out to a tax collector, assessed all the patrons bringing produce for sale. Most of the tax farmers were Jews who worked for the Romans.

Because fraud and force were integral parts of both the religious and political tax collection system, the common people held the collectors and publicans in utter contempt. Since the Jews never regarded the Roman rule as legitimate, taxes were viewed as outright robbery. The rabbis made no distinction between a tax collector, thief, or extortioner. Gentile rulers in Palestine were seen as robbers with no rights over the land or its people.[11] Even in the Gospels we find tax collectors categorized with sinners. Records indicate that the taxation was so oppressive that Syria and Judea begged for a reduction in AD 17. The suffocating nature of taxes and debts is also underscored by the fact that, when the Galilean

Zealots gained control of Jerusalem in AD 66, the first thing they did was to burn all the debt records stored in the Jerusalem archives to prevent future retaliation by the rich.

Very Rich and Very Poor

The historical picture that emerges in Galilee is not a three-tier economic class structure as in Jerusalem, but a structure of only wealthy land holders—usually absent—and poor masses struggling to eke out an existence under the weight of two tax systems. In Galilee the middle class was absent. The biographer of Herod Antipas, ruler of the area, says, "It can be safely concluded that there existed both the extremely rich and the miserably poor, the latter being the lot of the majority of the people."[12] The parables and sayings of Jesus also assume a two-class system of rich and poor.

The bite of Roman taxes was particularly irksome because, as political taxes, they were no longer going primarily to rebuild the temple as they did under Herod the Great. Now they were financing a foreign army and the luxuries of a faraway empire.

In this poor Galilean setting we find Jesus growing up. Two additional bits of evidence in the Gospels confirm His anchorage with the poor peasants of Galilee. Mary describes herself as a person of "low estate" in her song of exaltation (Luke 1:48). The prescribed offering for the dedication of a child in Jerusalem was a lamb and a dove. But Mary and Joseph brought only two doves which was the acceptable practice for poor families who could not afford a lamb. Although these two bits of evidence suggest that Jesus came from a poor family, He probably was not from the poorest of families. His father was not a day laborer or landless tenant. Like His father, Jesus was a craftsman—a skilled worker, probably a mason, carpenter, or cartwright. Thus he probably came out of the uppler echelon of Galilee's poor class.[13]

Even though He was a skilled craftsman, in His adult life Jesus identified with the poorest of the poor class.[14] He told enthusiastic followers that He had no place to lay His head. The foxes and birds were better off than He was (Luke 9:58). His disciples were caught on a Sabbath shelling grains of wheat in the field which were left for the benefit of the poor according to the Deuteronomic code. When grilled about paying Roman taxes, he asked for a coin indicating that His pocket was empty. He held no job after the beginning of His ministry. As with other rabbis, He received no pay for His teaching and was without any formal support beyond that contributed by the women along the way (Luke 8:3).[15]

Although He emerges out of poverty ridden Galilee, Jesus' social critique cannot be explained away by His poor economic environment. He was not merely a product of His cultural milieu. As a skilled craftsman He would not have been as vulnerable to revolutionary ideology as the very poor. He parted with His cultural background most significantly in His refusal to use the Zealot strategy of violence. The Zealot cause was the normal response of bright youngsters growing up under economic oppression in Galilee. Their dream was to someday burn the record of debts held in the Jerusalem archives. Although Jesus emerged in the middle of the revolutionary rhetoric he left it behind. He was not simply the product of economic oppression. To be sure He despised that as well as other forms of oppression since the new kingdom He announced shattered the demands of all other earthly institutions. His message announced that man is much more than an economic animal.

Living Bread

Certainly the temptation that Jesus faced with the bread was more than a taunt to ease His private hunger pangs. It was undoubtedly the urging to go back to Galilee and miraculously feed the masses. We cannot second guess all the dimensions of the test such as whether it meant picking up the mantle of Judas the Galilean and continuing the violent freedom fight to end Roman control and taxes. In any case, the bread represents the economic base of daily survival. The temptation of being a glorious miracle baker may have continued with Jesus during the feeding of the five thousand. In the final analysis, however, he rejected the live-by-bread-alone option. The Upside-Down Kingdom way has a lot to do with bread but instead of merely passing it out, the new way is rooted in a deep response to the saving acts of God among His people down through holy history.

Miraculously feeding the multitude was a short-term solution. Hunger would spring up again when the miracle baker died. Leading the masses in violent revolt against the rich landowners would not change the basic economic structure. It would merely place different people in the same depraved structure. The upside-down alternative for Jesus was to offer Himself as the permanent bread of life. Instead of a miraculous temporary solution or a change of actors in the play, Jesus offered a new alternative. His life, His way, His teaching are a new foundation for living—a new bread of life. As persons digest this bread they realize the temporalness and inadequacy of the old bread. They begin to use their material bread in new ways.

Near the midpoint of His ministry Jesus fed the five thousand and the four thousand the loaves and fishes. This was the sign—the revelation that He himself was the living bread—the long awaited Messiah (Mark 6—8). The breaking of the bread came just before the scene at Caesarea Philippi where Peter confessed that Jesus is the Christ. The crowd feeding was not an attempt to establish His identity as a miracle worker, for a few days later Jesus told the crowd that the only reason they followed was because they were fed (John 6:26). He understood that miraculous feedings were not the way to cultivate serious disciples. The feeding was performed because Jesus was moved by compassion when He saw the crowd's hunger and confusion (Mark 6:34; 8:2). It also became one of the first symbolic announcements that He was indeed the new bread, the Messiah of life. In the breaking of the bread He disclosed His messianic identity. John reports an extended discussion of the bread in Chapter 6 of the fourth Gospel. Jesus declares, "I am the bread of life." Miraculous manna falling in the wilderness did not save your fathers. "I am the living bread which came down from heaven. . . . If anyone eats of this bread he will live forever."

As He prepared for a violent crucifixion, Jesus ate the Passover meal with His disciples and, breaking the bread, He told them, "This is my body" (Luke 22:19). After the resurrection, the Emmaus road walkers suddenly recognized Jesus in the breaking of the bread (Luke 24:30). His messianic identity as Saviour of the world is revealed not by turning boulders into loaves but by allowing His life to be broken for others.

When the values of Jesus' Upside-Down Kingdom become the bread of life, the economic institutions of society lose their grip on their human slaves. Rich persons suddenly realize that there is new eternal bread. In that realization they begin sharing liberally so that there is even mundane bread for all. This is an upside-down way of feeding the hungry masses, not revolution by angry peasants, nor miraculous baking. Instead, rich persons moved by God's mercy and filled with joyous liberation from their economic taskmasters, stop hoarding and give liberally.

If the upside-down way of Jesus pulled the rug out from under the institutional feet of political power and religion, the yank was even harder on the rug under the economic structures of Palestine. Again and again, story after story, the punchline of Jesus penetrated the financial structures. Woe to you that rich are. . . . Blessed are you poor (Luke 6:20, 24). His life and teaching brought a straightforward condemnation on the institutional structures that trample over poor people to make rich people richer. As we shall see in the next chapter, the heroes of Jesus' Upside-Down Kingdom are not the rich landowners living plushly in Jerusalem but the poor, the maimed, and the weak. These are exalted in this upside-down way while the rich are sent away empty.

A close scrutiny of Jesus' mission shows that His new way undercut the leverage of three major social institutions of His day: political force, established religion, and conventional economics.

As often happens, these three institutional structures were closely interwoven together. The rich aristocracy of chief priests and Sadducees in Jerusalem owned large estates in Galilee which crushed small peasant farmers. They controlled the mighty Jewish supreme court—the Sanhedrin. This body, in turn, controlled the temple ritual and religious regulations. It was this same rich upper crust of Jerusalem which was in cahoots with the Romans. They wanted the Romans to stay so their property and plush living would be protected from the rebellious countryside bandits like Judas the Galilean. They wanted the Romans to use violent force to suppress Zealot violence. It was this Jerusalem crowd that shouted, "Crucify him, crucify him," for they perceived the new way of Jesus to be more dangerous—more upsetting in its totality—than the threat of the rebel leader Barabbas who led a revolt in the city. One bandit could be caught again and killed. But a new teaching, a new way of living which overturned the political, religious, and economic tables was too dangerous to the plush security and luxury of the Jerusalem elite.

And so the mountain, the temple, and the bread represent three real social institutions which Jesus rejected in His encounter in the wilderness. Since His alternative upside-down way sliced through the prevailing social structures of His day, it is reasonable to understand the temptation that

He denounced as symbols of the upright institutionalized patterns in the Palestinian social structure. It makes little sense to see Jesus struggling with His own personal problems like hunger when His entire mission was to flesh out new modes for living quite different from the prevailing and established patterns. This reading of the temptation gives us a new appreciation for the anguish which Jesus must have endured in the wilderness as He struggled with the powerful forces of politics, religion, and wealth in His day. It also enhances our understanding of the upside-down way God was introducing among His people showing a new power, a new temple, and a new bread. The closeness of this new kingdom in the minds of serious disciples defuses the power wielded by old kingdoms.

Questions for Discussion

1. How do you respond to the suggestion that the bread temptation went beyond Jesus' personal hunger?
2. Does it spiritualize a serious economic problem to merely say, "Jesus is the bread of life?"
3. Why is "bread" such a prominent symbol throughout the New Testament?
4. How do economic structures today contribute to hungry masses?
5. In what way are the temptations Jesus encountered similar to our own struggles?
6. What do the words, "In God We Trust," on U.S. currency mean today? Do they symbolize the meshing of political, religious, and economic institutions?

5
FREE SLAVES

Hometown Boy Lynched

Jesus gave an emphatic "no" to the three Rightside-Up Kingdoms. But what was this Upside-Down Kingdom which He was about to inaugurate all about? Mark (1:15) and Matthew (4:17) report that immediately after the temptation Jesus began going about announcing that the kingdom of God was here. Luke (4:16-30) begins his account of Jesus' work by describing His appearance at His hometown of Nazareth. Although Matthew (13:53-58) and Mark (6:1-6) agree that the audience was stunned by Jesus' appearance, they place the event later in the sequence of His ministry. Luke sees greater significance in this hometown ruckus. For Luke, Jesus' inaugural sermon in front of familiar faces unravels many of the mysteries of the new kingdom.

This is the decisive moment. Here is God in flesh. The long-awaited Messiah stands before us. Joseph's boy walks in. The leader of the synagogue hands Him the scroll. He unravels it to a section from Isaiah. But He doesn't read. He quotes it forcefully by memory. The synagogue audience hears the carpenter's boy, who grew up down the street, say that He is the anointed one—the Messiah. In the terse quote from the prophet He summarizes His identity and mission.

> The Spirit of the Lord is upon me, because he has anointed me
> to preach good news to the poor.
> He has sent me to proclaim release to the captives
> and recovering of sight to the blind,
> to set at liberty those who are oppressed,
> to proclaim the acceptable year of the Lord. Luke 4:18, 19.

Proclaiming liberty and announcing the favorable year of the Lord rings the Jewish bells. The people know what He means. They've heard these phrases again and again—releasing, liberating, letting go, restoring. Yes, yes—these are the words which frame their religious calendar. This is the language of the sabbatical and the Jubilee. This is what the Messiah—"the anointed one"—is all about.

A reading of Luke-Acts shows that Luke uses these words from Isaiah to map out the messianic purpose. Three elements stand out in Jesus' use of the Isaiah passage (Isaiah 61:1, 2). First, He reveals that He is the Messiah in the first person. Second, His role is to bring liberating good news to the poor, the blind, the slaves, and the oppressed. Finally, this is the proclamation of God's favorable year. Jesus omits the word of judgment at the end of the Isaiah passage but He concludes with dynamite: "Today this scripture has been fulfilled in your hearing." The messianic announcement is alive today in your presence. You are living witnesses to it. You are seeing it fulfilled before your very eyes!

The reception which Jesus' friends and neighbors give this message is one of the most fascinating stories of crowd reversal on record. At first they "spoke well of him, and wondered at the gracious words" but in a few moments they were filled with wrath—so angry that they took Him to a cliff at the edge of their city and tried to push Him over. We must let the riddle of the reversal wait for a later chapter.

The usual readings of this passage completely spiritualize its meaning. Jesus is typically understood as only proclaiming release to those who are the captives of sin, giving sight to those spiritually blind, and offering liberty to those oppressed by the bondage of evil. While this is true, the Old Testament background to this text enriches and expands its meaning considerably. André Trocmé shows that the "acceptable year of the Lord" refers to the Old Testament Jubilee.[1] Thus Jesus was actually announcing that the kingdom of God was a restoration of the Hebrew Jubilee. The Nazareth inaugural was a Jubilee proclamation. Not all New Testament scholars agree on this point.[2] In any event, the economic principles of the kingdom of God coherently flow together when they are viewed from the perspective of the Jubilee. The Jubilee model provides a handle for integrating and interpreting the economic teachings of Jesus. But first, we must explore the meaning of the sabbatical and Jubilee years.

A Hebrew Turnover

Three books—Exodus, Deuteronomy, and Leviticus—describe these very unusual Old Testament practices. Today we are familiar with a weekly cycle of six workdays and a rest day or sabbath. This pattern emerges from the creation story where God rested on the seventh day. The Hebrew calendar didn't stop with the weekly cycle. After six work days and a sabbath for rest, they also counted six work years and then celebrated the seventh year as a year of rest. This "Sunday" year was called a sabbatical year. This same idea operates today in many colleges and universities where a teacher is eligible for a "sabbatical year" after teaching at least six years.

The Jubilee year celebrated the end of a week of sabbatical years or the end of seven, seven-year periods of time. Just as the sabbath indicated the end of a week of days, the sabbatical year signaled the end of a week of years and the Jubilee ended a week of sabbatical years. Scholars are not sure if the Jubilee year fell on the forty-ninth year and coincided with the seventh sabbatical year or whether it actually was the fiftieth year observed after the last of the seven sabbatical years.[3] In any case the Jubilee year represented the largest unit of time in the Hebrew calendar. The term Jubilee means "a ram's horn." A special straight horn made from a mountain goat was blown on the Day of Atonement to signal the start of Jubilee festivities. The unique ram's horn blown exclusively by the priests was used only on the Jubilee year. An ordinary ram's horn was used other years.[4]

The sabbatical and Jubilee years established a chronological rhythm. Their religious practices, however, turned social life upside-down. In brief, three shake-ups occurred in the sabbatical year.

1. *Land* was given a vacation. Crops were not to be planted or harvested. Volunteer plants which came up by themselves were to be left for the poor. The Lord promised a plentiful yield on the sixth year, large enough for both sixth and seventh years. As the people rested on the sabbath after six days of work, so the land also was granted a vacation after six years of productivity (Exodus 23:10, 11; Leviticus 25:2-7).

2. *Slaves* were released on the seventh year. Most slaves in the Old Testament became slaves because they could not pay off their debts. After working for six years as a hired servant, they were freed in the seventh year. It is not clear if they were always released on the sabbatical year or not, but the principle of being let go after six years is certain (Exodus 21:1-6, Deuteronomy 15:12-18).

3. *Debts* were also erased in the sabbatical year. Since Israel originally had an agricultural economy, the debts were primarily charitable loans to needy persons rather than commercial loans. Charging interest on loans to other Hebrews was prohibited. On top of this kindness was the unbelievable teaching that the debts must be canceled every sabbatical year (Deuteronomy 15:1-6).

On the fiftieth or Jubilee year, a fourth shake-up was added to the land, debt, and slave restorations. The land itself was returned to the original occupants who owned it at the beginning of the Jubilee period.

> And you shall hallow the fiftieth year, and proclaim liberty throughout the land to all its inhabitants; it shall be a jubilee for you, when each of you shall return to his property and each of you shall return to his family. Leviticus 25:10.

This fifty-year upsetting of land ownership was designed to maintain the original pattern of land ownership instituted when the twelve tribes settled the Promised Land. The Jubilee turnover prevented anyone from permanently controling large sections of land at the expense of the poor. Although land was bought and sold during the forty-nine-year period, the Jubilee equalizer guaranteed the restoration of original land titles at least once in each generation. Actually the Hebrews didn't buy the land in the intervening years, they purchased the use of the land. As the Jubilee year approached, the price for the use of the land declined, since it was calculated by the number of harvests remaining before the Jubilee (Leviticus 25:13-16).

It is difficult to know just how conscientiously the sabbatical and Jubilee practices were kept. Numerous historical references outside of the Scriptures suggest that the practice of letting the land fallow on the sabbatical year continued until the destruction of the temple in AD 70 or even later. It is uncertain how conscientiously the slave, debt, and land restoration was observed. Even if the details of the sabbatical and Jubilee were not always executed, they definitely continued as symbolic markers of Hebrew time. Some information suggests at least partial observance of these practices. During the reign of Zedekiah, before the fall of Jerusalem to Babylon in 586 BC, the rich released their slaves. But a few days later, they deliberately recaptured them. Jeremiah was fuming mad at this disobedience.

> You turned around and profaned my name when each of you took back his male and female slaves, whom you had set free according to their desire, and you brought them into subjection to be your slaves. Therefore, thus says the Lord: You have not obeyed me by proclaiming liberty . . . behold, I proclaim to you liberty to the sword, to pestilence, and to famine, says the Lord. I will make you a horror to all the kingdoms of the earth. Jeremiah 34:16, 17.

The prophet considers the sabbatical violation one of the reasons for the impending destruction of Jerusalem (Jeremiah 34:18-22).

Nehemiah (5:1-13) around 423 BC rebuked the people for not observing the Jubilean ordinances after returning from captivity. He admonished the nobles and officials to free their slaves and return the land to its original owners. In the last chapters of Ezekiel, the prophet calls for the reestablishment of the Jubilee (Ezekiel 45:7-9; 46:16-18).

Although some scholars think the Jubilean land reform was never practiced, others believe it was periodically observed. One interesting bit of research shows that a leading Pharisee, Hillel, who lived during the time of Herod the great, near the birth of Christ, instituted the prosbul.[5] This was an ingenious legal device to eliminate the devastating effect of debt cancellation every six years. Creditors would certainly be slow to lend if they knew the approaching sabbatical year would wipe out the loans they were making. In short, people refused to lend money because they were afraid they would never see it again.

The prosbul allowed the lender to deposit a certificate with the courts when the loan was made. This paper prevented the obligation from being erased at the sabbatical year. The borrower also understood that the debt would be binding regardless of the sabbatical. The existence of the prosbul indicates that the sabbatical provision for debt cancellation was at least taken into account.

Level Pyramids

More important for understanding the Upside-Down Kingdom than the details of the Jubilee and historical confirmation of its practice are the theological principles which undergird it. There can be no question that the Jubilee vision called for a social revolution—an upsetting of the social applecart. As God's social blueprint for His people, the Jubilee dream put its finger on the three major factors which generate socioeconomic inequality. Control of the land represents access to the natural resources. Ownership of slaves symbolizes the human labor necessary for production. Borrowing and lending money points to the management of capital and credit. The use of these three factors—natural resources, human resources, and financial capital—are the keys to determining the amount of inequity in any society. Technology in the modern world is the fourth variable which completes the equation. Through the control and use of these commodities some individuals and groups become wealthy and others become poor. Abusive mismanagement of these variables has fermented the revolutions of history. A review of the underlying Jubilean principles shows the unique solution which God proposed to this incessant problem of social injustice.

1. *God's Ownership.* The message which rings clear again and again is God's ownership of the natural and human resources. Why shouldn't the land be sold perpetually? Because "the land is mine; for you are strangers and sojourners with me" (Leviticus 25:23). Why shouldn't slaves be held continually—why should they be released periodically? "For they are my servants, whom I brought forth out of the land of Egypt; they shall not be sold as slaves" (Leviticus 25:42, 55). The land and the people are the Lord's! They are not to be used in any careless fashion. The managers of land and slaves are not the final owners with absolute say. They are stewards responsible to God. The land and the people are to be

managed according to divine precepts. They dare not be used to build up huge economic pyramids and social dynasties. The practice of giving the land a vacation in the sabbatical or seventh year also fits this understanding. Since the land was the Lord's, it was not to be abused. On the seventh year it was to be given back—restored to God—its original Owner.

2. *God's Liberation.* Why were God's people called to participate in this unusual vision? Why were the debts to be forgiven? Why were the slaves to be liberated? Why was the land to be restored? Was this some human concoction designed as a safeguard to prevent rebellion and revolution? No! God's liberation was at the heart of it. His decisive act in the Egyptian Exodus provided the theological base for the Jubilee. Let no one forget; "you shall remember that you were a slave in the land of Egypt, and the Lord your God redeemed you; therefore, I command you this today" (Deuteronomy 15:15). "I am the Lord your God, who brought you forth out of the land of Egypt to give you the land of Canaan, and to be your God" (Leviticus 25:38). For 450 years you worked as slaves carrying bricks for the Egyptian taskmasters. Not long ago you were whipped and beaten slaves. You too cried out for freedom. I, the Lord your God, intervened on your behalf. I liberated and redeemed you from Pharaoh's enslavement. I freed you from bondage and brought you back to the Promised Land. Time and time again the memory of God's liberating act in Egypt flashes across the pages of the Old Testament.

3. *Jubilee Response.* The Jubilee is rooted in a joyous response to God's gracious liberation and deliverance. As the people recalled how God had redeemed them out of slavery, the only logical response was to pass that liberating freedom on, forgiving debts, releasing slaves, and redeeming the land. To the modern mind releasing one's slave sounds like a great act of benevolence. But the Jubilean prescription didn't stop with a self-righteous pat on the back. Simply freeing the slave

was not enough. "And when you let him go free from you, you shall not let him go empty-handed; you shall furnish him *liberally* out of your flock, out of your threshing floor, and out of your wine press" (Deuteronomy 15:13, 14a emphasis added). Why such generous mercy? Isn't it enough just to free the slave? Why this extra dose of goodness? "As the Lord your God has blessed you, you shall give to him" (Deuteronomy 15:14b). As God liberally redeemed you out of Egypt, so you ought to graciously liberate your brothers and sisters. Jubilee acts of social justice are not motivated by an interest in heavenly green stamps. They are the natural and joyful response to the good news of God's liberation.

4. *Jubilee Compassion.* The Jubilee respondent has one eye on history—on God's gracious acts of deliverance. The other eye looks forward and around him. Jubilee behavior is also prompted by compassion and care for those who are crushed down by the social and economic structures. The sight of trampled on, disinherited persons brings memories of their own slavery in the past. One of the reasons the land is to lie fallow is for the poor. "But the seventh year you shall let it rest and lie fallow, that the poor of your people may eat." (Exodus 23:11). "There will be no poor among you . . . if only you will obey the voice of the Lord your God, being careful to do all this commandment which I command you this day. . . . You shall not harden your heart or shut your hand against your poor brother, but you shall open your hand to him, and lend him sufficient for his need—whatever it may be. . . . You shall open *wide* your hand to your brother, to the needy and to the poor, in the land" (Deuteronomy 15:4, 5, 7, 8, 11, emphasis added).

The hearers are explicitly warned not to refuse loans to poor brothers even if the sabbatical year is near. Although the debt will not be repaid because of the sabbatical cancellation, "you shall give to him freely, and your heart shall not be grudging when you give to him; because for this the Lord your God will bless you in all your work and in all that you undertake" (Deuteronomy 15:10). So there is a double motive in the Jubilee forgiveness, a gracious response to God's liberation and compassionate eyes that see the human hurt around them.

5. *Upside-Down Revolution.* The Jubilee envisions a social turning over. But it's certainly a unique revolution. Revolutions often erupt at the bottom of the societal ladder because of economic injustice. Exploited peasants, angered by their oppression, grab pitchforks or machine guns and violently lash out at the rich oppressors. If they are successful, they gain power. More often they are crushed. Successful revolutionaries of today in turn become the oppressors of tomorrow as they continue to use the weapons of force. Jubilee is upside down. Here the flame of revolution breaks out at the top. Those in power, the rich and influential, are moved by God's grace. They see with compassionate eyes and join the Jubilee by periodically redistributing the control of natural and human resources. The socioeconomic pyramids are flattened out. Those at the top begin freely giving as God has given them.

6. *Institutionalized Grace.* The Jubilee demonstrates a keen awareness of human sin and greed. Without any controls, excessive pyramiding occurs. Without constraints and periodic leveling, the weak—at the bottom of the social ladder—are stamped into the dirt. The social structure of a society must have special provisions to defend and protect the helpless. Periodic and regular levelings are necessary to arrest the "bigger is better" mentality. The Jubilee is a splendid example of a society-wide—yes, an institutional—plan to harness personal desire and ambition. Benevolence cannot be left up to the personal whims and wishes of the rich. Such giving makes the rich feel better but does not alter the evil structural conditions which allow them to perpetuate their luxury at the expense of the poor. Regular and periodic level-

ing must be part of the very structure of the society if it is to have any consequence. It must be incorporated into the rules of the game, not left up to the fancy of each player.

Another part of the Jubilean genius is that it doesn't squelch individual initiative. It doesn't prescribe that all things should be held in common or that every one must have exactly the same amount. There is room for individual initiative. Personal aspirations have a place. But such things easily get out of hand. And so there must be periodic structural changes at regular intervals which equalize the disparities which otherwise would run rampant. As we have seen in the biblical record, this institutionalized grace is in response to God's grace since He has already taken the initiative. The Jubilee portrays the biblical vision of spiritual and social integration. There are not two separate compartments for religion and economics. The two are woven together into one cloth in the Jubilee model. Experiencing God's grace results in economic change. Refusing to participate in the economic turnover is considered sin and flagrant disobedience. Pulling the two apart prostitutes the biblical truth.

Meanwhile Back at Nazareth

The old words take on new meaning—good news for the poor, release for the captives, sight for the blind, liberty for the oppressed, announcing God's favorable year! The research of some New Testament students indicates that Jesus preached these words during an actual sabbatical year.[6] One scholar is even convinced it was actually the year of Jubilee.[7] Whether or not His announcement coincided with one of these sacred years is not crucial. The Old Testament embellishes the meaning of these words. Now they jump out at us in a new way. The Hebrew word for liberty is used only seven times in the Old Testament, but each time in conjunction with the year of liberty.[8] The literal meaning of a Jubilee proclamation was certainly good news to the ears in Nazareth. The poor could say good-bye to their debts. Those driven into slavery because of debts could return home. Those forced to sell land would see it returned again to their family. No question about it—this was very good news!

But there's more. This isn't just another old Jubilee proclamation. "The Lord has anointed me." This is a messianic announcement. Interestingly, when John sent his disciples to ask Jesus whether or not He was indeed the Messiah, Jesus didn't give a definite yes or no (Luke 7:22, 23). Instead he said to tell John that "the blind receive their sight, the lame walk, lepers are cleansed, and the deaf hear, the dead are raised up, the poor have good news preached to them." This is a catalog of the same kind of people that Jesus mentions in the Nazareth inaugural. This is not the first time such a list appears. In fact, we find the same type of persons mentioned in numerous messianic prophecies in Isaiah 35:5, 29:18, and 61:1. Jeremiah points out that references to the blind seeing, deaf hearing, and so on, are all age-old descriptions in the East for the time of salvation—the time when there will be no more crying, sorrow, or grief.[9] Jesus goes beyond all expectation by adding lepers and dead to the list—both of which are missing in Isaiah's passages. So to the alert Nazareth ears and to John's disciples He was using the messianic code words of the Old Testament to tell them that the Messiah is here! Salvation is dawning. The kingdom of God is near. It is at hand before your very eyes!

Restoration is the prominent theme in the Jubilee and the common thread which ties together both the Nazareth sermon and Jesus' reply to John's disciples. Things will be restored back to their original state. There are images of paradise here. No more sweat. No more debts. No poverty. No more work. Slavery ends. These images of the garden take us back to the Creation in the first chapter of Genesis. Things are rejuvenated, reestablished, restored back to their original state of garden perfection. Jubilee talk describes the

Messiah's work. He announces that as of now God releases, lets go, and forgives our debts—our sins. In Jesus Christ we can be restored to our perfectly created state of Genesis chapter one. He remolds us into the image of God. The chains of sin are cut. Our eyes are opened. We are released from the captivity of evil. This is true liberation. Now we can return to the Garden of Eden. Harmonious ties with God are reestablished. This is the function of the Messiah. As we repent He restores us back into the family of God. And so at Nazareth Jesus was announcing God's acceptable year of salvation. In Jesus Christ the sin debts are canceled and we can walk with God once again in the garden. The final punch line of the Nazareth sermon points to God's use of Gentiles in the Old Testament. It slices through Jewish pride. This new Jubilee restoration is not only for the Jews but for Gentiles as well. This is the proclamation of a universal Jubilee. This is an all-ethnic kingdom. This straw broke the Jewish camel's back. It was this fact that quickly changed the Nazareth crowd's reaction from applause to insidious anger.

This is good news. But we cannot stop here. What is our response to God's act? Now we remember that we are forgiven debtors. We are released slaves. One time we were oppressed. One time we were captives. Suddenly the reciprocal rule from Deuteronomy 15:14 makes sense: "As the Lord your God has blessed you, you shall give to him." It points to the New Testament chain reaction principle: Forgive as I have forgiven, be merciful as I have been merciful, love as I have loved, give freely as I have given to you. Our response to God's graciousness is to forgive others. His mercy moves us to cancel debts. We release our slaves in light of His great salvation act. In short, we pass the Jubilee on to others.

An underlying rhythm emerges out of the Jubilee experience. It echoes from the garden to the cross. The drummers of holy history pound out the four-beat message which reverberates down through the ages:

garden—Egypt—Exodus—Jubilee;
perfection—sin—salvation—mercy;
freedom—oppression—restoration—forgiveness.

The first beat reminds us of God's perfect creation in the garden. The reality of man's sin and oppression in Egypt follows. God intervenes with mighty acts of liberation to bring restoration and salvation. Man responds to God's salvation by extending mercy and forgiveness of Jubilee to others.

Just as the Hebrew response to God's liberating exodus had real social consequences, so must ours. It is not enough to sit and ponder the theological beauty of this. We must act. The biblical model means that now we start forgiving, not only interpersonal insults but financial debts as well. We bring release to those who we oppress socially and economically. We lower rents and raise salaries. This unconventional and overwhelming Jubilee response to God's merciful love is the New Testament expectation. In the Lord's Prayer "and forgive us our debts, as we also have forgiven our debtors" (Matthew 6:12), our granting forgiveness and accepting it are tied up in one moment. We become eligible to accept God's forgiveness only when we repent and are willing to grant it to others.

The Greek word "forgive" is the same word used in the Greek version of the Old Testament—the Septuagint—to describe the Jubilee which means liberate, forgive debts, send away. André Trocmé points out that the word "debts" in the Lord's Prayer refers specifically to a financial debt in the most material sense.[10] So we are to forgive not merely bad feelings but actual financial debts. Here, in the center of the Lord's Prayer, we find the Jubilee principle couched.

The parable of the unforgiving servant (Matthew 18:23-35) also underlines the Jubilee axiom. A king forgives the large debt of one of his servants. The forgiven servant grabs a fellow servant by the throat and demands a small debt which the fellow servant cannot pay. The forgiven servant locks the small debtor in prison. When news of the unforgiving treatment reaches the king's ears, he angrily throws the forgiven servant in jail until he can pay the original debt. The story concludes tersely with the Jubilee moral: "So also my heavenly Father will do to every one of you, if you do not forgive your brother from your heart" (Matthew 18:35). The principle of reciprocal forgiveness which arises from the Jubilee pervades New Testament teaching. The economic instruction of Jesus squarely fits the Jubilee model. In the Jubilee perspective the words of Jesus no longer appear weird or stupid. Now they sound like a reasonable and natural response to God's liberating forgiveness in our own lives.

The Dog's Tail

We have seen how the Jubilee linked together the spiritual and social spheres of life. Although inextricably tied together, they do represent two different starting points. In fact, the way they mesh together is at the bottom of much philosophical controversy. Social scientists have observed that our ideas are shaped by the characteristics of our social and material environments. The chicken and the egg question of whether the ideas we think influence our economic patterns or vice versa draws the line of philosophical battle. The philosophers and theologians tend to line up on the one side and contend that our beliefs and opinions influence our socioeconomic behavior. On the other side, some social scientists, particularly the Marxists, argue that the ideas and thoughts which we think are merely a reflection of our economic position in life. In other words economic forces and material patterns determine the thoughts and beliefs which we hold dear. For instance, a person born into a wealthy situation often comes to believe that riches here and now are a sign of God's blessing. In contrast, persons born into poverty frequently believe that God's blessing will come as pie in the sky bye and bye.

To say it succinctly, this is the question of the relationship between religion and economics, the spiritual and the material, faith and the pocketbook. It's the question of the dog and the tail. Does our faith wag our pocketbook or does our bank account wag our convictions? What controls what? This is a gross oversimplification, of course. There is no simple causal relationship where the pocketbook completely and always controls the belief system or vice versa. But undoubtedly there is significant interaction between faith and finances. As a sociologist I'm convinced that economic factors in our life such as our salary, the income of our friends, the value of our house, and our social status are factors which powerfully influence the way we look at things. These socioeconomic factors in our life provide a set of glasses through which we view life. They also provide the hotbed which incubates theological beliefs to support and legitimate our economic position. These material variables influence how we read the Bible and fertilize religious beliefs which conveniently support our economic position. In short, the pocketbook wags our beliefs a great deal of the time.

This contradicts the biblical pattern. The scriptural vision calls for a faith which influences pocketbooks. All of us are shaped by the socioeconomic factors in our life and none of us can jump out of our social environments. But we can listen to and obey the biblical message which urges us to bring our economic decisions under the jurisdiction of our faith.

The Jubilee provides the Old Testament solution to this dog-tail problem. Here the faith of a people in their God, who graciously delivered them from slavery, motivated them to wag their economic involvements. Here God's acts of salvation in holy history moved the community to forgive debts, free slaves, and return land. The fact that people sometimes refused to follow the Jubilee prescriptions attests to the powerful strength which economic loyalties can have over faith. Nevertheless, the biblical model is clear: faith should wag pocketbooks. The Old Testament principle is completely restored in the teaching of Jesus to which we turn in the next chapter.

Christian obedience today does not mean that we try to duplicate all the details of the Jubilee. We no longer live in a theocracy where civil and religious legislation are interwoven under God's direct Kingship. It is impossible for a small group of Christians to impose this kind of economic philosophy on the larger society. Restoring land to its original owners is of little assistance to families who have never owned land in the first place. Nor does it correct the injustices of industrial society which are built around the inequitable distribution of technology, capital, and natural resources other than land. Allowing wheat to stand every seventh year in Nebraskan wheat fields won't feed the hungry in New York and Bombay. The basic theological principles undergirding the Jubilee, however, do provide a uniquely biblical view which can relevantly inform the Christian's economic philosophy. The biblical model of Jubilee ought to be the economic norm within the corporate life of the church. And it provides a distinctly biblical perspective to guide the Christian community's behavior in the larger economic system.

Questions for Discussion

1. How do the principles of Jubilee economics contrast with capitalism and socialism?
2. In what ways are Jubilee principles relevant to our financial involvements today?
3. List examples of spiritual and economic integration in your own life.
4. What difference should our salvation experience make in our financial management?

5. Do Christians generally manage their finances in a different way than non-Christians?

6. How could Jubilee principles be applied to the economic life of your congregation or fellowship?

7. Identify some examples where economic concerns control our religious beliefs.

6
LUXURIOUS POVERTY

Perpetual Jubilee

The kingdom of God is upside-down economically. It stands in stark contrast to the prevailing western economic philosophy. I was amazed a few years ago when I realized for the first time in my life how much Jesus had to say about finances. Before then I always assumed that He merely muttered a few peripheral sayings about money. Luke, in particular, makes economic conversion a fundamental aspect of the new kingdom. We will primarily follow Luke's record with cross-references to the other Gospels.

Jesus makes it clear that He expects forgiven and converted people to live an upside-down economic life. He holds up the Jubilee model as the new way for His disciples. People on the way with Him respond financially to God's great love for them by sharing with those in need around them. One cannot conclude that Jesus was condemning private property nor that He was calling for a new Christian commune. But His message did strike at the heart of the economic structures of His day. His gospel was a harsh judgment on the financial practices in Galilee and Judea. We must remember that wealth doesn't simply drop out of the sky. It is a commodity in a system of norms and social rules which control its acquisition and use. In speaking out against wealth Jesus questioned the accepted economic norms which allowed a great disparity to emerge between the affluent and the poor. He never says that material things are evil or sinful in and of themselves. But He does warn that they are dangerous. They quickly assume a demonic character which unseats the rule of God in our life. We will look at six dangerous characteristics of wealth which Jesus lays before us.

Beware: The Strangler

Tucked away in the parable of the sower is a sermon on the threat of riches to kingdom citizens. Jesus or the early church clarified the riddle. The seed is the Word of God which, in its growth, symbolizes the emergence of the kingdom. The seed that falls among the thornbushes is choked. "And as for what fell among the thorns, they are those who hear, but as they go on their way they are choked by the cares and riches and pleasures of life, and their fruit does not mature" (Luke 8:14; Mark 4:18, 19; Matthew 13:22). The seeds sprout. There is growth and new life. But the vitality is quickly smothered by prickly thorns. The cares, riches, and pleasures of life suffocate the new plants. They strangle the shoots. The synoptic writers all use the word choke. The throbbing spiritual life is gagged. Fruit buds appear; but there is no harvest. The seed never develops to maturity. The point is straightforward. Jobs, houses, swimming pools, snowmobiles, stock markets, skis, clothing, cars, and stereos can abort the growth of the kingdom in our lives. They can divert us from the work of the kingdom and squelch the harvest.

Beware: The Worrier

Yesterday brings guilt. Tomorrow brings worry. Jesus correctly perceives a tendency of wealth when He says it generates anxiety. It provokes fret. Will we be secure tomorrow? How can we protect our property? What if the stock market crashes? Could the burglar alarm fail? The ownership of property immediately brings concern for its defense and protection. In Luke (12:22-34) and in Matthew (6:19-21, 25-33) Jesus urges the disciples four times not to be anxious about food and clothing.

> And do not seek what you are to eat and what you are to drink, nor be of *anxious* mind. For all the nations of the world seek these things; and your Father knows that you need them. Instead, seek his kingdom, and these things shall be yours as well.
>
> Fear not, little flock, for it is Your Father's good pleasure to give you the kingdom. Sell your possessions, and give alms; provide yourselves with purses that do not grow old, with a treasure in the heavens that does not fail, where no thief approaches and no moth destroys. For where your treasure is, there will your heart be also. Luke 12:29-34.

The correct translation of the Greek word for anxious used in the text means "do not make anxious efforts for."[1] This is not simply a brain problem. It's a call to stop floundering around after fashionable clothes and sirloin steaks. This is how pagans act. "The nations of the world seek these things."

Not so the disciples of Jesus. They are not to be preoccupied with such insignificant things. They are to concentrate 100 percent on the kingdom! God will see that they are cared for. In the context of the sabbatical year when they had planted no crops, the instruction takes on new meaning in Yoder's paraphrase.

> If you work six days (or six years) with all your heart, you can count on God to take care of you and yours. So without fear leave your field untilled. As he does for the birds of heaven which do not sow or harvest or collect into granaries, God will take care of your needs. The Gentiles who pay no attention to the sabbath are not richer than you.[2]

Hearing the words in the sabbatical year context assures us that they're no prescription for laziness. Their counsel remains very relevant today. Amassing things distracts us from the kingdom. We are not day laborers—hired servants who have to worry about our job—we are children of a caring Father. The focal point of this whole discourse is the poor. Hoarding goodies is the pagan way. Sell and give alms to the poor. The upside-down way is giving to the poor. The Jubilee principle rides again. Children of a loving Father who joyfully gives them the kingdom respond by selling their possessions for the sake of the poor. The instruction to sell doesn't come because property is wrong or because poverty is a virtue—it's an act of compassion on behalf of the poor.

This same spirit permeates the Beatitudes when Jesus tells us to give to him that begs—and to lend without expecting a return (Luke 6:34, 35; Matthew 5:42). Persons who have their heart in the kingdom won't be tantalized by excessive profits. When the kingdom is our treasure, we switch from hoarding to giving. When we focus completely on the kingdom and liberally share our wealth, we not only restore and liberate the poor but also ourselves! We are freed from fretful anxiety. We are released from the bondage of worry.

Perhaps the number of insurance contracts sold each year is an indicator of the amount of corporate anxiety in a society. Worry isn't inherited. It's a child of possessions. Children don't worry. A four-year-old child listened to a record designed to elicit emotional responses from children. Listeners were encouraged to respond sponstaneously to questions such as "What are you sad about?" and "What are you mad about?" When the child heard, "What are you worried about?" she came sobbing to Mommy saying, "I don't have nuthin' to worry about." A few days later she announced that she "finally found something to worry about." Jesus' observation about entering the kingdom as a child means that we believe that our Father cares about tomorrow.

The pithy saying from Matthew's Gospel sums it up. "Therefore do not be anxious about tomorrow, for tomorrow will be anxious for itself. Let the day's own trouble be sufficient for the day" (Matthew 6:34).

Beware: The Blinder

In one of His most moving and powerful parables Jesus tells us that the trappings of riches blind us. Moreover, He warns that our pocketbooks have more to do with heaven and hell than our hymnbooks.[3]

> There was a rich man, who was clothed in purple and fine linen and who feasted sumptuously every day. And at his gate lay a poor man named Lazarus, full of sores, who desired to be fed with what fell from the rich man's table; moreover the dogs came and licked his sores. The poor man died and was carried by the angels to Abraham's bosom. The rich man also died and was buried; and in Hades, being in torment, he lifted up his eyes and saw Abraham far off and Lazarus in his bosom. Luke 16:19-23.

Usually known as the story of Lazarus and the rich man, a better title might be, "Surprised by Hell." The story is probably aimed at the rich Sadducees living luxuriously in Jerusalem who doubted the resurrection. It also may be Jesus' answer to the incessant requests for a sign. In any case the teaching is clear. The rich man lives in a large house and throws parties every day. He's exquisitely outfitted in purple robes and the most expensive Egyptian underwear. He is not a robber or a cheat. He has not acted illegally to gain his riches. He has simply taken advantage of the economic system of his time, fully complying with civil law. His wealth may have come through inheritance, family connections, hard work, or chance. In any case, he was an upright and decent rich man. He had not swindled anyone.

At the edge of his fenced-off estate lay a poor beggar suffering from a skin disease. Lazarus, the only character named in any of Jesus' parables, means "God helps."[4] Day after day he reached out for chunks of bread which the guests would toss to him after using them as rags to wipe their hands clean after feasting. Clarence Jordan points out that the Greek word for "beggar" is related to the word for "spit." Lazarus was a "spit upon" person despised by the party thrower. The rich man was embarrassed to have a beggar spoil the lovely decor of his party atmosphere. But not the dogs. They had more compassion than the wealthy one. For the dogs symbolized the unsaved, the Gentile outcasts—worthless scavengers. The upside-down moment dawns. The rich religious Sadducee spits on the beggar in contempt. But the dogs, of all things, show compassion by using their saliva for healing.[5]

Suddenly the world turns upside down! The rich man roasts in hell and old spit-upon Lazarus sits in the bosom of Abraham. The right hand of Abraham was the place of honor—the most prestigious seat in the congregation of the righteous.[6] The tables are turned. High is low and low is high. Lazarus used to reach up to the rich man for crumbs. Now the rich partier reaches up to Lazarus for a drop of water. Echoes of Mary's Magnificat ring in our ears. "He has filled the hungry with good things, and the rich he has sent empty away" (Luke 1:53). The message is clear. The rich man who was blinded by luxury and refused to Jubilee is now severely punished. The huge gulf symbolizes his awayness from God. God had not forgotten the weak and spit-upon Lazarus. But this is not a comfort story for beggars.[7] The parable doesn't plead for the poor to patiently wait for pie in the sky. No, instead the ending of the story sharply focuses on the five rich brothers who are still living.

Now the rich man has compassion and begs Abraham to let Lazarus rise from the dead and warn the quintet. Abraham refuses and a second time the toasting rich man begs for a miraculous messenger to rise from the grave and warn his brothers. Each time Abraham says, "They have Moses and the prophets; let them hear them. . . . If they do not hear Moses and the prophets, neither will they be convinced if some one should rise from the dead" (Luke 16:29, 31). They've known about Jubilee since their childhood. Their ears have heard the laws regarding sabbaticals and Jubilees read Sabbath after Sabbath. The message is obvious. No special sign will be sent to warn the living rich. Those who refuse to practice Jubilee, and flagrantly violate God's reign, will be judged. The sad story ends on this harsh note. Scrumptious feasting and a lavish lifestyle blinded the vision of the rich man. He was so wrapped up in the good life that he couldn't see the sores or hear the cries of despair. How much more serious for those who have not only Moses and the prophets but in addition Jesus, Paul, James, and church history. He that hath ears to hear let him hear!

Beware: The Boss

The sermonic conclusion to another parable informs us that riches not only blind, they also boss us. Jesus tells of another rich man who had a steward managing his estate (Luke 16:1-9). The owner discovered that the steward engaged in fraud. The boss asked for a complete inventory of his goods and then planned to fire the cheat. The steward quickly called in some of the master's debtors and reduced their debts. The boss commended him for this and even Jesus held the cheat up as an example of piety. Many commentators have been perplexed by this story. The Jubilee perspective and knowledge of the financial practices of the time clarify the riddle. J. Duncan Derrett provides extremely helpful insight because of his intimate knowledge of the economic laws surrounding the story.[8] At the heart of the story is the fact that the steward was charging interest on the loans he had made to the debtors. Interest was forbidden in the Old

Testament because it was considered usury by the law of God. Derrett shows with convincing documentation how the Pharisees had established ways to allow a hidden interest which was even condoned by the Jewish civil courts.

Particularly with commodity loans of wheat and oil, a hidden interest could be charged if the borrower was not making the loan out of "immediate necessity." If he was desperately poor and in drastic need, then interest was prohibited. Non-necessary loans were absurdly interpreted so that hidden interest could usually be charged, thus violating the law of God. For example, if a man had "one drop of oil" and wanted to borrow more oil, then his loan would not be one of "immediate necessity" since he already had one drop of oil! Thus, he could be charged interest on his loan. Since the rule of "immediate necessity" applied primarily to commodity loans like wheat and wine, monetary loan repayments were often translated into commodities since this allowed interest to be charged. The interest was never written into the contract, since this would grossly disobey God's law.

Back to the story. The steward is in a crunch since he'll soon be jobless with no references and a shady reputation. In the bind he decides to forgive the borrowers the amount of interest which he unjustly added to their loans. Apparently the steward himself would have gained the interest and by canceling it he lost a considerable sum. He didn't have the power to forgive the entire debt since the principle was owed to the master. "Our steward, then, lending at interest to Jews was morally a transgressor but legally secure, so long as his contracts hid the fact that the loan was usurious."[9] The loans were probably converted to commodities of oil and wheat to cover up monetary debts in order to collect interest.

The steward acted righteously by releasing the interest percentage on the loan. According to the law of the land, the steward could have forced the debtors into slavery if they defaulted on their interest payments. But the interest was not the property of the master, according to the law of God. The owner may even have been ignorant of the usurious nature of the loans. Under the oral law of the Pharisees, if the steward forgave interest even without the owner's authority, the owner was required to accept the steward's decision. In fact, the boss had nothing to lose and all to gain. He would now appear as a caring and forgiving creditor and wouldn't have gained the interest anyway himself since it was headed for the steward's wallet. The owner does commend and ratify the decision of his steward to act righteously (Luke 16:8). Then comes the upside-down moment; "the sons of this world are wiser in their own generation than the sons of light".

It was the Pharisees who had devised these ingenious ways to get around the law of God because they were "lovers of money." The worldly steward acted righteously by canceling the interest, while the ingenious Pharisees who were supposed to be sons of light intentionally set up economic structures which violated the law of God so that they could become rich. The unrighteous mammon refers to the prohibited interest. If they cannot be faithful in a little thing like loaning money without interest according to the law of God, how can God trust them to be faithful with the more important riches?

The parable launched Jesus into a biting sermon: " 'No servant can serve two masters; for either he will hate the one and love the other, or he will be devoted to the one and despise the other. You cannot serve God and mammon.'

"The Pharisees, who were lovers of money, heard all this, and they scoffed at him. But he said to them, 'You are those who justify yourselves before men, but God knows your hearts; for what is exalted among men is an abomination in the sight of God' " (Luke 16:13-15).

The steward was caught between two masters. The laws of God forbid interest, but the law of man permitted usury. The demands of the two masters were in contradiction. This fraudulent steward realized the incompatibility and decided to serve the law of God. In upside-down fashion, the bad guy ends up as hero. Mammon is the Aramaic term for "wealth, money, property, or profit."[10] The fascinating truth here is that Jesus elevates money to divine status. He places it right up on par with God. It more than anything else can act like a god. He doesn't choose knowledge, physical skill, appearance, family nobility, nationalism, or occupation. It is wealth and property which most quickly act like deities in our lives. They begin to control and direct us. The *Wall Street Journal* or the Dow Jones Average can become our obsession. We become engrossed with a new CB radio and begin serving it. Just as a child is completely devoted to playing with a new toy at Christmas, so the adult can become a captive of material pursuits. He bows down and worships profit and material luxuries and they begin to manipulate and dictate his life. Serving God and wealth are mutually exclusive. They are never bed partners. Wealth can be used to serve God's ends, but the profit addict is not a servant of God. It is this warning that permeates Jesus' teachings. He cautions that dangerous mammon can easily slip in and replace God as the dictator of our life. This profanity is particularly irksome when the service to mammon is covered up and veneered over with pious sounding God talk.

Jesus' prophetic sanitizing of the temple was aimed precisely at the religious cover-up of profiteering that oppressed the poor. "My house shall be called a house of prayer for all the nations, but you have made it a den of robbers" (Mark 11:17; Matthew 21:13; Luke 19:46; John 2:16). The business merchants operating in the temple were not doing anything illegal according to civil law. They were exchanging pure money for offerings and selling animals for sacrifice at a high profit. They had concocted a "legal" economic system which was robbing the poor. Jesus calls them "robbers" who engineered a whole system to exploit the poor in the name of religion.

The Pharisees who were doing precisely this with their secret interest provisions sneered at Jesus' rebuke. He laid it on the line by declaring that the wealth which impresses men is a downright abomination in the eyes of God (Luke 16:15). The pursuit of profit, an easy buck, and secure financial status—all at the top of the western success ladder—fall at the bottom of the Upside-Down Kingdom. Mercy and compassion are the new yardsticks. Prevailing cultural values of success are inversely related to the way of God.

Beware: The Damner

Wealth can have a damning effect on our lives. Jesus underscores this point in a story about a rich fool (Luke 12:13-21). Example stories like the rich fool and the Good Samaritan are not parables or allegories which hold the secrets to some general principles of Christian behavior. They specify exactly what a person should or should not do. Someone from the crowd runs up to Jesus. He asks for legal advice. His older brother won't share the inherited family farm with him. He begs Jesus to intervene and straighten out the stingy brother. Jesus refuses and tells a story instead. Apparently Jesus detected a spirit of covetousness in the younger brother who wanted to make sure he got his fair share of the farm.

The forty-nine-year Jubilee pattern protected the inheritance of the poor. Since the land was to be returned about once each generation, no family could accumulate large tracts and pass them perpetually on within their own tribe. Typical inheritance practices give distinct advantages to the children of the rich. Perhaps Jesus was not only identifying this man's greed, but also pulling the rug out from under the inheritance practices which gave this man a free farm while others had none. Jesus warns, "Beware of all covetousness; for a man's life does not consist in the abundance of his possessions" (Luke 12:15).

Again we find an inversion between kingdom values and societal standards. After the box is covered six feet under, the gossipers ask, "What was his estate like?" "How much did he leave?" Successful people are those who acquire and leave large financial portfolios. We reverently and covetously cheer the wealthy entrepreneur. The voices of our society tell us that financial success *is* the yardstick which determines the significance and importance of a person. Abundant possessions *do* equal an abundant life. We find just the opposite values in the Upside-Down Kingdom. Here the size of the investment portfolio is not an acceptable criteria for evaluating the significance of a person's life. Covetousness is an attitude. It's a mind-set glued to excessive profit and privilege. It can infect the poor as well as the rich. Both are equally vulnerable. Attitudes do lead to action. Greedy thinking eventually builds big barns.

Then comes the rich fool story. A rich farmer has good yields. He expands his storage space and locks up the grain. He makes plans for partying. That night God calls him a fool and demands his soul. Jesus ends with inverted words, "So is he who lays up treasure for himself, and is not rich toward God" (Luke 12:21). The barn that this fellow built is not a holding shed to keep grain until threshing, but a warehouse or store to permanently keep the threshed grain.[11] Rather than practicing the Jubilee by sharing his extra, he hoards it like a fool. He's not moved by compassion or care for the poor—only by selfish avarice. We can be sure that this wasn't a righteous sabbatical preparation of the sixth year's yield. This was selfish expansionism at the cost of the poor. His selfish motive is clear: "Take your ease, eat, drink, and be merry" (Luke 12:19, 20).

In the midst of the party God knocks at the nitwit's house and calls him a fool. To us "fool" means stupid or a little crazy. The biblical definition is harsher, for the fool is one who says there is no God (Psalm 14:1). He lives as though

God weren't around. The rich man's barn was his god. He was a practical atheist trapped by riches. In practice he denied the existence of God. In Matthew's Gospel (5:22) the person who calls his brother a fool is liable for the judgment of hell fire. This is no playful nickname. When God dubs him a fool, He means he is eternally damned. His refusal to practice the Jubilee, and his captivity by wealth, have damned his soul. Stacking up his own treasure made him a pauper in God's sight. Again an inversion strikes. Those who pile it up down here are very poor in God's kingdom. In God's eyes the rich person should give away freely—so freely that he appears poor by this world's standards. That person is the treasure himself. He has saved his own soul from the damning effects of wealth.

Beware: The Curse

We have seen the Jubilee's focus on the poor. The words of Jesus we reviewed bring sharp stings of indictment on the rich. The contrast between rich and poor is sharpened in the Beatitudes. Here Jesus disburses awards to the poor and spanks the comfortable. As usual, His perspective is upside down. All societies sanction their members as a way of controlling their behavior. Positive sanctions, or rewards, are given when persons successfully follow the societal norms. They receive awards, diplomas, pictures in the paper, or stars on their chart for eating vegetables. Negative sanctions, punishments like imprisonment and fines, are given to deviants who break social norms. Since monetary success is a basic American and Canadian cultural value, there are juicy rewards for the successful.

They receive private estates, public citations, prestigious board positions, honorary degrees, household servants, and excessive power. In short, they are held up as idols by public opinion. Not so in the Upside-Down Kingdom. Jesus comes on strong.

> Blessed are you poor, for yours is the kingdom of God. . . . But woe to you that are rich, for you have received your consolation. Luke 6:20, 24.

The sanctioning system is flipped over. The rich are surprised with a cursing and the poor with a blessing. The normal pattern of rewards is inverted. The poor, who are normally rebuked for being lazy, welfare bums, are suddenly exalted. The despised, forlorn, weaklings are the recipients of God's happy blessing. The usually applauded rich are cursed. The shoe fits today. The rhetoric of patriotic slogans proclaims, "God blessed America." Patriotic songs, presidential prayers, and bumper stickers herald America as the nation blessed by God. This usually means that the United States has a high standard of living, a rising gross national product, and enjoys the best luxuries of pleasure. These material things are seen as blessings from God. The biblical perspective reverses this. As we have seen throughout the teaching of Jesus, material wealth is more of a curse than a blessing. Poverty which is cursed by the wealthy is blessed by the biblical words. The heresy of patriotic nationalism turns the biblical blessings into curses and vice versa.

Does this mean that raw poverty is a virtue? Do poor people automatically enter the kingdom? The term "poor" in the biblical context has at least three meanings. First of all, it refers to the materially poor—those destitutes who have insufficient housing and clothing. The term "poor" occurs more than sixty times in the Old Testament and usually refers to material poverty.[12]

Second, in the broader material sense, the term refers to those who were generally oppressed—the captives, slaves, sick, destitute, and the desperate. These are the down-and-outers who cannot defend themselves. They hopelessly depend on the mercy of the powerful. Jeremias reports that Jesus' followers consisted primarily of the disreputable, the uneducated, and the ignorant whose religious deficiency and moral acts blocked any hope of their salvation according to the Pharisees' formulas.[13] His followers are often described as the "little ones," "the simple ones," and "the least ones."

The third connotation of "poor" comes out of an Old Testament tradition which saw the poor as the humble in spirit—those who are poor toward God. These stand before God as beggars with outstretched hands pleading for mercy with contrite and broken spirits. It was this poorness before God which Matthew highlighted in his version of the Beatitudes, "Blessed are the poor in spirit, for theirs is the kingdom of heaven" (Matthew 5:3). Matthew underscored inner spiritual poverty, while Luke clearly had the materially poor in mind.[14] His beatitudes consist of a quartet of blessings and woes. (See Luke 6:20-26.)

Blessed are	**Woe to**
You poor	You that are rich
You that hunger now	You that are full now
You that weep now	You that laugh now
You when men hate you	You when all men speak well of you

What does all this mean? There's no doubt that Luke is thinking of those who are really poor, really hungry, actually crying, and persecuted. First of all, this is a prediction of material reversal. Those who are at the bottom of the social ladder for Jesus' sake—the hungry, poor, crying, and despised—will some day be at the top. Rather than meaning that poverty automatically equals eternal life, Jesus stresses that those who follow in His way may literally need to become poor for His sake. When they walk along with Him they will face persecution. The rich who refuse to practice the Jubilee will be punished for violating the law of God. Those who detach themselves from the demonic power of possessions are the new rich of His kingdom.

A second meaning is that the poor in their physical and social impoverishment are closer to the kingdom than those caught in the bondage of wealth. It is easier for them to enter because they aren't bound by property and prestigious reputations. The rich are distanced from the kingdom, for they must wrestle themselves loose from the clamps of mammon. As we shall soon see, riches block the kingdom's entrance. The uneducated, sinners, prostitutes, children, uninvited guests, and publicans enter the Upside-Down Kingdom more readily than the sophisticated, the righteous, the strong, the rich, and the pious. The poor have little to give up. They simply walk in. They are grateful. They are the ones who know what it's like to have debts forgiven. The haughty, arrogance of the rich often barricades them from the love of God.

Jesus' word to the poor is that they shouldn't consider their lack of wealth a sign of divine disapproval. This was the common Jewish interpretation. The advent of salvation is signaled by the transformation of destitutes: the blind see, the lame walk, the lepers are cleansed, and the oppressed are released (Matthew 11:5; Luke 4:18, 19; 7:22). The poor are included as the final sign in this messianic list: "The poor have good news preached to them." The good news was that God welcomed them in Jesus Christ. Social outcasts, yes! But they were no longer bums in God's sight. As far as God was concerned their poverty was not the result of divine punishment. They were just as welcome as anyone else into the kingdom. That was good news indeed! They were royal guests of the kingdom. It was probably this good word to the poor that required Jesus to add: "Blessed is he who takes no offense at me" (Matthew 11:6; Luke 7:23). Healing lepers and curing the sick carries no offense. Pharisaic ears were insulted when Jesus redefined the plight of the poor and welcomed ignorant destitutes into the kingdom.[15] The kingdom is not biased against the rich. They are not automatically kicked out. They also are welcome if they shuck off the dictates of wealth, obey God's economic laws, and conspicuously practice the Jubilee.

Jubilee Refused

We have surveyed six warnings of Jesus regarding wealth. Now we turn to three characters who stimulate discussions about mammon. The rich young ruler episode unfortunately is often interpreted out of its context (Luke 18:18-30). The impact of Jesus' dialogue with this bright fellow is sharpened when it is seen in contrast with Zacchaeus. Two brief stories fall between the rich ruler and Zacchaeus. A comparison of Zacchaeus and the ruler dramatizes their differences.

The adjective rich has been used to describe the wealthy persons which we've met so far. It's not strong enough though for this young upstart. He was *very* rich. He had everything that counts—youth, wealth, and power. Possessing these three attributes simultaneously put him at the top of the social pile. We can only speculate about how he became rich at such a young age.

Why does he stop Jesus? He wants to know what he should do to inherit eternal life. This is the basic question which haunts our existence. It was asked one other time in the Scripture and that time Jesus responded with the Good Samaritan story. As in the Lazarus account, eternal life is once again linked squarely with the question of wealth. Once again we have a sincere and conscientious fellow. This is no cunning robber.

In fact, this fellow has been raised correctly—religiously. He knows God's commandments. He's studied in the synagogue. He's gone through the religious institutions—Sunday school, Bible school, youth choir, Christian camp, and the church youth organization. He knows his theology. He has memorized his denomination's creed and doctrine. He accepts orthodox theology. He not only knows all this stuff, but he "observes it." He practices the commandments right down the line. He doesn't steal. He hasn't gotten rich illegally.

Jesus responds to the eternal life question by pointing out a deficiency in just one area. He needs to sell *all* his possessions before he can follow Christ. Why? Because it's wrong to have them? No! Because they should start a common treasury? No! Why should he sell out? Because the poor are hungry and needy. Today we would counsel him to invest it and give the poor the interest. Jesus detects that wealth has captured the young man's heart. Selling out will refocus his attention on the heavenly kingdom. It is important to note that Jesus not only tells him to sell but also invites him to "come, follow me." We should accent the "follow" rather than the "sell." This is an invitation to join the people of the kingdom and selling out in this case was a necessary prerequisite. Although his decision isn't reported, it appears negative since the counsel of Jesus makes him sad. He decides to forfeit eternal life. Jesus doesn't always counsel persons to sell *all* that they have. But in this case He does.

Jesus summarizes the event with harsh words. "How hard it is for those who have riches to enter the kingdom of God! For it is easier for a camel to go through the eye of a needle than for a rich man to enter the kingdom of God" (Luke 18:24, 25). The hardness of this teaching shows up in the fact that some later scribes changed the manuscript to make it more reasonable. One later edition said that getting a rich man into heaven was like pulling a cord or rope through a needle. Another version said it was like getting a camel through a small gate. Neither of these are legitimate interpretations.[16] Jesus probably meant a camel and a needle. It certainly fits with His other teaching on wealth. The immediate outburst of the crowd was, "Then who can be saved?" The answer: "What is impossible with men is possible with God" (verse 27). This doesn't mean that God will miraculously drag rich people through the kingdom's gate. Rather, it means that by the grace of God even a rich man can be freed from the demonic powers of wealth. Even a rich man can be converted, turn around, and practice the Jubilee—as we shall soon see. So in this story we have good theology—orthodox beliefs and proper doctrine—but no obedience. Here there's no Jubilee, no compassion for the poor—only stuffy orthodoxy.

Luke bridges between the sad ruler and Zacchaeus with two short stories. Jesus tells the disciples about His impending doom on the cross. They don't understand. They can't figure it out. Those who should have known didn't. Perhaps they reflect the blindness of the rich ruler. Next is the story of a blind beggar hunched over outside of Jericho. He can't see. But he understands who Jesus is and yells for mercy. Jesus heals him. Now he sees. The people glorify and praise God. Luke is getting us ready for Zacchaeus.

Jubilee Embraced

Zacchaeus might have been short, but he ran a sizable business (Luke 19:1-10). Jericho wasn't a small farm village. It served as Herod the Great's winter capital because of its balmy weather. It was a large city with pools, parks, and typical Greco-Roman buildings. It was a wealthy city because the surrounding irrigated area was extremely fertile. The rabbis spoke of the "fat lands of Jericho." The area also had the distinction of cultivating large groves of balsam trees. They sold for an enormous price, often bringing their weight in gold.[17] Furthermore, Jericho was the gateway for a trade route that ran between Jerusalem and the whole Gentile area east of the Jordan.

Zacchaeus was rich because he was the chief tax farmer (collector) for this district. A team of subordinates collected the taxes for him. It was a lucrative job in a lucrative area. Zacchaeus had apparently outbid other contenders to secure the license to collect the Jericho taxes. Most tax collectors used force and fraud to make a financial killing. The underlings cheated the people and the main tax farmers like Zacchaeus embezzled from their subordinates whenever possible. Tax collectors were hated and despised—not only because they were Jews working for the Romans but mostly because they cheated and used brute force to take money or possessions. They were in the cellar of the house of social prestige. They were not allowed to be judges nor could they serve as a witness in court. They were in the same boat as a Gentile slave. Civil and political rights were denied to them, even rights permitted to seriously blemished bastards.[18] Money from a tax collector couldn't be given for alms because it was tainted. Eating and associating with a tax collector was thought to contaminate the righteous.

It would have been unthinkable for a Pharisee to lunch with Zacchaeus. The people sneered at him. Perhaps they nicknamed him Zacchaeus out of contempt. There's a pun in his name which actually means "the righteous." He is anything but righteous. Yet Jesus lunches with him, unlike the rabbis and scribes who would have joyfully spit in his face. Jesus deliberately contaminates Himself with the food from the table of this detestable outcast. They eat together in a large mansion—one of the finest in Jericho, built on the excessive profits Zacchaeus has squeezed from the poor. We don't know the content of their talk, but a miracle happens. Zacchaeus is moved by Jesus' care and compassion—so moved in fact that he decides to practice Jubilee. The neighbors and passersby are called together in the front lawn. They are startled and flabbergasted to hear crabby old Zacchaeus say, "Behold, Lord, the half of my goods I give to the poor; and if I have defrauded any one of anything, I restore it fourfold" (Luke 19:8). The people cheer. This must be a hoax. They can't believe the miracle that's happening before their eyes. It just can't be true.

We don't know what happened to Zacchaeus' bank account. Depending on how much he returned because of fraud, he may have been wiped out completely. Or he may have had a pile left over. In any case Jesus affirms his action. "Today *salvation* has come to this house, since he also is a son of Abraham. For the Son of man came to seek and to *save* the lost" (Luke 19:9, 10, emphasis added). This man has been saved! Now he is part of the people of God. He is in the royal family as a son of Abraham. This is what the day of salvation is all about. What is impossible with man is possible with God. This rich man by the grace of God has walked through the needle's eye.

Things are quite upside down. The rich young ruler has his theology down pat, but there's no obedience. Zacchaeus has a lousy theology—probably none, but he practices Jubilee. The ruler calls Jesus a "good teacher" but the cheater calls him "Lord." The ruler is trying to obtain eternal life, but he refuses to share and can't squeeze through the needle's eye. The swindler, Zacchaeus, probably never even thought much about life eternal, but his new care for the poor widens the needle's eye. The religious one runs up to Jesus to theologize about eternal life. In contrast Jesus initiates a contaminating lunch with a sinner who is moved by His compassion. The rich ruler has good attitudes but no acts. The cheat has a change of attitude which produces economic action. In the first story economic concerns stagnate faith. But in the second story faith controls economic interest. We have here two contradictory responses to the gospel, two opposite reactions to the poor. On the one hand, good theology, no Jubilee, and condemnation; but on the other hand lousy theology, Jubilee, and salvation.

Upside-Down Jubilee

We conclude Jesus' teaching on wealth with a case of inverted Jubilee. Near the end of His ministry, a day or so after cleaning out the temple den of robbers, Jesus returns to the temple. He is in the large room of the temple treasury where offerings and gifts are placed in large gold and silver vessels. Again we find a comparison of the rich and poor.

> And he sat down opposite the treasury, and watched the multitude putting money into the treasury. Many rich people put in large sums. And a poor widow came, and put in two copper coins, which make a penny. And he called his disciples to him, and said to them, "Truly, I say to you, this poor widow has put in more than all those who are contributing to the treasury. For they all contributed out of their abundance; but she out of her poverty has put in everything she had, her whole living." Mark 12:41-44; Luke 21:1-4.

In the verse immediately before this account of the widow, Jesus condemns those "who devour widows' houses and for a pretense make long prayers. They will receive the greater condemnation" (Mark 12:40).

The widow in Palestinian society was an outcast. She had no inheritance rights from her husband's property. When he died, the oldest son acquired the property. If there was no son, she might be married by a brother of her deceased husband. If the brother refused or if there was none, she would return to her father's house or to begging. Widows, like other women, had no role in public or religious life. They often wore black clothing to signal their plight. Evidence from the prophets' message in the Old Testament shows that widows were often oppressed by the rich.

We have just seen Jesus condemning the scribes for devouring widows' houses. Apparently the scribes had developed some religious legislation which forced widows to lose their houses. This economic injustice was glossed over with pretentious long prayers. After searing the scribes, Jesus turned to highlight a widow's faithfulness. The rich, probably Sadducees and nobles from the aristocratic Jerusalem families, are putting "large sums" into the offering plate. These are impressive amounts, probably in the prescribed form of pure Syrian silver coins. The widow comes and she is poor. She drops in two copper coins which equal a penny. The copper lepton was the smallest Greek coin in circulation. It took 128 of these leptons to equal one denarius which was a day's wage. So the widow is dropping in 2/128 of a day's wage! Jesus is impressed, so impressed that He calls the disciples together for a lesson. The widow, He says, has put in more than all of these rich persons together. How can this be? She put in everything she had, but they skimmed off the top of their abundance. The actual amount of money was insignificant. What counted was what was left over for consumption. The rich were still very rich, even after a sizable offering. The poor widow gave her capital rather than a self-righteous tithe. The proportion of our wealth that we give is the critical issue—not the raw amount.

Jesus again is striking out against the rich. He also affirms the Jubilee attitude of the poor widow. Certainly she could have found some convincing religious excuses for not giving the last two leptons in her purse. This is upside-down Jubilee when the poor give with greater sincerity than the rich. Jesus' instruction in Matthew (5:40) to give your cloak as well as your coat if someone sues you is directed to a poor man. This advice is for the poor debtor who had given his coat as a sign of his positive intent to repay a loan. The creditor shows up and demands repayment which the poor man can't make. In such a case he should be willing to give even his cloak. Jesus not only expects the rich to Jubilee, but also affirms the benevolence of the poor. They as well as the rich can be caught by covetousness and also need the joy of detachment.

This concludes our survey of the six warnings and three character studies focusing on wealth. These nine components summarize Jesus' economic message. The amount of material on the wealth theme is astonishing. No other concept than the kingdom of God itself reappears more frequently in the Gospels than the warnings about wealth. We obviously cannot conclude that the Christian's economic practice is a peripheral fringe of the gospel. It stands at the very core of the kingdom way. Conversion which does not involve economic change is not authentic conversion. The inverted or upside-down message reverberates again and again:

> Blessed are you poor . . . woe to you that are rich. Luke 6:20.
>
> What is exalted among men is an abomination in the sight of God. Luke 16:15.
>
> Lazarus goes to Abraham's bosom, the rich man ends up in torment. Luke 16:22, 23.
>
> So is he who lays up treasure for himself, and is not rich toward God. Luke 12:21.
>
> For all the nations of the world seek these things. . . . Instead, seek his kingdom. Luke 12:30, 31.
>
> The rich young ruler seeks eternal life, but salvation visits Zacchaeus' house. Luke 18:18—19:10.
>
> Do not lay up for yourselves treasure on earth . . . but lay up for yourselves treasures in heaven. Matthew 6:19, 20.
>
> No one can serve two masters; for . . . he will hate the one and love the other. Matthew 6:24.

The economic values of the kingdom are upside down in contrast to the dominant values of modern life. Jesus not only delivers a harsh condemnation of Palestinian economic structures, He also calls us to join the perpetual Jubilee of God's kingdom which even today looks upside down in the midst of contemporary culture.

Questions for Discussion

1. Discuss instances when material possessions in your life have fit the warnings which Jesus left. When have they been a "Strangler," "Worrier," "Blinder," "Boss," "Dam-

ner," or "Curse," in your experience?

2. Which of these six threats is most serious in your life?

3. Do you personally identify more with Lazarus or with the rich man?

4. What economic practices today produce a Lazarus?

5. What strikes you most in the comparison between Zacchaeus and the rich young ruler? Which one are you most like?

6. In your own words what was the central message of Jesus' economic teachings?

7. How do our typical financial inheritance practices relate to the Jubilee vision of Jesus?

8. Identify and discuss persons and/or organizations which practice Jubilee principles today.

7
RIGHT-SIDE-UP DETOURS

In the midst of affluence the economic instruction of Jesus strikes us as hard teaching indeed. It is one area of the faith-culture relationship where the prevailing social values often warp our faith. Our commitment to the present economic order often causes us to bypass the bulk of biblical teaching on wealth and distorts how we read the Scripture. Some verses and teachings are lifted out of their context and incorrectly used as proof texts to legitimate or "bless" our personal economic philosophy. In addition to misinterpreting Scripture in order to rationalize affluence, we use other nonbiblical but nevertheless "sacred" sayings to support our accumulative financial practices. I will identify ten detours—ten examples where our economic philosophy controls our theological beliefs. In other words, these ten bypasses permit us to self-righteously slide around the substance of Jesus' economic message. In most instances these evasions take an isolated verse or a proverbial wisdom saying and use it to maneuver around Jesus' call for economic conversion.

Detour One: What About the Parable of the Talents?

This is one of the most frequent excuses which I hear. This parable is found in both Matthew's (25:14-30) and

Luke's (19:11-27) Gospels. An irony here is that this parable which directly follows the Zacchaeus story in Luke is used to justify precisely the opposite of Zacchaeus' behavior. The misinterpretation of this parable often runs along the following lines. God has given each of us different kinds and amounts of abilities or personal talents. This includes our personal skills such as singing, managing, and counseling. The talents also refer to our capital assets such as cash, property, and stocks. We will be held accountable for how we use these personal attributes and material resources. God will reward us for expanding them and using them to their fullest capacity. In similar fashion, punishment will fall on those who sit on their resources. It follows then that if making money is our gift, we should make money like mad. Capital assets and property should also be multiplied as rapidly as possible. This type of logic is often used to justify profiteering and to squelch giving to the poor. Matthew's Gospel explicitly quotes the master as telling the unfaithful steward, "You ought to have invested my money with the bankers, and at my coming I should have received what was my own with interest" (Matthew 25:27).

Just because Jesus uses money—probably the equivalent of a 100 day's wages—as the key symbol in the story does not mean that the point of the parable is literally about financial stewardship. The actual objects in a parable can never be taken literally as the norm for Christian behavior. Usually they communicate a hidden meaning or principle which emerges out of the everyday story. We don't say that the parable of the sower means that the Christian today should actually sow grain, nor do we say that the parable of the lost sheep implies that Christians should raise sheep! On the other hand, example stories such as the Good Samaritan in contrast to parables are intended to demonstrate specifically how a Christian should act. "Go and do likewise" (Luke 10:37).

What is the point of the talent story? It is clear that the merchant or nobleman entrusts his servants with a commodity and holds them accountable for their use of it. When he suddenly returns, there is a crisis. Each servant is judged according to how he cared for the master's property. The commodity in the story can only refer to our knowledge of Christian faith. Perhaps it was directed to the scribes or the Jewish people in general. How had they cared for the faith and Scriptures which had been entrusted to them? They were now in the process of being judged by Jesus on their stewardship of the law. Were they good stewards of the commandments? Had they preserved and interpreted the law of Moses properly?

The early church interpreted the parable to mean that Jesus was going away and upon His return He would judge them on how they had expanded and multiplied the ideas of the kingdom. In fact, Luke (19:11) reports that the reason Jesus told the parable was because some of the followers thought the kingdom would appear immediately when they arrived in Jerusalem. Luke suggests that Jesus is going away and at his second coming will judge His followers according to how they spread the teachings of the kingdom. As Clarence Jordan puts it, we are to "trade" with kingdom ideas.[1] We will be held responsible for using our knowledge of the kingdom to its fullest. The more we know about the secrets of the kingdom, the greater will be our accountability. Rather than a story which justifies the acquisition of wealth, we find the opposite. The more we know about the upside-down economic way of Jesus, the greater our obligation to live it.

The story of the rich man and Lazarus rings clear. The rich man knew about Moses and the prophets. He understood the Jubilee. He had been given a talent, knowledge of God's economic way, but he buried it. He sat on it. He didn't feed the beggar Lazarus. He was utterly punished on the day of judgment. Following the story of Zacchaeus, the parable of the talents suggests that we are responsible and will be judged for how we live the truth of the Zacchaeus story. Will we allow the lordship of Jesus Christ to open our pocketbooks? This same interpretation applies to the wisdom saying at the end of the parable and in Mark 4:25, "For to him who has will more be given; and from him who has not, even what he has will be taken away." This cannot mean he who has money will make more. Rather, he who multiplies his kingdom knowledge will be given more and he who wastes his kingdom ideas will lose them completely.

Detour Two: Seek the Kingdom and Get Rich!

After teaching about anxiety in both Matthew's and Luke's Gospels, Jesus instructs the disciples to "seek first his kingdom and his righteousness, and all these things shall be yours as well" (Matthew 6:33; Luke 12:31). I have heard it said that this is biblical proof that if we really focus our energies on the kingdom, we will become rich. Or another way to say it is that riches are a sign of God's blessing. The more affluent someone is the more they must be seeking the kingdom. We have already seen that Jesus viewed riches more as a curse than as a blessing.

What does it mean that kingdom seekers will also have the material things of life as well? In the sabbatical context, Jesus was simply telling the people that God will continue to provide an adequate six-year yield to cover their needs in both the sixth and seventh years. If they obey His command, He will care for them. The "things" to be provided here are food and clothing—not luxurious houses and estates. God will provide for their bare necessities. When this passage is read in the sabbatical setting there is no promise here of getting rich off the kingdom. I believe it is true that a business venture or a household managed in harmony with God's laws of honesty and integrity will usually be successful. However, if the manager or owner truly allows the rule of God to operate in his life he will not hoard any gain but will follow the biblical examples of conspicuous sharing. In fact, the accumulation of a material stockpile is a good barometer that the teachings of the kingdom are not understood and are not being lived.

Matthew counsels us to seek the kingdom and His "righteousness" which could be interpreted as His "justice." Seeking the kingdom doesn't mean that bread will mysteriously fall out of the sky. Nor does it mean that we will automatically get rich. To pursue the kingdom in order to get wealthy is certainly a perverted motivation. Concentrating on the kingdom will certainly mean that profit which does emerge will always be shared in Jubilee fashion.

Detour Three: Leave and Gain!

A similar evasive route is found near the end of the rich young ruler story. Jesus concludes by saying, "Truly, I say to you, there is no man who has left house or wife or brothers or parents or children, for the sake of the kingdom of God, who will not receive manifold more in this time, and in the age to come eternal life" (Luke 18:29, 30; Mark 10:29, 30; Matthew 19:29). Matthew and Mark include land in their list of things which are left for the sake of the kingdom. In numerous discussions, I have heard it said that this means Jesus will multiply our property if we follow Him. A pastor warming up his congregation for an offering promised that God would literally return to them $100 for every dollar they gave. Such perverted motivation of "give to get rich" utterly destroys the Jubilee spirit of giving.

In the first place such an interpretation would also anticipate a multiplication of wives, husbands, and parents in this age. What Jesus means to say here is that when we join the kingdom we join the family of God. Even though disciples may sell property or leave their homes, they will find warm welcomes in other Christian homes as they travel. They will discover a network of new sisters, brothers, and parents in the kingdom who welcome them with beds and teapots. This, I think, is the meaning of the passage. The persons who say this means God doubles our wealth if we follow Him usually are the people who have not literally left any houses or lands in the first place. They are still sitting on their property and trying to find an isolated Bible verse to justify multiplying their holdings.

Detour Four: Remember the Poor Are Always with You!

All four Gospels report the story of the woman pouring expensive perfume on Jesus (Matthew 26:6-13; Mark 14:3-9; Luke 7:36-50; John 12:1-8). There is considerable variation in the four accounts; except for Luke, the writers report that the disciples or onlookers condemned this waste of almost a year's wages. They wondered aloud why the perfume wasn't sold and the money given to the poor. Jesus responded by saying, "For you always have the poor with you, but you will not always have me" (Matthew 26:11).[2] Here is a clear case of Jesus fatalistically acknowledging the perpetual existence of the poor and showing the priority of worship over social concern—or does He?

Interestingly, Jesus quotes directly from Deuteronomy 15, the chapter containing Jubilee and sabbatical instructions. Earlier in the passage God tells the Hebrew people that if they obey Him there will be no poor in their land. But He goes on to say that if they harden their hearts there will be poor. As long as greed and selfishness continue the poor will be among them. Does this justify a callous looking the other way which neglects the poor? Just the opposite, "For the poor will never cease out of your land, therefore I command you, You shall open *wide* your hand to your brother, to the needy and to the poor, in the land" (Deuteronomy 15:11, emphasis added). In light of His continual plea on behalf of the plight of the poor, it's hardly conceivable that in this one verse Jesus is contradicting the bulk of His teaching by telling us to tighten our pocketbooks since after all the poor will always be around and there's not much we can do about it. Rather, He is saying that since greed and ambition will continue to govern the lives of people and their social systems, there will always be poor. They are a natural product of greedy systems. The observation of the fact does not justify its perpetuation. In light of this reality, how much more we need to care and give and be sure that we are not part of structures and organizations which trample the poor.

Derrett has shown through a detailed study of the Jewish law that pouring the perfume was not an act of worship but one of charity.[3] A prostitute could not give her offering in the temple because it was contaminated by her profession. Contaminated earnings and ointment could however be used to prepare a corpse. The preparation for burial took precedent over feeding and clothing the poor. Jesus said that by "pouring this ointment on my body she has done it to prepare me for burial" (Matthew 26:12). This immoral prostitute takes the most important tool of her trade—perfume—and uses it to perform an act of charity on Jesus' body. The perfume which once seduced other bodies is now joyfully given to prepare the body which will be broken for the sins of the world. Upside-down indeed! Dashing the perfume over Jesus' body symbolized her rejection of her old life and the spontaneous joy of forgiveness, for she had many sins. Matthew and Mark move directly from this story to Judas' purchase of the body of Jesus for thirty pieces of silver, initiating His death. It is not possible to twist this story of joyful forgiveness into a prescription for callousness toward the poor.

Detour Five: It Just Depends on Your Attitude!

This is undoubtedly the most frequent way our culture

locks our purses. Often at the end of a discussion on Jesus and wealth someone will summarize the talk by saying, "Anyway it's our attitude that's important. As long as we have the right attitude, things will work out okay." Now obviously attitudes are important. They are a good starting place. Poor people can be just as materialistic, if not more so, than rich people. Jesus taught that wrong attitudes are just as bad as wrong behavior. His comments along this line were aimed primarily at correcting the Pharisees who had lots of good-looking surface behavior but rotten internal attitudes.

Jesus didn't intend, however, to teach that good attitudes are enough or that they are a satisfactory replacement for good behavior. They are the right place to start, but Jesus clearly intends for us to go beyond thinking. He condemns acts which accumulate wealth; the rich fool with a barn and the rich man who threw crumbs to Lazarus. He commands acts which distribute wealth. A number of times He tells the disciples to sell. Zacchaeus is described as a child of God because of his act. The change in Zacchaeus' attitudes led to an immediate change in his economic behavior. The rich young ruler may have had good attitudes, but they didn't feed the poor. Having warm feelings in our heart, good intentions in our head, and proper attitudes in our mind doesn't clothe and feed the poor. We can have nice attitudes and still enjoy luxury. Behavior is the test. Jesus calls us to an upside-down kind of compassion that results in economic action.

Detour Six: What About Stewardship?

This pious word is used as a cover-up for a lot of impious economic behavior. Oddly the word "stewardship" isn't on the lips of Jesus when He discusses wealth. Instead He insistently warns us of the dangers of mammon and calls us to economic compassion. The idea of stewardship implies that a steward looks after an owner's property. In the Hebrew, it means "man over the house"—an official who controls a large household for the master. I think it's proper to use the term stewardship to describe the Christian's relationship with property, since this reminds us that God is in fact the Owner of the property. But what do we mean by stewardship?

It's helpful to distinguish between the wishes of the owner and the wishes of the steward. The steward is responsible to see that the property is managed according to the master's wishes. The steward's wishes are subordinate to the owner's. The problem with a lot of Christian talk about stewardship is that we use the term to whitewash our own use of property with little regard to the biblical understanding of property. According to our logic, stewardship means that we should take whatever resources we have and multiply them as fast as possible, and hang on to them until the grave. We certainly shouldn't give them away, since, after all, they really aren't ours. We need to hang on to them for God's sake.

This distorted logic perverts a proper view of stewardship. We should begin with God's vision for the use of natural and social resources. We have seen in the Old Testament Jubilee and in Jesus' teachings that God wants His resources to be widely shared. They are not to be used to elevate some persons and to put others down. They are to be given freely to those in need. This means that good stewards of God's resources will generously share and distribute them. We are not stewards of God's resources when we stockpile, protect, defend, and multiply them for personal gain. The use of the term stewardship for this kind of behavior is profanity. Good stewardship means that we are tight or frugal when calculating our own needs but joyfully loose when responding to others. Spending lavishly on ourselves is not good stewardship, but lavish sharing with others is!

Detour Seven: Give a Tithe!

Tithing often serves as a convenient and self-righteous diversion from the economic thrust of Jesus' message. It can be a mechanical rule which justifies luxurious living for persons receiving sizable salaries. We are not explicitly instructed to tithe in the New Testament. Paul and Jesus both encourage liberal giving—even capital as we have seen in the case of the poor widow. Tithes were an integral part of the Old Testament system of sacrifices and offerings. The inadequacy of tithing as a rule for giving is obvious. A person earning $10,000 a year gives $1,000 and retains $9,000. The person earning $100,000 gives $10,000 and can live extravagantly on $90,000. The unfortunate problem with tithing is that it focuses our attention on how much we give rather than on how much we keep. God doesn't care much about what we give. He's primarily concerned about what we hang on to. It's not important that one family gives $1,000 and another gives $10,000. What is important is that one family struggles along to make ends meet with $9,000, while another family self-righteously spends $90,000 lavishly because, after all, "they have tithed."

Such token tithes are not examples of good stewardship, compassion, or Jubilee. They are religious maneuvers which are an abomination in the eyes of God. We need to concentrate on lowering our standard of living and then give the rest away. Perhaps the term tithe is not useful and should be purged from our vocabulary.

Ron Sider, in his excellent book, *Rich Christians in an Age of Hunger,* proposes a graduated tithe.[4] In his plan a family establishes a yearly baseline budget of say $8,000. A regular 10 percent tithe is made on this basic figure. A 5 percent increase is added to the tithe for each additional thousand dollars of income above the baseline. A $9,000 income would be tithed 10 percent on the first eight thousand and 15 percent on the last thousand. When the income reaches $26,000 all of the last thousand dollars would be given since the graduated tithe has increased to 100 percent. At the $26,000 income figure a family following Sider's scheme would have given $11,150 and retained $14,850 for personal use and savings. This proposal certainly moves us beyond kindergarten tithing. It would revolutionize Christian giving.

Even under this plan the tithing family earning $26,000 has another time as much money at their personal disposal as the family with an $8,000 income. The Jubilee model takes us beyond elementary tithing to a graduated tithe or, better yet, graduates us from tithing completely so that we give all above our baseline budget.

Detour Eight: Live Within Your Means!

This advice which emerges out of a tithing mindset suggests that living the good life is okay as long as we can afford it. This norm of "living within our means" suggests that if our means are meager, we must follow an austere budget. But if our means are large, we have a license to consume freely. The "live within your means" maxim is obviously a necessary rule for the lower income family. It can, however, become convenient verbage which blindly endorses an affluent lifestyle for higher income persons. It is not a specifically religious rule of thumb, but it's a nice-sounding cultural belief which most people take for granted. In this quiet way it blinds us to the Jubilee model.

Detour Nine: Maintain the Witness!

Here is one of the more sinister arguments used to justify evading the Jubilee model. It's the notion that a high standard of living is necessary in order to communicate and "witness" effectively to affluent persons. In order to reach uppity-up people with the gospel we need to communicate to them with their own symbols. We obviously can't make a meaningful witness to the Mercedes crowd if we drive a VW. They won't take our message seriously until we get a Grand Prix or Continental. The people who advocate "luxury evangelism" would certainly not encourage stealing in order to establish evangelical rapport with legal offenders. Yet they use this kind of logic to justify an affluent lifestyle. They distort "evangelism" to rationalize an extravagant lifestyle. In the process, the good news is diluted and contaminated to the point that it's no longer good news.

Witnessing from this kind of posture calls others to a simple "yes" to Jesus in their heart with no expectations for social and economic conversion. This is cheap salvation. When the gospel becomes inoffensive, it's no longer gospel. People are not released from the grips of economic bondage and social fads. Instead, they trust in a false gospel which makes their service to mammon appear righteous. The witness of the gospel is that Jesus frees us from the bondage of other gods in our life. Maintaining a high standard of living in order to "effectively" witness is not only an abominable cover-up in the sight of God, it also leads others to a cheap and erroneous faith.

Detour Ten: Children of the King!

A final detour sign reminds us that we are after all children of a King. God has promised that He will reward and bless His children if they are faithful to Him. Since earthly kings live in extravagant palaces, Christians have the right to live luxuriously to demonstrate that they are indeed members of God's royal court. Children of a king should dress and eat in regal fashion. It is true that Jesus is our King. But that doesn't give us a permit to enjoy the good life of affluence. Just the opposite. If Jesus is indeed Lord and King of our life, we will conscientiously obey His commandments to share our wealth. He most certainly is our King, but his kingship is upside-down in contrast to earthly kingdoms. He does promise to "bless us" to provide wholeness, peace, and joy, but He never promises to make His children financially rich.

Meanwhile Back Home

What does all this mean? If we accept the message of Jesus as authoritative and bypass the subtle cultural detours, how do we implement upside-down economics? We have found that the imminent rule of God in the lives of believers is the key to the economic preaching of Jesus.[5] The nearness and closeness of the reign of God robs the economic demons of their power. We have seen the Jubilee principles threaded throughout the Gospels. As men experience the forgiveness of God, they are able to forgive. As they learn of the goodness of God, they no longer fret and worry about their bare necessities. Because they have been freed from sin, they can liberate their debtors. Because God cared about them, they have a new and intense care for others. One time they were beggars, strangers, slaves, and debtors. Now the warmth of God's love moves them to compassion when others hurt. Their compassion has feet. The love of God in their heart changes their economic behavior. Mercy becomes the new yardstick for a successful life instead of accumulation, conspicuous giving instead of conspicuous consumption. At the bottom of this upside-down way is the sum of God's law. Loving God with all your heart means loving the neighbor as much as oneself. Loving the neighbor as much as oneself means caring for him economically—sharing, giving, considering his economic welfare just as important as one's own. The liberating detachment and looseness of the new way strips the old economic demons of their grip.

Hard Question

As usual, this is nice theology but what does it mean? We cannot construct six easy rules for upside-down economics. Jesus doesn't give us specific answers, but He is the catalyst for asking the right questions. He moves us beyond absolute rules and regulations by insisting that we practice a perpetual Jubilee. Jesus doesn't categorically reject private property nor does He insist on communal ownership. Much of His teaching assumes the fact of private property. A person cannot lend or give to help those in need if he has no property. At times we may need to sell all, like the rich young ruler, but at other times, as with Zacchaeus, the Jesus way may level financial pyramids but not call for a complete sellout. Jesus doesn't insist on a sellout nor does He require that we all buy in together. What He does insist on is that we care about the poor as much as we care about ourselves.

He calls us to question the prevailing economic assumptions in every culture. Although His teaching was directed primarily toward individuals, His words and actions undercut the commonly accepted economic values and practices which upheld the Palestinian financial structure. Just because someone worked hard to earn money didn't mean that He had a right to spend it however He pleased. Just because money could be gained legally didn't make it's acquisition moral. Just because the religious leaders put their blessing on economic practices didn't make the procedures holy or right. His continual call for Jubilee was a judgment on the economic structures which permitted huge disparities between the rich and the poor in Palestine. He incessantly warned that the strength of economic forces can be a powerful god which captures and jails us before we know it.

And so we need to question the taken-for-granted assumptions afloat in our culture. Is it morally right to pay only the minimum wage even if it's legal? Is it right to charge the prevailing professional fees even when they are within the law? A minimum wage and exorbitant professional fees may operate against the Jubilee principle by perpetuating an economic structure which keeps poor people poor. Should we sell our house to the highest bidder just because that's the conventional practice? Is getting the "best price" we can manage really "good stewardship"? Selling it for a lower figure to a poor family might be more in the spirit of Jubilee than holding out for the "best price" from an "entrepreneur" who already owns five houses. Is charging the highest commission consistent with the way of Jesus? Is it actually "good stewardship" to try to squeeze the last nickle out of every deal? Should we charge the going rate of rent if we don't need it just because that's the way things are? In many subtle and unconscious ways we are captives of an economic system which easily distorts our faith. We dare never assume that just because "that's the way things are" means that they are right or Christian.

I'm Not Rich

Jesus used the terms rich and poor almost flippantly. They apparently didn't need definition or clarification for His audience. In a two-class society with virtually no middle class, the rich were obvious. Most Christians who take the time to read and study Jesus' comments on the rich don't take them too seriously since they unconsciously assume that they themselves certainly aren't rich. A moment's reflection makes it obvious that the term "rich" is a relative word which is socially defined. We don't determine "richness' with absolute standards. We are rich compared to whom? We tend to think that middle classers need not worry about Jubilee since Jesus only talked about the really rich.

Social scientists have discovered that happiness doesn't automatically increase as wealth increases. Happiness comes when people feel that they have enough money to meet their perceived needs. What we think we need is of course socially determined by the people around us. If we don't think we need much we can be happy with a relatively small income. On the other hand, a high salaried person may be very unhappy with an income that doesn't meet what he or she considers a "bare bones" budget.

When I think about rich people, I think of people like Ray Kroc, the genius behind McDonald's hamburgers who has piled up a fortune of over 600 million by most estimates. Or take someone like John Donald MacArthur, a billionaire who owns more than 100,000 acres of Florida real estate.[6] I think of the Rockefellers, the H. L. Hunts, the J. Paul Getty's, the Kennedy's. I also think of places like Palm Springs, California, where Ex-President Gerald Ford is building a "simple and unpretentious" home for $620,000. It certainly is a modest house compared to most of the other places in this posh retirement community like Joey Hrudka's $3 million dream house and Frank Sinatra's $1.8 million estate. I also think of top executives who receive $500-700 grand a year. And then there are million dollar sporting stars. And Robert Redford earned a $2 million salary for appearing in "A Bridge Too Far." His contract required three weeks of work with an option on a fourth one.[7]

These are rich people in my book. I certainly don't think of myself when I think of rich people. My salary is nothing compared to that kind of money. I've always considered myself poor until a few years ago when I was traveling in Honduras and visited a Christian brother. He took me to his banana plot a mile-and-a-half up the mountain. I counted as we walked. He literally had over fifty patches on the only pair of trousers he owned. It suddenly hit me that I was rich—very rich indeed—with at least a dozen pair of trousers and more shirts.

The problem with a relative definition of "rich" is that we all tend to look up the social ladder and compare ourselves with persons above us. We certainly aren't rich compared to the person who gets $5,000 a year more than we do. No, we aren't rich in contrast to the guy with three more pairs of shoes than we have. By looking up the ladder, we are never rich—never wealthy. Staring up the ladder always makes us look poor. Thus, the biblical message doesn't speak to our situation except to make us hope that the rich guy on the rung above us will drop a few leftovers down and not tramp on our fingers too much. But that's wishful thinking because he's probably not looking down in the first place. He's busy feeling poor himself compared to the people above him.

Again the Jubilee perspective is helpful. The reminder that once we were slaves, once we were captives, converts our focus from up to down. The biblical spotlight focuses downward. Pagans look up the ladder. The Gentiles climb the ladder seeking after these things. When we look down, we always look rich. Then the Jubilee message fits. Probably no readers of this book are a Lazarus. But there are Lazaruses in our communities—persons who don't receive the minimum daily requirement of calories. Even on the conservative side about half a billion—that's 500 million!—people in the world are gradually starving, receiving less than the baseline requirement of calories. Another half billion get enough calories but are short on protein. In 1975 the world population shot past the four billion mark, and we are scheduled to number five billion by 1986. At least one billion, or about one fourth of the worldwide village is hungry.[8] Few readers of this book are part of the one billion malnourished citizens of the world. Compared to them we are rich. Even in the United States 12 percent of the population lives below the poverty level of $5,500 a year for an urban family of four.[9] It's time we start reading our Bibles as rich Christians. We are the rich man—not Lazarus. Those of us living in North America are on a rich lifeboat floating in a sea of starvation. Using the gross national product as a comparative indicator, one third of the world's population gobbles up 87 percent of the world's resources while the poor two thirds of the four billion are left to scrap for a meager 13 percent. Even when the respective standards of living are taken into account and "real" purchasing power is calculated, the average American is fourteen times richer than the average Indian and seventeen times wealthier than the average Kenyan.[10] We can only read the Bible as rich persons when compared to poor persons on the local, regional, and international level.

Patches

We can begin by consuming less. Many of our so-called necessities are status symbols which we polish to maintain a respectable image among our peers. We can eat soybeans instead of steak. We can buy used or factory reject furniture instead of new. We can drive VW's instead of Mercedes. We can keep the temperature at 68 degrees instead of 76. We can wear patches instead of the latest fashions. We can buy clothing at the Salvation Army instead of at Gimbels. We can buy retreads instead of new tires. Such behavior is not frugal or miserly, it is merely the beginning of responsible stewardship of the God-owned nonrenewable resources. It may mean jeopardizing our social reputation and our plastic image of respectability.

All persons need friends who provide a warm social mirror of support and affirmation for their behavior. Our self-image and our sense of being "okay" emerge from how we think other people view us. I am what I think you think I am. If I think that other people think I am an oddball, I immediately feel inadequate and begin to think of myself as weird. All of us want others to respect us and to think well of us. To gain that acceptance we are often forced to buy and conspicuously display the status symbols of our social group. Outdated clothing, small cars, black and white TVs, and stay-at-home vacations violate the rules of social acceptance in middle-class culture. Ironically, the fashion show expectations peak in the pew at 10:00 a.m. on Sunday morning. Fashionable dress is too often a prerequisite for acceptable worship.

Deviant behavior is punished by smirks, gossip, ridicule, and avoidance. Few individuals have the emotional and psychological strength to live upside down economically on their own. The rejection and ridicule hurts and can destroy us. For this reason we need Christian friends who can affirm upside-down economic values. All of us are social beings—dependent on others for our sense of worth and value. It is important that we select and create circles of friends—reference groups—which affirm and support kingdom values. This network of Christian friends doesn't need to be structured formally into a commune, but they do need to aggressively reinforce each other's attempts to live out a Christian lifestyle. Only in the warmth of such a Christian counterculture is it possible to withstand the demonic forces of the admen.

Curtailing our consumption patterns is certainly not a magic solution to world hunger. Buying less steak at the local supermarket will not automatically put more protein into third world countries. As Christians we must act responsibly by consuming less, not because that is an effective international solution to hunger, but because it is the morally right thing to do. We will be judged not by our grandiose solutions to world problems, but by our personal obedience to our present knowledge. Second, it is easy to be tempted to do nothing because we think that our small act will be of no consequence. It is true that one more baby, one more big car, and one less steak will make no significant difference. The problem is that with several hundred million other people thinking the same thing the corporate consequences of our behavior are devastating. One million pieces of litter and 50 million more gas guzzlers and 30 million more babies do make a whopping corporate difference. The "my behavior won't make a difference" line does not excuse us from moral responsibility. Individual acts, however, are not enough. We also must act collectively through organizations such as Bread for the World which influence legislation and political policy. Above all we must have a global perspective which makes a difference on the local level.

Living the Jubilee

The negative attitude toward riches in the teaching of Jesus does not mean for one moment that we should run away from the business world. He didn't leave us with an economic manifesto of withdrawal. He doesn't call us away from industry. He doesn't teach us that the handling and management of money and property are wrong. He tells us instead that the economic reign of God in our life should make a difference in our acquisition, management, and disposal of wealth. The freedom from economic bondage breaks out and surprises the prevailing assumptions. The expression of the Jubilee takes different forms, depending on our position in a particular economic structure. When we are the rich man in a structured relationship, it means sharing beyond expectation to the persons below us.

As employers, we practice Jubilee by paying above-average wages joyfully. Instead of trying to squeeze the maximum labor out of each employee at the minimum price, we release them from slavery by generously sharing profits, providing dignity in work, and encouraging stock ownership in the company. This is not a prescription for bankruptcy—nor is it a carelessness about the bottom line. It is, however, a commitment to the Jubilee perspective which calls for a redistribution of profit to those who have earned it. Funneling all the profit into the hands of a few leads to a pyramiding which contradicts the Jubilee spirit. We must continually ask where profit comes from. Does it come at the expense of poor employees? Where is it going? Does its distribution conform to a Jubilee vision, or does it hoist a few persons to the top of the economic ladder and hold the rest at the bottom?

We must continually recall the biblical injunction that the people and the material resources are the Lord's. They are not to be exploited for selfish gain. People are to be valued—not possessions—and possessions should be used, not people. The Jubilee industry will aggressively work to employ the socially disadvantaged, ex-offenders, racial minorities, and youth without prior work experience. Jubilee companies will go beyond the minimum federal quotas for hiring minorities. For me personally, Jubilee economics means paying the secretary who types for me more than the prevailing clerical wage. I am the rich man in that particular relationship. In professional services the Jubilee approach may mean a graduated payment scale for clients by income. It may mean charging lower fees than the prevailing fee structure to all clients. We cannot simply assume that it is moral for professionals to collect a $50,000 a year salary from clients who earn $10,000 on the average. Embracing an exploitive economic structure is inconsistent with the Jubilee way. The Jubilee professional will not exploit such an economic structure, even if it is legally permitted. Thus, when we are the rich person, we express Jubilee to those below us with joy.

Such upside-down giving which goes beyond conventional and legal expectations is the witness that we have entered the kingdom. It is a powerful sign—with greater credibility than any sermon—that King Jesus is also King of the bottom line. We need to find creative ways of "giving" and using our property for the sake of the poor. In our community a pretrial bail association posts property bail so that poor persons don't need to sit in jail for months before their trial. Homeowners provide their properties as bail for this program. Property or savings accounts can be used as collateral for disadvantaged persons lacking credit who want to buy a home or start a small business. If we love our neighbor as much as ourself we must be willing to sign our name on his dotted line and take the consequence if his payments default.

We are in some economic relationships as the rich person and in others as the poor person. When I tip a waitress, I'm probably the rich guy, but when I relate to my employer I may be the poor guy. When we are the poor person in an economic relationship, we can still express a similar sense of freedom from financial captivity, although the expression of it may take on different form. Instead of clamoring and banging on the office door for a raise, we can quietly accept our wage. When raise time comes, we may even offer to continue working at the old rate. If the raise is imperative for our family budget, we can accept it graciously. If it's not needed, we may turn it down. We can freely tip beyond expectation. We can offer to pay more than the established price for a product or service. This is not carelessly wasting our money, nor is it poor stewardship. It's an upside-down witness to our freedom from economic bondage. We can add a tithe to the monthly rent or mortgage as a sign of our liberation. Freely giving and sharing the Jubilee spirit in our economic structure is not always possible. Inflation and our yearly budget may gobble up every cent. As we cut out frivolous luxuries and work at a more austere standard of living, we are able to give "surprise tithes" when tithing isn't expected as a witness to our Savior's love. This pocketbook witness directed to both our rich and poor neighbors is a most powerful sign of God's love and economic liberation.

The Signs of Upside-Down Giving

It is probably clear by now that one way of Jubilee giving is not to take money from poorer people in the first place. But lowering fees and increasing employees' salaries means that we will have less money to control. We will have less to give in the offering plate and less deductions to claim on the income tax form. Although the saying may be trite, it is true that money is power. Giving is a real form of social power. Church agencies, schools, and benevolent organizations eagerly identify generous givers and quickly begin wooing them. Our normal tendency is to support the organizations which promote our particular brand of faith and theology. Unfortunately, giving can turn us into power brokers who wheel and deal influence to push our pet programs through. It is obvious that people will support and promote programs which benefit them and trumpet their favorite ideology. Giving to receive a plaque or a building namesake is not Jubilee giving. There is little witness in this kind of giving. It's merely the old power broker mentality in sweet religious garb.

There are five upside-down characteristics of Jubilee giving. Jubilee sharing is primarily directed toward the poor—those who have been crunched by economic disparities. Jesus again and again directs us to give to the poor. Had we been in His shoes we would have probably told people to give to the temple. Jesus doesn't ask for contributions to His cause. He is concerned solely with the plight of the poor, not with religious propaganda, for He understands that the most powerful Christian witness is the witness that comes when our giving is unattached to the strings of propaganda. The old worldly mentality contributes money in order to peddle our own pet religious ideas.

Second, Jubilee giving includes other Christians in the decision-making process of the where and how of giving. It's not wheeling and dealing by rich prima donnas to buy seats on boards, honorary degrees, and subtle influence. Jubilee giving is a corporate expression of love where the poor in the church have an equal say in the giving process. The members of our house fellowship contribute their tithes and offerings to a common fund which is then dispersed by group consensus. Through this procedure, the giving power is disbursed and equalized among members. Third, Jubilee giving assumes that one form of giving is not to take money from others in the first place. Trying to make as much as possible in order to give as much as possible is foreign to the Jubilee spirit. Not taking money from poorer persons which could be legally ours is a bonafide form of giving which protects the dignity of the individual more than paternalistic gifts.

Fourth, Jubilee giving doesn't send checks to every compassion fund which places pictures of children in Christian magazines. There is a keen awareness that money is only a part of the need. People, time, institutions, motivation, dignity, and education must be included in the Jubilee care package. Simply dishing out money is not enough. The compassion needs to be intelligent, orderly, sophisticated, and humane. It must go beyond Christmas baskets to jobs, low interest loans, credit, security, educational projects, and housing. Finally, Jubilee giving must be squarely rooted in the story of God's love. There must be a continual witness to the biblical story of Jubilee articulated by Jesus. Without the biblical perspective financial aid can simply push persons up an economic ladder in a rat race more vicious at the top than at the bottom. Jubilee giving proclaims the good news of forgiveness in Jesus Christ. Giving that doesn't bring a message of spiritual liberation is little more than do-good paternalism which only encourages new ways of worshiping mammon.

Questions for Discussion

1. Can you identify other detours by which economic concerns may lead us around the biblical material on wealth?

2. Which of the detours is most prevalent in your personal experience and in the life of your congregation?

3. List some of the accepted assumptions about economic life which may be inconsistent with our Christian faith.

4. Do you agree that certain financial practices may not be moral even if they are legal? Discuss some examples.

5. How did you arrive at your definition of "richness"?

6. Is it proper to pay employees more even if it means that a Christian employer will need to give a smaller offering to the church?

7. How do you respond to the idea of "surprise tithes" and the five signs of upside-down giving?

8. Discuss the questions raised on pages 151-152.

8
IMPIOUS PIETY

The Tradition of the Elders

We have already seen that Jesus refused to seek the endorsement of the religious establishment by miraculously parachuting from the pinnacle of the temple. That rejection and His insistence on living God's law of love among men precipitated a head-on clash with the religious authorities. Why? Jesus lived in an Old Testament world. He supported the teachings of Moses. He didn't come to destroy the law. He fulfilled it. He completed its best intent. He didn't knock the Mosaic law; he didn't even scorn or poke fun at it. If He affirmed the law, why was He so abrasive with the religious leaders? We find the answer in His attitude toward the oral law. Jesus endorsed the written Torah—the five books of Moses—but he was irreverant toward the oral law. His deliberate violation of the oral law generated bitter tension between His movement and the Pharisees. It is impossible to grasp the nature of the conflict without a brief understanding of the oral law.

At the time of Jesus there were actually two Torahs. The written Torah—the five books of Moses—was accepted by both Sadducees and Pharisees as the holy law of God. This contained the commandments given to Moses on Mt. Sinai.

There was also an oral Torah—a verbal unwritten law—which was passed on by word of mouth from generation to generation. The scribes had developed the oral law and by the time of Jesus the Pharisees fervently advocated it. The oral law went through three different stages. The first step known as the *Midrash* emerged after the Jews returned to their homeland from Babylonian captivity. The Midrash was a verse-by-verse commentary on the written Scripture. After each verse came an explanation or interpretation. For example, in Leviticus 19:13 the written law says, "You shall not oppress your neighbor or rob him. The wages of a hired servant shall not remain with you all night until the morning." The Midrash commentary following this verse says: "This applies also to the hire of animals, or of utensils, or of fields. So too does a man violate the law if he withholds a hired man's wages even if the employee did not come to him to ask for the wages. The Bible says 'with you' (namely the responsibility rests upon you, the employer). A wage earner hired for the day must be given pay for the following night; one engaged for the night, for the following day."[1]

In this fashion the Midrash was a vast verse-by-verse commentary on the five books of Moses. It's amazing that such an extensive commentary could be retained and passed on orally from generation to generation. Ezra the scribe and his associates used the midrash method in their public reading of the law in 444 BC.

In the two centuries before Christ the second stage of the oral law emerged. This contained the bulk of Jewish legal teaching and folklore for the four centuries between 200 BC and AD 200. Sometime near the end of the second century AD the oral traditions were gradually written down in a form known as the *Mishnah*. This stirred great controversy since many rabbis considered writing the law down the same as burning it. Eventually this corpus of legal and wisdom lore was expanded into what we know today as the *Talmud*. Most important for our purposes is the oral law which prevailed during the time of Jesus.

The oral law or "tradition of the elders" (Mark 7:5) was not a verse-by-verse commentary on the written Scripture like the Midrash. Instead, the oral law was organized by topics. Although it was not tied verse by verse to the biblical text, its purpose continued to be the illumination and interpretation of the written word. At first the oral tradition was subordinate in authority to the Scriptures but eventually it was said that the oral law itself had been given to Moses on Mt. Sinai by God and preserved carefully in His divine providence down through the generations. The oral tradition soon assumed equal if not greater authority than the written word because it spoke to the specific application of the law to everyday life. Both Judaism and Christianity accept the Old Testament. The Talmud, a collection of oral laws, is the distinctive book of Judaism comparable to Christianity's New Testament.

The scope and detail of the oral law is unbelievable—especially in light of the fact that it was completely memorized by the scribes and rabbis. A written compilation of the Mishnah on my desk has 789 pages of small print![2] No wonder a scribe's entire life was devoted to its study and memory.

The contents are organized into six major divisions called "orders." Each order contains seven to twelve subdivisions called tractates. These tractates are broken down into a total of 523 chapters. Finally each chapter contains approximately five to ten legal paragraphs.[3] The Mishnah covers the whole gamut of any conceivable question which might arise regarding religions and civil legislation. Can laborers on top of a tree or wall offer a prayer? Can one open up quarries or wells during a sabbatical year? If one is naked and makes a dough offering from wheat or barley in one's house does that make the offering unclean? Is tying a knot considered work on the sabbath? Can a man divorce his wife for burning a meal? What is the proper death penalty for someone who blasphemes—burning, stoning, beheading, or strangling? Is a man ceremonially unclean if he touches a mouse? If an unclean bird sat on the eggs of a clean bird would the eggs remain ceremonially clean? If a dog eats the flesh of a corpse and then lies at the door of a house does it make the house unclean? On and on for 789 pages the Mishnah spells out the oral tradition of do's and don'ts for Jewish culture.

In the scribe's mind there was no contradiction between the oral and written law. In meticulous fashion the oral law expressed the spirit of the written law for the civil affairs of everyday life. Religious insight penetrated the most mundane issues. This oral tradition which accumulated like a holy snowball contained the answer to any hypothetical question which might ever be asked. The memory capacity of modern computer's lose their awe in comparison to the immense mental storage ability demonstrated by the scribes.

The Progressive Pharisees

The Pharisees—unlike the Sadducees—insisted on applying the oral law to everyday life. Their intent was good. The Pharisees believed that religion should cover all of life. By careful study and examination of the Scriptures they thought it was possible to prescribe right conduct for every circumstance. They didn't want the Law of Moses to become a static book unrelated to life.[4] In contrast, the Sadducees vigoriously claimed the authority of the written law but they refused to let it address the real issues of their day. They could accept and embrace the Roman presence because their written law was a crusty old document. The Sadducees readily accepted the influence of Greek and Roman culture because the dusty books of Moses seemed so ancient and irrelevant. Their strict adherence to only the written word excused them from serious everyday obedience to the law. It permitted them to piously operate the cult of the temple and at the same time flirt with Greco-Roman culture.

The Pharisees on the other hand were concerned about faithful practice. Obedience to the oral law which had accumulated over the centuries signified their conscientious adherence to the Mosaic covenant. In particular they emphasized the laws pertaining to ritual purity and to tithing. They observed the regulations set up for the temple priests with the optimistic vision that someday all the people would follow their example. Unfortunately the term Pharisee has taken on a negative conotation suggesting hypocrisy and formalistic self-righteousness. We must remember that in the context of their times they were definitely the progressives who were sincerely seeking to implement the Mosaic vision in the corporate life of Judaism. The Essenes ran off to caves near the Dead Sea and established a communal life withdrawn from the center of society. The Zealots were slitting throats, hoping to eradicate the Romans. At the opposite extreme the Sadducees were working hand-in-glove with the Romans to maintain the status quo for financial benefit. The Sadducees were the political, economic, and religious conservatives. Of the four groups it was the Pharisees who were really working at the true Jewish agenda. They were the ones living in creative tension. They had not retreated to Dead Sea caves nor had they sold out to the Romans. They lived in the center of Jewish society frowning on those who carelessly disregarded the laws of purity but not self-righteously withdrawing. In this tension between retreat, rebellion, and compromise they sought to maintain the Old Testament vision of a nation of priests.

Many Christian readers of the New Testament don't pay serious attention to the struggle between Jesus and the Pharisees. They read the New Testament as though they were one of the disciples eagerly following in the footprints of Jesus. We fail to understand that many if not most of us would have joined the ranks of the Pharisees had we lived during Jesus' time. The task of translating the tradition to daily practice would have excited us. It is time that we begin listening to the message of the Gospels as Pharisees, for we are the ones who have created institutions and programs to flesh out our own Christian tradition. The words of Jesus directed to the Pharisees can inform us about the nature of our relationship to organized religious institutions today.

Jesus finds Himself in conflict with the Pharisees for a number of reasons. Their influence was stronger in the rural geographical areas in which He traveled. He appealed to the masses and crowds of common people who were also the Pharisees constituency. Thus He threatened to erode their base of social power. He directly challenged their strict observance of the Sabbath and ritual cleanliness. His infractions of the Sabbath and purity norms signaled a radical rejection of the oral law. Although He affirmed and amplified the written law, His rejection of the oral law, His "profane act" in the temple, and His "blasphemous announcement" that God was His father brought Him to the cross.[5]

Irreverent Jesus

Jesus' irreverence is a fascinating question in New Testament study. Why was He so disrespectful of Jewish religious ritual? Why did He openly and deliberately disobey the civil laws of His time? In at least four ways He intentionally violated Jewish rules of piety: sabbath misbehavior, disrespect for ritual cleansing, associating with irreputable persons, and cleansing the temple. We will look at the meaning of each of these profane acts and then summarize Jesus' verbal critique of the Pharisees.

The violation of Sabbath norms was the most irritating and flagrant act. The Sabbath rest was instructed in all the Old Testament accounts of the Ten Commandments. From the time of God's rest in creation it symbolized the respectful fear and worship of God. It was one of the distinctive features of Hebrew faith which set the Jews off from other peoples. The Sabbath was reserved exclusively for sacred worship and praise. Transgressing Sabbath laws was no joking matter. In fact it was so serious that the death penalty applied to violators. If a person received a warning after one violation and then deliberately violated a Sabbath ordinance for the second time he got the Jewish electric chair—stoning.

All four Gospels report Jesus' Sabbath deviance. Matthew and Mark each record two violations: harvesting grain and healing (Matthew 12:1-14; Mark 2:23—3:6). Luke pens four Sabbath disturbances—the first two similar to Matthew and Mark and then two additional healings (Luke 6:1-11; 13:10-17; 14:1-6). John (5:2-18) reports the Sabbath healing of a man who had been sick for thirty-eight years. Matthew, Mark, and Luke report the same five-step sequence for the first two infractions. Jesus first of all defends His disciples for shelling grain on the Sabbath. Here the offense is not stealing, since travelers and the poor were permitted to help themselves to grain that was left standing in the field. The insult is working (shelling the grain) on the Sabbath. Second, the Pharisees discuss the violation with Jesus and according to Jewish law warn Him. Third, they put Him under surveillance (Mark 3:2) to see if they can catch Him in a second offense punishable by death. Sure enough, even after a warning, He deliberately profanes the Sabbath again, this time by healing. It's not an emotionless act. Mark says, "He looked around at them with anger, grieved at their hardness of heart" (Mark 3:5). In the final step, the Pharisees make plans to destroy Him after the second illegal performance. Jesus then withdraws from the area apparently fleeing for His life.

Luke reports two additional Sabbath healings. Why is Jesus so audacious? Why does He continue this disrespectful behavior? Why does He play with death? Why does He strike out at the heart of the oral tradition jeopardizing His own life?

When people were sick for thirty-eight years why didn't He politely wait at least one more day to heal them? What's one day compared to thirty-eight years? Rather than waiting courteously, He deliberately offends the Pharisees with these outrageous acts on the Sabbath. Caught in their own judicial system, their only plausible response is to plan His execution. He knows full well the penalties of the law, yet He mocks them in spite of a warning and continues to heal.

In striking out against the Sabbath, Jesus was stabbing at the heart of the oral tradition. Although the Ten Commandments forbid Sabbath work, the oral law contained an unbelievably meticulous system of tiny rules specifying proper Sabbath observance. In printed form the Mishnah contains thirty-six pages spelling out the boundaries of Sabbath behavior. These pages are broken down into 243 legal paragraphs. One paragraph lists the thirty-nine major kinds of work which were prohibited: sowing, ploughing, baking, spinning, tying a knot, writing two letters (alphabetical), erasing two letters, putting out a fire, lighting a fire, striking with a hammer, and on and on.[6] Numerous paragraphs discuss in intricate detail other prohibitions associated with each type of work. For instance, tying camel drivers' knots and sailors' knots were forbidden but not a knot for a hair net, shoe, or belt. It was just as wrong to untie a knot as to tie one. However, persons were permitted to tie a knot which could be opened with one hand since this wasn't considered a knot. Territorial space was divided into four areas: public, private, neutral, and free. The Sabbath rules dictated the type of material that could be moved from one place to another on the Sabbath. If a person threw anything from a private to a public space or vice versa he was guilty of a Sabbath infraction. But if he threw something from a private space to another one with a public space in between he was not guilty.[7]

If a person wrote two letters of the alphabet with either left hand or right hand using an ink which leaves a lasting mark, he was guilty. If a person wrote with fruit juice, or in dust or sand, he was not guilty since it left no lasting mark. It was permissible to write one letter on a roof and another on the ground since they couldn't be read together. The sabbath rules go on and on covering activities such as warming up food, leading an animal, wearing false teeth, carrying a loaf of bread, making beds, throwing objects into the sea, folding garments, closing a shutter, bathing, preparing food, borrowing, and renting. The detail is absolutely amazing.

Ingenious devices were created to get around some of the Sabbath legislation. Persons were not permitted to walk more than 3,000 feet on the Sabbath. To circumvent this, individuals could "establish residence" at the end of their Sabbath day's walk a day in advance. They established residence the day before the Sabbath by carrying two meals to a place 3,000 feet from their home. One meal was eaten there and the other one buried—thereby "establishing residence." Then on the Sabbath day the person could travel 3,000 feet from his permanent home to his "newly established residence" and then he could go an additional 3,000 feet beyond his new residence. In other words, this legal detour allowed him to travel a maximum of 6,000 feet.[8]

The Sabbath represented the height of institutionalized Jewish religion of the day. It symbolized the whole complex of ritual, norms, and prohibitions spelled out in the massive oral tradition. By violating Sabbath norms Jesus was undercutting the authority of this complex network of orthodox legislation. His succinct commentary on His Sabbath deviance infuses His illegal acts with meaning. "The sabbath was made for man, not man for the sabbath; so the Son of man is lord even of the sabbath" (Mark 2:27, 28; Matthew 12:8; Luke 6:5). The profound point here is that the Sabbath was originally intended to serve man. It was made so that men might be refreshed after six days of sweat. The Sabbath was designed to serve man's physical, emotional, and psychological needs. Man was the master and the Sabbath was the servant.

But over the years this relationship reversed itself. Things turned upside down. As the oral law grew and accumulated, the Sabbath rules also grew. Soon the Sabbath rose up as the master. People became enslaved to it. They no longer ruled the Sabbath. It had stopped serving them. Now each Sabbath day they served it by dutifully obeying its hundreds of detailed regulations. Instead of giving them rest it provided them with new things to worry and fret about. Instead of looking forward to the rest of the Sabbath, people now looked forward to their manual labor during the week when they were free of Sabbath burdens. This religious institution symbolizing all of the oral law, once so good in its intention and purpose, was now oppressing the people.

The second part of Jesus' comment is that He is lord of the Sabbath. He is lord even of these religious regulations and practices which take on such a sacred aura over time. Religious institutions and rituals become even more coercive than regular social norms. First of all they are done in the "name of the Lord." They beg for obedience because they are said to incur God's wrath and eternal punishment. The death penalty for Sabbath violations was not seen as a vicious act by mean men. It was the wrath of God spewing forth on belligerent criminals.

Jesus announced that He was Lord of these religious practices which coerced people even more severely than regular social norms. Jesus was the Master of these traditions. He would not bow down and worship them. He wouldn't tip His hat to them. The moment that they became idolatrous and refused to serve man, they should be torn down. He would not permit them to capture and enslave God's people, for they were to serve God and Him alone. In both the grain shelling and healing incidents Jesus allowed human need to take precedence over religious dogma. Religious institutions dare not stand in the way of feeding and healing people. In fact Jesus suggested that the Pharisees took better care of animals than of persons. They would pull an ox out of a pit on a Sabbath but they prohibited a doctor from touching a sick man. For the Pharisees religion was ritual. Jesus turned religion upside down by calling it loving service.

Dirty Hands

Jesus also irritated the Pharisees with His disregard for their ceremonial washing before meals. Matthew (15:1-20) and Mark (7:1-23) report similar accounts of an occasion when Pharisees and scribes from Jerusalem came sixty miles north to Galilee to interrogate Jesus on this issue. Luke (11:37, 38) includes a brief report of a Pharisee who hosted Jesus for a meal and was astonished to see that He ate without washing. The ceremonial washing with water before each meal was an important mark of the conscientious Pharisee. This cleansing was not specifically for personal hygiene but originally was a ritual duty prescribed for the priests whenever they ate the tithe or priestly heave offering—a 2 percent tithe of the fruits of the field. The Pharisees washed themselves without fail, hoping to accomplish their vision of a nation of purified priests.[9]

It is difficult for us to understand the pious Jew's paranoia for uncleanness. Old Testament law divided objects, persons, places, and animals into two categories—clean and unclean. Camels, badgers, swine, vultures, eagles, and winged insects—just to name a few—were all considered unclean. Cemeteries were taboo. Clean objects could be contaminated if they were merely touched by a contaminated person or animal. In the Mishnah 185 pages are devoted to laws of defilement and purity. It boggles the mind to think of all the possible ways objects and persons might become defiled.

The Pharisees stressed eating with the right people—those who obeyed the purity laws—and they held to the tradition of their elders that required washing hands before eating. This was necessary to sanitize any religious contamination which they might have accidentally acquired during the day. In reply to their criticism that He neglected the purifying rinse, Jesus came down hard. "You leave the commandment of God, and hold fast the tradition of men. . . . You have a fine way of rejecting the commandment of God, in order to keep your tradition!" (Mark 7:8, 9). Quoting Isaiah the prophet, He told them that they worship with lips but not heart and they teach the ideas of men as though they were the doctrine of God. In short the Pharisees had elevated the oral tradition to divine status. Not only were they allowing it to master them but they worshiped it as well. They gave it precedence over the Word of God and even used it as an excuse for not obeying God's will.

Their practice of taking a vow called corban was an example (Mark 7:10-13). Rather than allowing a child to support His parents financially, the Pharisees encouraged persons to consecrate their property to the temple in the corban vow. Once the property was dedicated to the temple it could not be used to support the parents and eventually would be donated to the temple. Cutting off their financial support crushed the parents. The Pharisees encouraged this "devout" act of corban at the expense of human suffering.

Jesus harshly critiqued the laws of uncleanness when He said that defilement results from things which come out of the mouth, not those that go in. Words and social acts such as murder, adultery, fornication, theft, false witness, and slander defile a person, not food that's eaten (Matthew 15:18-20; Mark 7:20-23). In a few sentences He condemns the oral tradition which had not only taken on an idolatrous character but which also prevented obedience to God's Word. In fact Jesus says one is completely cleansed by doing acts of charity which flow from the heart (Luke 11:41). In the time of Jesus, the words and traditions of men had asserted a divine status superseding God's supreme law of loving one's neighbor. It was more important to obey the oral gossip than to love the neighbor. The human religious apparatus operating in the name of God in fact prevented the observance of God's law of love.

Dirty Friends

A third aspect of Jesus' behavior which really peeved the Pharisees was His free association with unclean persons. Tax collectors and sinners didn't observe the rules for ritual purity and were considered thoroughly contaminated. Such persons were shunned by the bleached Pharisees who refused to talk and eat with them. Jesus excluded no one. He acted forgiveness by eating with the irreputable people of His day. He invited them to meals (Luke 15:2) and joined in their parties (Mark 2:15; Matthew 9:10). In the background the Pharisees rumbled and grumbled infuriated by his unorthodox behavior. They mocked Him saying, "Behold, a glutton and a drunkard, a friend of tax collectors and sinners" (Matthew 11:19; Luke 7:34).

Jeremias points out that in Palestinian culture inviting a man to a meal is a sign of honor. It signals peace, trust, brotherhood, and forgiveness; sharing a table means sharing life. In Hebrew culture table-fellowship symbolized fellowship before God. Eating a piece of bread broken with others around a common table meant a corporate sharing of the blessing spoken by the master of the house at the beginning of the meal. Jesus' wining and dining with the religiously unclean is not merely a sign of His compassionate care but also represents their inclusion around the heavenly banquet table—their welcome into the community of salvation.[10] By lodging with Zacchaeus and by inviting tax collectors to join His disciple ranks, Jesus was overtly violating the norms of religious etiquette. People were more important than pious rules. In fact, in an ironic note Jesus indicates that He came to save the sick. The healthy don't need a physician (Matthew 9:12, 13; Mark 2:17). The satire here is that the religious ones who really are sick think they are healthy and reject the Physician. But the ones who really are sick know that they are in need and party with the Physician.

The religious piety which masters, and becomes idolatrous, is also exclusive. It sorts all of life into profane and sacred boxes. A tight web of holy rules protect the "righteous" from the contaminating influences of the evil ones. From inside the protected holy box the self-righteous sneer at the pagans whom they've effectively barricaded out. Jesus blurred the fine lines which box off sacred and profane areas. By embracing sinners He made it clear that the new kingdom welcomed all regardless of their piety or sin.

Fumigating the Temple

Sabbath defilement, ritual irreverence, and hanging out with sinners was abrasive to the staunch upholders of the oral tradition. Jesus' final act of judgment pricked a different group: the Sadducees. This political party operated the large temple in Jerusalem. The rich Sadducean elite benefited immensely from the income which the temple generated. In His final act of defiance Jesus symbolically rebuked the temple hierarchy. In chapter three we saw the temple at the center of Hebrew worship. Yahweh's presence in the holy of holies made it the most sanitized spot in Palestine. It was one thing to strike out against the oral traditions of the Pharisees in rural Galilee. But it was quite another thing to level an attack on the nerve center of religious, political, and economic power all in one. Angered Sadducees enjoyed their cozy Roman connections. A cohort of 500-600 Roman soldiers stood by in the Jerusalem fortress of Antonia watching for any ruckus in the temple area.

All four Gospels report Jesus' decisive act. With the full awareness that His behavior would be understood as profane and blasphemous He moved deftly. "He entered the temple and began to drive out those who sold and those who bought in the temple, and he overturned the tables of the money-changers and the seats of those who sold pigeons, and he would not allow anyone to carry anything through the temple. And he taught, and said to them, 'Is it not written, "My house shall be called a house of prayer for all the nations"? But you have made it a den of robbers.' " (Mark 11:15-17). The money changers were set up in the outer courts of the temple called the court of the Gentiles. Here they exchanged common coins for pure money to be used for temple offerings. The animal jockeys sold sheep and goats for sacrifices to pilgrims coming home from a distance. The court of the Gentiles, designed so that even Gentiles could come and offer a prayer, had turned into a lucrative cattle market and bank. Tables cluttered the area. The stench of animal dung filled the air—not a very conducive prayer room atmosphere!

It is impossible to know whether Jesus just chased a few sellers out or whether He completely eradicated the area. A major disturbance would have certainly activated the Roman cohort, but perhaps they also feared the crowd as the chief priests and scribes did (Mark 11:18). Regardless of the scope of Jesus' cleansing it certainly was interpreted as outrageous profanity in the hallowed courts of God. This flagrant act of deviance cost Jesus His life. It was more than just opening up the outer court so that Gentiles could pray.[11] It went beyond merely refocusing temple activities away from the money changers back to the holy of holies.

Mark sandwiches the temple purging between two slices of a fig tree cursing (Mark 11:12-14; 20-26). Before entering Jerusalem for the dramatic act, Jesus spotted a fig tree. He was hungry and reached for figs. There were none. He cursed the tree. The next day, after the temple episode, the disciples pointed out that the roots of the tree had withered. The fig tree represents the temple, the center of Jewish cultic practices. As the curse on the tree shriveled its roots so the prophetic purging signifies the shriveling of the temple's functions. Jesus' outrage in the temple provided a prayer place for Gentiles and signaled the new kingdom's international advent. Regardless of the scope of the purge, whether complete or symbolic, it also suspended the function of temple ritual. With the money changers gone there was no pure, untainted money for offerings. With the animal sellers in disarray there were no animals for sacrifice. Jesus' prohibition on carrying vessels through the temple disrupted the ritual ceremonies.

We have here the Prophet with rich symbolism striking at the nerve center of Jewish religion. He shuts the temple down.[12] It no longer operates. He points to a new age, a time when a new offering will be made, a body. A permanent sacrifice will be given. Each person's heart will be a vessel for the Holy Spirit. In Jewish eyes this is a vulgar act. But the Prophet is fearless of the 600 Roman soldiers and the Sadducean authorities. He acts definitively, judging the heart of Jewish religion which has perverted itself by squeezing out the Gentiles to make room for profiteers. He is not only Lord of the Sabbath and Lord of the oral tradition. Now He is also Lord of the temple—terminating its sacrificial ritual in preparation for the new kingdom. Jesus has returned to the temple not as a miraculous parachuter but as Lord of its functions. In a single moment He critiques perverted religion and points to the new age.

The purge was more than overturning tables. Flipping a few tables in a local Jerusalem inn would have been inconsequential. Given the social definition of the sacred area, the table episode was no less than a deliberate attack on the rich Sadducean elite who operated the temple. The Sanhedrin—that mighty and supreme Jewish law court—met a few blocks down the street. Jesus had boldly challenged the authority of the priestly families who operated the temple with lucrative success. Out in rural Galilee a little blasphemy and Sabbath naughtiness might slip by occasionally, but not in the sacred temple, not by the doors of the mighty Sanhedrin, not under the nose of the high priest and chief priests. It would absolutely not be tolerated. In Mark's Gospel the plot against Jesus' death now flares up again more openly than anytime since the second Sabbath violation back in Galilee. The chief priests and scribes are bent on destroying Him. Institutionalized religion cannot permit such outlandish irreverence. Jerusalem, the place of life and worship, soon becomes the place of death and revenge.

Naughty Pharisees

If the Pharisees and Sadducees thought Jesus was wrong, the feeling was mutual. As if four irreverent acts were not enough, Jesus also scolded the religious leaders with a verbal avalanche of criticism using both direct indictments and parables. While most of Jesus' talk and behavior condemned the religious leaders, apparently a few of them accepted Him or at least befriended Him. Some amiable Pharisees warned Jesus that Herod Antipas wanted to kill Him (Luke 13:31). The Pharisee Simon entertained Jesus in his house (Luke 7:36). Nicodemus, a Pharisee who perhaps sat on the Sanhedrin, chatted warmly with Jesus one evening (John 3:1). It is difficult to unravel an objective picture of what Jesus said to the Pharisees since the Gospels were written at a time of struggle between the Pharisees and the early church. The Gospel accounts probably reflect some of this contention between Judaism and the emerging church.

Public Piety

At the root of His fiery attack on the religious establishment was the social worship of the Pharisees. They offered their sacrifices on the altar of social status. The demands of God didn't matter. What counted was how their religious behavior was perceived by others. They were interested in social profit. Would their prayers, fasting, and tithes enhance their status in the eyes of their peers? In Matthew (6:1-6) Jesus, while not mentioning the Pharisees specifically, debunks their clamoring for social applause. "Beware of practicing your piety before men in order to be seen by them; for then you will have no reward from your Father who is in heaven" (Matthew 6:1). Two kinds of public piety were particularly irksome to Jesus. Trumpets were blown in the streets and synagogues when the religious leaders gave a tithe so "that they may be praised by men." They also prayed long and boisterous prayers in the synagogues and on street corners to be "seen by men." The public audience saw these performances as acts of genuine piety.

The Pharisees also vied for the best seats in the synagogue, and wore big religious ornaments for ostentacious display. They sewed long fringes on their robes and wanted the seats of honor at feasts. They preferred dignified greetings in the streets (Matthew 23:5-7; Luke 11:43; 20:46). Mark (12:40) and Luke (20:47) both report that the scribes made long prayers for the sake of social display. The tone and language of their prayers fit the prescribed norms for pious prayers. All of these deeds, Matthew (23:5) says, were designed for the social audience, done "to be seen by men." Luke calls them lovers of money who justify themselves before men (Luke 16:14-15). Such social religiosity oriented toward the applause of others is an abomination in God's eyes.

John (12:42, 43) says that some of the authorities who believed in Jesus were afraid to admit it because "they loved the praise of men more than the praise of God." In Matthew's Gospel Jesus lumps the scribes and Pharisees together and comes down hard on them.[13] They are like filthy cups which appear clean on the outside. They are like polished tombs which reek with stench on the inside. "So you also outwardly appear righteous to men, but within you are full of hypocrisy and iniquity" (Matthew 23:28). In the three synoptic Gospels Jesus warns His disciples to watch out for the leaven of the Pharisees (Matthew 16:11, 12; Mark 8:15; Luke 12:1.) Leaven symbolizes a spreading internal growth. Luke calls the leaven of the Pharisees hypocrisy. Mark interestingly makes it the leaven of the Pharisees and the leaven of Herod. The same contagious hypocrisy breeds in both the religious and political establishment.

The religious authorities take their reference groups seriously. They don't enjoy ridicule any more than the rest of us. Applause and affirmation sound sweet in their ears as well as in ours. They want others to perceive them as godly, upright men, but inside they stink.

Gobbling Up Widows Houses

The garbage inside the Pharisees is more than bad thoughts. They talk but don't walk; preach but don't practice; theologize but don't obey. Their internal filth lies in the fact that they no longer allow God's love to flow out of their lives in gracious acts and deeds. They are consumed with the details of keeping pots clean and forget the agony of the sick and poor. In a satirical comment on the Pharisees Jesus advised the crowd and His disciples to "practice and observe whatever they tell you, but not what they do; for they preach, but do not practice" (Matthew 23:3). On another occasion after the chief priests and elders had questioned Jesus' authority, He made the same point in a biting parable (Matthew 21:28-31). A man had two sons. He told both of them to go work in the vineyard. The first one said, "No, I won't," but afterward he repented and went. The second son said, "Yes, Dad," but never went. The scribes and Pharisees were always mouthing, "Yes, Dad," in impressive ways but they never made it to the vineyard.

They were the brothers of the rich man in the Lazarus story who had Moses and the prophets but yet refused to practice Jubilee. The Pharisees were extremely conscientious in observing ceremonial cleanliness and meticulous in tithing. They carefully tithed even the smallest of herbs grown in the garden—mint, dill, and cummin. But in their preoccupation with such irrelevant trivia they forgot the heavy matters of God's law—justice, mercy, and faith. They foolishly look like a man trying so hard to strain a mosquito out of his tea that he overlooks swallowing a camel (Matthew 23:23, 24; Luke 11:42). They preach ritual observance of minute regulations but at the same time they foreclose widows' houses (Luke 20:47; Mark 12:40). Their pious voices sound nice in public but underneath they have created economic structures which callously take away the homes of widows. With the practice of corban they thwart the law of love by removing financial support of the elderly with a religious vow (Mark 7:9-12). Not only does their verbiage produce no action; their sweet God-talk is used to cover up economic injustice while they go merrily on their way tithing the herbs in their gardens.

How Great Thou Art

Careful observance of religious dogma breeds pride. The Pharisees were like the man who got up each morning and sang "How Great Thou Art" to the mirror. In a pithy parable Jesus condemns their arrogance.[14] A tax collector and a Pharisee walk to the temple to offer their prayers probably at 9:00 a.m. or 3:00 p.m. (Luke 18:9-14). The devout one finds his usual prominent place and offers his prayer of thanks. He is thankful that he isn't a cheater, he isn't unjust, and he doesn't run around with other women. Finally peeking out of the corner of his eye he adds that he is especially thankful that he's not contaminated like this tax collector who robs the poor. Then he offers his righteous deeds to God. Now while the law calls for an annual fast on the Day of Atonement he voluntarily fasts on his own every Monday and Thursday. He gives tithes on everything he buys from shopkeepers and merchants. Even if the products have been tithed previously by the grower, he still tithes to guarantee that everything he uses is holy. This man represents the epitome of Hebrew orthodoxy. He is at the top of the religious ladder.

The tax collector, considered a robber without civil rights and ostracized by decent people, can't even reach up to the bottom rung of the ladder. He stays at the edge of the temple court, not venturing into a prominent spot. In contrast to the proud Pharisee, the tax collector doesn't even lift his hands heavenward. His eyes don't so much as glance Godward. Instead he pounds his chest, a sign of deep contrition. He cries out to God in despair, overwhelmed by the gulf separating him from the divine. Repentance for this man doesn't mean smiling nice tomorrow. It means leaving his profession and starting over again. More than that, it dictates a fivefold repayment to all the people he has cheated. He himself doesn't know how many people he has swindled. This is an impossible situation and so he cries for mercy. Unexpectedly, the status reversal strikes like lightening. Not the devout Pharisee, but the penitent tax collector is commended. This social bandit, this patriotic traitor, has found favor with God. The Almighty has accepted his sacrifice of a broken and contrite heart. He went down to his house justified. This was upside down indeed in the ears of Jesus' audience. The point hit home. Those who arrogantly trust in themselves and despise others reject God even in the midst of their religious motions. The insight is perceptive. Self-centered worship sneers at others. Instead of taking a serious personal inventory it derives a false piety from social comparison. This barbed parable stung the haughty Pharisees sharply.

Keep Out

Condescending pride turns heaven into an exclusive club for the elite. Shunning the irreputable and smirking at their irreverance wasn't the Pharisees' only sin. In addition, a steel barricade of trivial rules effectively barred sinners from the table of salvation. Jesus detested the erection of this exclusive spirit in the scribes and Pharisees. "They bind heavy burdens, hard to bear, and lay them on men's shoulders; but they themselves will not move them with their finger. . . . Woe to you, scribes and Pharisees, hypocrites! because you shut the kingdom of heaven against men; for you neither enter yourselves, nor allow those who would enter to go in" (Matthew 23:4, 13-15; Luke 11:45-52). In contrast to the hundreds of rules which crushed the devout Jew, Jesus offered a light load, "For my yoke is easy, and my burden is light" (Matthew 11:30). While constructing their religious institutions, so well-intentioned to translate the five books of Moses into nitty-gritty affairs, they had inadvertently thrown away the key to the kingdom of heaven both for themselves and for others. They had locked themselves inside the synagogue of their own ritual and sealed out others who might have entered. Jesus diagnosed this problem accurately in the parable of the tax collector and publican. He noted that ceremonial religion not only accents pride in ritual performance but also creates an unbridgeable social chasm between the practitioner and the outsider.

The Last Will Be First

Many of Jesus' parables are intended as a defense or vindication of the gospel. His life and His acceptance of sinners was the presentation of the good news. The religious leaders not only snidely shoved the tax collectors and prostitutes out of the kingdom, they were also indignant about Jesus hobnobbing with persons leading an immoral life such as swindlers and adulterers. The term "sinners" also referred to those deprived of civil rights such as office holding and serving as a witness in a trial. Such persons included tax collectors, shepherds, peddlers, tanners, and pigeon racers.[15] Jesus' message in numerous parables is clear. Even if the religious establishment tossed these people out of the kingdom, God loves such impious folk and Jesus communicates that care through His acts of table fellowship despite the flack from leading Pharisees. They might slam the door shut in the face of sinners, but God surely doesn't. He warmly wraps His arms around them and hugs them. Furthermore, the smug religious rejection of Jesus and the sinners is no flippant matter. In fact, things just might turn upside down and they might find themselves hanging on the outside of the door while repentant sinners are feasting inside with the prophets.

Yes, God cares for these social castoffs. Jesus compares God to a father who, after waiting day after day at the end of the lane for his disobedient son to return, hugs and kisses him and then throws a party in his honor (Luke 15:11-24). God is also like a woman who sweeps every crack of her house searching for a lost coin (Luke 15:8). He can also be compared to a shepherd who trudges over the hill country looking for a weak lamb caught in the thorns (Luke 15:3-5). Or you can think of Him as a farmer who cared so much about the laborers who only worked an hour that he gave them a full day's wage even when they surely didn't deserve it (Matthew 20:1-16).

Jesus demonstrates this kind of overflowing acceptance when He wines and dines with sinners. The parables also had a sizzling sting for the religious heavyweights. Your attitude is just the opposite of God's. You are like the elder son who grumbles at the sight of a party thrown for his own brother (Luke 15:25-32). You are like the farmhands who worked all day and then griped after receiving the contracted wage because the latecomers received the same pay (Matthew 20:11-16). In fact, you are like the tenants of a vineyard who refused to give one of the owner's servants some of the wine from his own vineyard. You killed other servants he sent and finally you had the daring audacity to kill his only son (Luke 20:9-16). Suddenly the tables are turned. The owner will give that vineyard to others. This upside-down theme of eschatological reversal permeates other parables. The unexpected happens. The religious leaders forfeit their kingdom card. Sinners have a seat at the party.

The biting stories continue. You are like the special invited guests to a banquet who refuse to come when the dining begins (Luke 14:15-24; Matthew 22:1-10). Because of your stubborness God invites others to replace you at the feast. He welcomes the poor, maimed, blind, and lame from the city streets. Then He goes to the countryside and invites others to come. All of these spiritual and social outcasts which you spit on He gives a royal reception. Then the moment of judgment strikes! "For I tell you, none of those men who were invited shall taste my banquet" (Luke 14:24). In another picture of impending crisis for the religious hierarchy, Jesus clarifies the upside-down reversal. The judgment will surprise the staunchest defenders of the faith. They will say the Lord ate and drank in our presence but the Lord Himself will reply, " 'Depart from me, all you workers of iniquity!' There you will weep and gnash your teeth, when you see Abraham and Isaac and Jacob and all the prophets in the kingdom of God and you yourselves thrust out. And men will come from east and west, and from north and south, and sit at table in the kingdom of God. And behold, some are last who will be first, and some are first who will be last" (Luke 13:27-30).

Jesus concludes the parable of the two sons directed at the Pharisees with these terse words: "Truly, I say to you, the tax collectors and the harlots go into the kingdom of God before you" (Matthew 21:31). After blasting the scribes for devouring widows' houses and making long prayers for a pretense, Jesus indicates that they face not only exclusion from the kingdom, but "they will receive the greater condemnation" (Mark 12:40; Luke 20:47). The stalwarts of Jewish faith have had access to Moses and the prophets. They were given a talent—knowledge of God's law—but they buried it and covered it up with oral tradition. It was covered over so well that sinners couldn't hear God's call. In fact the man-made traditions repulsed them and drove them far from God. Jesus restores the day of grace. His table fellowship with the social throwaways signals the dawn of God's salvation. These who are impious and ignorant of religious ceremony accept the warmth of God's love. They don't stumble with haughty arrogance; they embrace God's welcome.

This is tragically upside down. The ones who worked so hard to translate the written Torah into everyday affairs are left behind. Their fervor and enthusiasm for ceremonial piety thwarts God's law of love. Now they themselves who had fought so hard for religion are in jeopardy. They are due the greater condemnation while forgiven prostitutes and repentant tax collectors enter the kingdom. These newcomers might be a motley looking and irreverent crew, but their righteousness exceeds the righteousness of the Pharisees (Matthew 5:20). One of their crowd, Zacchaeus, returned stolen goods. A prostitute who anointed Jesus repented and was forgiven much. The tax collector at the temple beat his breast. The younger son ran home. In contrast to the religious elite, these novices were sorry for their sins and walked in on the kingdom's red carpet. The tragic message finally penetrated the skulls of the righteous. The words hit home! "When the chief priests and the Pharisees heard his parables, they perceived that he was speaking about them. But when they tried to arrest him, they feared the multitudes, because they held him to be a prophet" (Matthew 21:45, 46; Mark 12:12; Luke 20:19).

The Wine and the Skin

What does all this mean for us today? How do kingdom and church intersect? Jesus described the inbreaking of the kingdom on the old order with two stories (Mark 2:21, 22). Always wash a patch before sewing it on an old garment.

Otherwise the patch will shrink after the first laundering and rip the old cloth worse than ever. Store new, fermenting wine in flexible new wineskins. Bubbling wine poured into brittle old skins will crack them open and drain away. The wine is the essential, the primary substance. The skin is secondary. We can't drink and enjoy skins! Nevertheless, the skin is necessary to store and transport the wine.

In picturesque words Jesus pinpoints the tension which exists between the new wine of the kingdom and old religious structures. The kingdom wine which Jesus poured out cracked the brittle skins which the Sadducees, scribes, and Pharisees had preserved. The oral law's skins were so old and brittle that virtually all the wine leaked away. Sinners couldn't even smell wine; all they could see were the brittle old skins. New animal skins in which fresh wine is stored are soft and pliable. As the wine ferments they expand and contract. Today, we must distinguish between the kingdom and the institutionalized church.[16] The kingdom that Jesus announced points us to something greater than ourselves and our own structures. The New Testament does not make the kingdom synonymous with the church.[17]

The relationship between the kingdom and the church has been a thorny one down through church history. In general there have been three solutions to the problem. Some theologians, particularly those in the tradition of C. I. Scofield, hold that the coming of the kingdom was postponed because the Jews rejected the message of Jesus.[18] The church is viewed as an interim arrangement which calls people to salvation now so that they can particpate in some future kingdom. The kingdom will only be actualized and realized, according to this view, when Christ rules in an earthly millennium. A second resolution to the church/kingdom relationship has been the sectarian community model where the kingdom of God is understood to be identical with a sectarian people and their institutional structures. The distinctive boundaries and practices of the community itself are thought to contain the kingdom of God. The third alternative lies somewhere between the two extremes and is the conventional reformation perspective. In this spiritualized model the kingdom is understood as operating in the realm of personal and private experience. In reaction to Catholic ritualism, the reformers viewed the true church or kingdom as hidden and invisible. It occurred in a universal, mystical way but could not be identified in external or social forms on the local level.

The shift from "kingdom" to "church" language from the Gospels to the Epistles largely results from moving from a Jewish to a Greek cultural base. This should not be understood as a major discontinuity or radical change in God's plan as the promoters of the first option suggest.[19] The sectarian model promotes exclusivism and isolation. If the community structures are actually the kingdom of God, who dare criticize or modify them? This particular model is especially vulnerable to Pharisaic self-righteousness. The spiritualistic model is inadequate because of its de-emphasis of the social and political aspects of the gospel which we find so prominent in the life of Jesus. As we have already seen, entrance into the kingdom made specific, tangible, and external differences in social life.

Part of the problem in distinguishing between kingdom and church is the large number of words that we often use loosely such as church, denomination, church institution, and people of God. Most discussions of church/kingdom relationships usually refer to three distinct phenomena. A careful distinction among the three realities of kingdom, church, and structure helps to get us out of the quandry.

We have already said that the kingdom refers to the rule of God in our hearts and relationships. God Himself was "at hand" in Jesus, living in the midst of people and calling them to Himself. Today God rules through the presence of His Holy Spirit. The Spirit teaches us about kingdom ways and ideas. In the wine and the skin parable the wine symbolizes the dynamic power of God infiltrating our lives. Following Clarence Jordan's suggestion, Norman Kraus proposes that we can also think of the kingdom of God as a movement.[20] The God movement is the dynamic power which gathers people together under the lordship of Jesus Christ.

The term "church" can be used to refer specifically to the assembly of persons who allow God to reign in their hearts and relationships. The church is the body of Christ composed of individuals living in obedient discipleship to the way of Jesus. Or we might say that the church is the community of believers or the people of God.

Finally come the structures and organizations. The people of God need vehicles to meet their own needs and to serve others. These social vehicles or servant structures are created by the church for both of these purposes. Servant structures include such organized church activities as denominations, schools, worship traditions, Sunday school, mission agencies, and committees. Howard Snyder calls these social structures the parachurch.[21] These are the social skins, the servant structures which the church creates to do its work but they are not the church or the kingdom. We can think of the kingdom as the wine, the powerful rule of God. The church is composed of the people who respond to the reign of God. Servant structures or skins are then created by the church to accomplish both its internal and external mission objectives.

The kingdom transcends the church in two ways. It existed before the beginning of the church and will continue to be God's kingly domain at the end of the church's earthly existence. The kingdom is also larger than the church in the present world and attests to the ultimate lordship of Christ over all peoples, principalities, and powers even though they do not now recognize His reign. The church or the body of believers presently submit to the rule of God. The structures of the church are designed to manifest and express kingdom ways but they can quickly become brittle and stifle the flow of the wine. The organized structures of the church are human creations and must constantly be evaluated to see whether or not they are indeed servant structures. These formalized institutions are functional because they are designed to serve the people of God, but they should not be viewed as normative or final.

This threefold distinction of kingdom, church, and structure provides a historical continuity between the kingdom and the church. The church began and existed alongside the kingdom as persons accepted the rule of God in their lives. The kingdom has visible social and political characteristics both in the body of believers who declare Jesus as King and in the structures they create to accomplish the mission of the kingdom. Furthermore, since the organizational patterns and structures are viewed as human creations, and not seen as synonymous with the kingdom itself, they are less easily deified. The moment we identify church structures with the kingdom they take on a sacred quality. Church programs and policies then assume divine characteristics parading God's stamp of approval which no one dare question. The church structures reflect and embody the kingdom but they are not the kingdom nor the church itself. The kingdom is present in the lives and relationships of people, but the programs and patterns of the church are humanly created responses to the kingdom.

Although expressing the essence of the kingdom, the religious social structures which we create are culturally relative but not culturally determined. The shape of their structure should flow from the Spirit of the kingdom rather than from the culture of their context. While it is true that these religious structures will vary considerably in different cultures, they should not be mere reflections of their culture. There will be many legitimate cross-cultural forms of church structures.

These diverse skins should be culturally relevant but not culturally determined. The kingdom message found in the biblical story is their designer and fabricator. The seduction of the church occurs when its institutional forms are shaped by prevailing cultural values rather than by kingdom perspectives.

Sacred Cows or Servant Structures?

The vision of the kingdom continually breaks in upon us through the Holy Spirit. It takes shape in new buildings, new projects, and in new task forces. These organized church programs soon solidify and become rigid. In their first-generation outburst of enthusiasm, new groups are spontaneous and charismatic in their organizational structure. As with any other group, spontaneous church patterns eventually become routinized. They are cemented into the minds of the members as "the way things are." They soon take on a sense of "rightness." No longer are they viewed as one of numerous ways of doing church. Now the second generation thinks they are the *only* way of doing kingdom work. Structures once created seek their own legitimation. They perpetuate themselves. Their developing momentum is hard to arrest.

The Pharisee temptation is always with us. The one-time spontaneous expression of love solidifies as the organization grows in size and age. The constitution gets longer, the red tape grows thicker, the symbols approach idolatry, the procedures increase in rigidity, evangelism is shortchanged for ethnicity, and status quo maintenance is more important than adaptation to new needs and new members. Exclusiveness emerges in the form of an elite club with its special code words and symbols. Outsiders feel left out. Pride rules the roost. Other denominations and strange patterns of church life are despised. In short, the once charismatic patterns become a wall instead of a door to new life. The way of love is smothered by status quo maintenance and social status protection. It's time for new skins.

The genius of the gospel is its seed of self-criticism found in the method of Jesus. Each generation of Christians experience the Pharisee tendency to sacralize its programs and to hang onto its original rituals. Jesus showed us that none of these humanly created structures are sacred. There are no sacred places, organizations, times, objects, doctrines, or social positions.[22] The pulpit or altar area in a church building isn't any closer to God's heart than the rest rooms. The unfortunate use of the term "sanctuary" encourages the tendency to see the church building as a sacred place deserving special reverence. Barefeet, cutoffs, and long hair, are not welcome. Howard Snyder has shown how religious buildings often witness to our immobility, inflexibility, lack of fellowship, pride, and social status.[23] Jesus' act in the temple declared once and for all that the buildings which house the body of believers are not sacred nor are they due any special reverence. They can be dedicated as one of the many tools for proclaiming and celebrating the kingdom news. But they should always be the servant of the gathered body. It's easy to succumb to the temptation of allowing the building to master the people by dictating pious rules and restrictions for its use and shutting out the tax collectors and prostitutes who direly need it. When that happens the building needs to be fumigated and returned to its subservient status of serving kingdom priorities.

The same loving irreverence must apply to doctrine, objects, social positions, and programs. The creed which provides a denomination with a unique historical identity can also become an idolatrous manifesto which supersedes biblical authority. The chairman of the board of elders may have wise counsel but he is not sacred. The pastor may contribute special insight and understanding but that doesn't elevate him to saintly status for awe and worship. Symbols of faith—

the cross, the candles, the altar, the basin—are just as mundane as other everyday objects. They point us to spiritual meanings, but they have no reverential status in and of themselves.

White Elephant Sabbaticals

The sacred cows which are more difficult to detect are institutionalized programs and projects. In time these humanly developed agencies and patterns of interaction rise up and master us. Initially they were constructed to meet our needs and to communicate the gospel in effective ways. The structured patterns found in Sunday worship services, yearly calendars, youth programs, mission boards, doctrinal practices, educational agencies, and social service projects—all of these institutional forms—can become especially coercive since they are the "Lord's work." This is not a plea for anarchy. I don't mean to suggest for one moment that organizational structures are wrong or unnecessary. We need social institutions and patterns of behavior and we will always have them. I do plead, however, for periodic institutional sabbaticals. When programs and projects no longer serve their original purpose or when they begin to master us, we need to bury them or at least push them back into their servant role.

The seventh or sabbatical year in the Hebrew calendar provided a time not only for rest but also for reflection. Perhaps it would be appropriate every seventh year to call a sabbatical rest for all the committees, commissions, and agencies which constitute much of institutional religion today. During this seventh year, extensive study and evaluation could assess if these programs should continue. Perhaps some should receive a major overhaul. Others might be allowed to proceed in their previous fashion. This seventh year interval would allow sufficient time to test a program but at the same time it would not let it run on ad nauseam.

In industry the bottom line effectively terminates unprofitable ventures. In social science, evaluation research of government programs is booming. Too often the church's white elephants plod on and on. Since they are the "Lord's work" no one dares tamper with them. Service to others and to the community of faith is the bottom line for burying church activities. When pastors have to urge and cajole and beg members to participate in a particular program or to attend a certain service, then it's time for an institutional funeral. When members of a congregation feel obligated to attend services, those structures have become masters. When structures serve the true needs of people, participation comes joyously and spontaneously.

Jesus is Lord of the "sabbath" institutions which we create to incarnate the kingdom in this world. As Lord His Spirit and the perspectives of His kingdom continually critique our humanly devised wineskins. The lordship of Christ over these organizational structures prevents them from perverting the nature of the gospel and prohibits them from asserting themselves as masters over our lives. Too often church members have forgotten the fact that Jesus is Lord of the Sabbath. They have equated their own church structures with the kingdom and serve church institutions like slaves.

How do we evaluate servant structures? The following questions help assess the servant posture of church structures. (1) What are the specific needs which this program is meeting? (2) Do people need this particular project so much that they'd recreate it if it were terminated? (3) Is it congruent with the spirit and purposes of the gospel? (4) Does it in any way promote an exclusive self-righteous posture? (5) Do people enjoy and eagerly participate in it? (6) Is flexibility built into its very structure? (7) Is there a designated time for serious evaluation of its functions? (8) Is there an effective decision-making process to declare an "institutional funeral" if necessary? (9) Is this structure radically committed to serving the sick and poor in the Spirit of Jesus? (10) Is it clear that this structure is not sacred and that the people of God have the authority to declare its moratorium?

The church is always caught in the tension between the traditional solutions of the past and the fermenting wine of the ever new kingdom. It's a tension between form and love, structure and gospel, organization and meaning. The symbols of the past threaten to become idolatrous. The old rituals assert themselves as absolute. The Spirit of the Jesus who violated Sabbath rules, avoided purity rituals, ate with sinners, and purged the temple is Lord of our structures today—judging them, critiquing them, and guaranteeing that they are pliable skins for the new wine. Hidden in the excruciating pain of judgment is the germ of renewal, the spark of revitalization which assures that there will always be new and vital skins for the kingdom's ferment.

Questions for Discussion

1. Do we have any equivalents of the oral law today in church life?
2. How do you reconcile the "irreverence" of Jesus with His message of love?
3. Are any of Jesus' criticisms of the Pharisees relevant for church people today?
4. In what sense might we be Pharisees?
5. Can you distinguish between kingdom, church, and structure in your own religious context?
6. Identify some sacred cows or brittle skins in your own congregation and denomination.
7. Discuss your response to the proposal for institutional sabbaticals.

9
LOVABLE ENEMIES

The Foolish Father

Among the other things that are topsy-turvy in the Upside-Down Kingdom, martial law is suspended. Agape or utterly unselfish love becomes the new rule of governance. This is an upside-down kind of love that goes beyond personal passion, sweet friendship, and benevolent do-goodism. Agape supersedes self-interest. But it is more than unselfish feelings; it is a love which acts. It concretely loves even enemies.

The whole idea of agape starts with the Head of the kingdom. This King is like a father. His subjects are not slaves but children. They don't address Him with, "Yes, Sir, Your Majesty," but fondly call Him, "Daddy." In this new order they don't perform good deeds just to accumulate rewards or merits. Here they love generously because they have been overwhelmed by a hugging Father. The Father's love is the catalyst for their abundant expression of love. What kind of a Father is this who can trigger off such a loving chain reaction? What kind of a Dad is this that stimulates such outbursts of love among His children?

Jesus described this Father in a parable about a man with two sons (Luke 15:11-32).[1] This story is good for at least three sermons, each focusing on one of the main characters. Our study must be limited to asking what kind of a Person is God like? Jesus suggests He is like the foolish father in this story. According to Jewish custom, the younger of two sons was entitled to one third of the property. The wealth could be passed on in two ways: by a will at the time of the father's death or by a gift during the father's lifetime. In contrast to Western culture, even if the son received the property as a gift during the father's lifetime he did not have the right to dispose of it until after the father died. Children were expected to honor their parents by obeying them and maintaining them financially. The sin in this story from the perspective of Jewish culture focuses primarily on the son's gross disrespect for the father rather than on his vices in the foreign country. Here is a son treating his father like he's already dead. This young upstart is violating civil understandings by leaving the father and squandering the property so that it can never be used to support the father again. In Jewish culture this was the rudest treatment a son could give his father.

To add insult upon insult the son ends up tending swine which was a prohibited Jewish occupation. Unclean pigs were thought to be the abode of devils. This son not only engages in this degrading occupation—he even puts himself on the same level as the pigs by wanting to eat what they eat. It's not difficult to imagine the great social embarrassment which the son's rude behavior caused for the father. The scribes in the synagogue sneered at him. Surely he was stupid to give the son the property in the first place. He was the laughingstock of the village for playing into the hands of his son. His reputation, esteem, and pious image were utterly destroyed. Certainly a father who raised this kind of son was not fit to give leadership or counsel in the synagogue. To vindicate himself, such a father could at least show his peers that he strongly disapproved of such behavior. At least he wouldn't look the other way and put his stamp of approval on rampant disobedience. He could legally disown the son and declare him permanently severed from his household. Although this is how we might expect a typical father to react, this is not the response of the father in Jesus' parable.

The father which Jesus describes doesn't defend himself. He doesn't retaliate to protect his social status. Nor does he go running after the son with a search party. This father allows the son freedom to go and to come. The freedom is couched in a deep love for the son which is stronger than the father's own needs for social approval. It is this father who patiently waits for his son to return. He looks longingly up the street every day—waiting, hoping, and expecting.

Finally the son "comes to himself." (This is a descriptive phrase in the Aramaic language suggesting repentance.) He returns home expecting harsh treatment from his father. He knows how fathers react when they are publicly disgraced. He expects the worst, so he comes confessing, begging to be accepted as a servant at the bottom of the household.

We might expect a number of responses from the typical Jewish father who sees his son walking home with pig dung on his feet. It would be reasonable to refuse him entrance and declare him legally an outsider. A fair reception would ask the son at least to shave and wash before beginning a thorough discussion of the problem. It would be understandable for the father to investigate the details of the son's deviance and then decide appropriate action. Justice would prescribe some sort of punishment to make sure that the son at least "learned his lesson." A time of probation with the son serving as a slave on a trial basis to prove his sincerity would certainly be a commonsense approach.

The father rejects all of these fair and reasonable solutions. In a foolish manner he welcomes back the disrespectful son with eight red carpets. (1) He runs to meet him. He doesn't coolly wait until the son knocks at the door. His compassion compels him to run. He responds immediately to the son's initiative. It was contrary to custom for an older person to run. The father had no idea what the son would say and by running prematurely he even risked encouraging the son's bad behavior. (2) The father hugs the boy. This was another break with the social rules of etiquette, since embracing was considered undignified for an aged person. (3) A kiss—the biblical symbol of forgiveness—follows. The father wipes the slate clean. The son is welcome back from the pigpen—not as a slave, not as a hired servant, but as a son. In fact, the father's next signs of welcome herald the son as an honored guest. (4) The best robe is put around him. This fine garment was a mark of high distinction. It was reserved for royal guests—not for disobedient sons. (5) The signet ring symbolized authority. He is not accepted back as a stigmatized parolee. He is given the emblems of power and prestige. (6) The shoes which the servants place on his feet clearly indicate that he is not a slave. Freemen wore shoes. Slaves went barefoot. This reinstated son would be served by the servants. (7) The fat calf was killed instead of the son who should have been killed. Steak was reserved for special occasions. The son who yesterday ate with pigs, dines today on steak. (8) There is music and dancing instead of a woodshed. This is a time to celebrate the resurrection of a dead son. It's party time.

The older son is offended by the gracious foolishness of the father. The older boy is concerned about justice, equity, and fairness. Where is the punishment which is due this younger son who squandered the father's security? While the elder son contemptuously refers to his own brother as "this son of yours" the father responds warmly with "my dear child." The older son reacts to the situation with conventional logic. The foolishness of the father's love infuriates him.

God is like an upside-down father. He forgives generously as we repent and forgive. He is like a father who rewards his pork-eating son with steak. He is like a father who doesn't spank a son who disgraces him but instead elevates him to the highest position "of most honored guest" in his household. He is like a man who asks no questions even after his son treats him like a corpse. This is limitless, unconditional love with no strings attached.

Having a Father like this moves one to action. Such enormous love overwhelms. Like the man who found a treasure in the field, the Father's children are swept off their feet with great joy in the presence of such incomprehensible forgiveness. This dramatic act on the part of the Father energizes a long chain reaction. The children get caught up with this love and pass it on. They are merciful as He was merciful. As He loved, they love. Because the disciple has been forgiven, He can forgive. This gratitude for God's vast acceptance is the motive for action in the Upside-Down Kingdom.

In contrast to the Pharisees who ran a religion of achievement where every act was calculated to produce heavenly green stamps, Jesus abolished reward motivation.[2] Although He sometimes uses the language of reward, it is clear that He doesn't intend it to be a motivating force. In contrast to the Pharisees, Jesus instructs His disciples to forget the alms they have given (Matthew 6:3-4). While He uses the term "reward" He presupposes that the disciples have already detached themselves from chasing after merits. His disciples do good as a response to God's grace, not to achieve spiritual brownie points. They are to forget the good deeds they have done. The father may compensate them sometime in His own way. But they shall never calculate His response or use it as a motive for passing on His love.

In fact at the last judgment those who are praised for visiting prisoners, clothing the naked, and welcoming strangers are surprised because they forgot that they had even done these things (Matthew 25:37-40). They certainly weren't pasting up gold stars for each good deed accomplished. The reformation emphasis on justification by faith alone has correctly straightened out the books on the fact that works do not save. However, the onesided thrust of justification by faith alone has sometimes led us in the direction of degrading works of love. There are different kinds of "works." The self-centered rituals which the Pharisees concocted obviously are like filthy rags since they were done to earn merit. Such ego-exalting ceremonies shut others out of the kingdom of heaven. It's a completely different breed of "works" which serves others. When done in response to God's goodness, these deeds become the arms of God's caring hug in this world. The motive makes a crucial difference. Acts which are meritoriously performed to earn salvation are as filthy rags. The same act in response to God's love is a sweet offering on the altar of worship.

Get Off Your Donkey

Stressing the suffering love of Jesus often results in a distorted Jesus. Emphasizing his nonresistant acceptance of the cross sometimes yields a portrait of a meek Jesus passively standing in front of the cross with His hands tied behind His back. Suffering in the face of violence is one side of the Torah of love but it also has many other sides. Love—the single ordinance of the Upside-down Kingdom—is not only expressed by stooping under crosses. In the previous chapter we saw an active Jesus who cared enough about others that He engaged in civil disobedience of Sabbath laws and purity regulations. Jesus clarified the assertive nature of kingdom love by telling another story.

It starts out as a believable story. A man is walking down the winding road from Jerusalem to Jericho. The Jewish audience assumes that the road walker is a fellow Jew. The countryside from Jerusalem to Jericho was barren land infested with Zealot bands and robbers living in caves. A robbery came as no surprise to the hearers. It was also typical for priests and Levites to ride home on this road after performing their week of duties in the Jerusalem temple. The crowd understood that priests and Levites who maintained the ritual purity laws could be contaminated if as much as their shadow touched a dead person. Since this traveler was stripped and beaten it was entirely plausible that a priest would not want to touch him if he was dead or nearly so. The audience expects the story to have an anticlerical punch line, which like many of Jesus' other parables criticizes the Jerusalem religious hierarchy. In contrast to the incompassionate religious leaders, they anticipate a lay Israelite to be the good guy in the story who rescues a battered fellow Jew.

The story line has an unbelievable surprise. Not a Jew but a Samaritan turns out to be the good guy. Why is the appearance of a Samaritan so shocking to the audience? The first century AD was a time of bitter tension between the Jews and Samaritans. There may have been as many Samaritans as Jews in Palestine during the time of Jesus.[3] They lived in Samaria which was sandwiched in the middle of the country between Judea and Galilee. The Samaritans emerged about 400 BC as a result of mixed marriages between Jews and Gentiles. The Jews regarded them as half-breed bastards. The Samaritans constructed their own temple on Mt. Gerizim north of Jerusalem. They had their own version of the five books of Moses. They even claimed that their temple was the true place of worship and insisted that their priests had pure blood ties back to the royal priestly line in the Old Testament. To the Jewish mind, Samaritans were worse than pagans because they at least knew better. Jeremias says that Samaritans were at the bottom of the ladder of social stratification. They were hated and despised by Jews.[4] The Scripture attests to the belligerent racism between the two groups. John (4:9) says the "Jews have no dealings with Samaritans." When Samaritans refuse to give Jesus lodging, James and John are so angry that they beg Jesus to destroy the village with fire (Luke 9:51-56). Jewish leaders call Jesus a "Samaritan" as a derogatory nickname, equating it with someone controlled by a demon (John 8:48).

When Jesus was about twelve years old some Samaritans sneaked into the Jerusalem temple at night and scattered human bones over the temple porch and sanctuary. This outrageous act escalated the Jewish/Samaritan hatred. Jews would not eat unleavened bread made by a Samaritan nor an animal killed by a Samaritan. Intermarriage was absolutely prohibited. One rabbi said, "He who eats the bread of a Samaritan is like one that eats the flesh of swine."[5] Samaritan women were considered perpetual menstruants from the cradle and their husbands perpetually unclean. Any place where a Samaritan laid was considered unclean as was any food or drink which touched the place. The saliva of a Samaritan woman was unclean. A whole village was declared unclean if a Samaritan woman stayed there. Another rabbi said the Samaritans "have no law or even the remains of a law and therefore, they are contemptible and corrupt."[6] Galilean Jews on pilgrimages to Jerusalem were frequently attacked by Samaritans. To the devout Jew the Samaritans were considered worse enemies than the Romans because they espoused a rival religion in the middle of their country and persistently harassed Jews.

Jewish ears were shocked to hear Jesus say that a Samaritan—an enemy—stops to aid the victim. It's like telling a group of Americans during the Vietnam war that a North Vietnamese farmer helped a wounded American soldier after two U.S. Army chaplains walked by him. If Jesus merely wanted to teach about neighborly love, the third person could have been another Jew. Or the victim might have been a Samaritan who was assisted by a Jew. To select a Samaritan for the good guy is absolutely unthinkable. Jesus was literally turning their social world upside down. The good guys, priests and Levites, who are supposed to be examples of piety, turn out to be the bad guys. The bad guy who was unclean and defiant of Jewish religion turns out to be the good guy. John D. Crossan points out that the effect of this unthinkable surprise in the story turned their world upside down and radically questioned its presuppositions. This instruction on kingdom love overturned prior values, dogmatic judgments, established conclusions, and conventional assumptions.[7] Suddenly the audience was faced with contradictory facts. Jewish leaders were acting without compassion. A Samaritan behaved like a loving neighbor even when he wasn't under obligation. The priest and Levite, representing the Jewish temple, are coldly incompassionate because of religious regulations on defilement. The Samaritan, representing the rival temple, is also concerned about ritual contamination; but he forgets the ceremonial prescriptions and acts compassionately.

Oil and wine were forbidden objects when touched by a Samaritan. The Jerusalem temple contained sacred oil and wine which were stored in a holy place and used as sacrificial elements. This sacred oil and wine could only be touched by the officiating priests. In the parable a contaminating enemy defiles the sacred emblems, using them as crude ointment and antiseptic to heal a Jewish enemy. This is true worship—genuine sacrament! The Samaritan lavishly pours them on his enemy without even tithing them according to proper Jewish procedure.

With this shockingly upside-down and astonishing parable Jesus answers the Jewish lawyer's questions, "How do I inherit eternal life?" and "Who is my neighbor?" There are only two times in the Gospels when Jesus is directly asked about acquiring eternal life. In the first instance the rich young ruler is directed to sell out to the poor and follow Jesus. On this occasion Jesus urges us to start acting like this Samaritan. Jesus chose this stigmatized enemy to demonstrate the nature of kingdom love to a sophisticated Jewish theologian.

The parable informs us about the nature of agape love. (1) It indicates the ridiculous nature of the lawyer's question, "Who is my neighbor?" Disciples love indiscriminately without asking whether or not they're obligated to love someone. The agents of agape don't draw lines of responsibility and exclusiveness. Upside-Down Kingdom citizens never ask about the social characteristics of their object of love. They don't inquire about the past history of their clients nor do they question whether the client deserves assistance from them. The answer is simple. If even an enemy is redefined as a neighbor, then certainly anyone less hostile than an enemy deserves agape assistance. In other words, the question, "Who is my neighbor?" is absurd since the story affirms that everyone including my enemy is my neighbor. The term "neighbor" is all-inclusive in the Upside-Down Kingdom. The categories of friend and enemy are meaningless since everyone is a neighbor. We act like a neighbor even to those whom we have no obligation to act neighborly toward—even to enemies whom we can rightfully hate. Agape love responds to persons, not to social categories. Jesus reverses things by asking the lawyer in essence if he is acting like a neighbor.

(2) Kingdom love is not stymied by religious or social conventions. Religious and social norms which might justify callous disinterest are suspended. Agape penetrates the socio-religious barricades which wall people off into prisons, mental hospitals, addiction centers, and inner-city ghettos. (3) Agape is inconvenient. The priest and Levite "saw and passed by on the other side." The Samaritan saw, had compassion, and got off his donkey. He placed the victim on his donkey and walked alongside. Agape was physically inconvenient. It is also inconvenient to get off the occupational donkeys which carry us to comfortable security. (4) Agape is risky. The whole thing might have been a frame-up with the robbers hiding nearby waiting to pounce on any "Good Samaritan" who came along. By walking instead of riding,

the Samaritan was also making himself much more vulnerable to armed attack. (5) Agape takes time. In addition to stopping and bandaging the victim, the Samaritan merchant was slowed down by walking instead of riding and by his stop at the inn.

(6) This act of love was financially expensive. The Samaritan paid the innkeeper for twenty-four days of lodging and offered a blank check to pay for any additional costs. If this were a case of a Jew helping a Jew, a civil court would have supported the helper's plea for repayment. But since a Samaritan is involved, there's no possibility that a Jewish court would support any request for reimbursement. Here is a Samaritan freely lending finances without hope of return. This is precisely what Jesus prescribes in his formal instruction: "Lend, expecting nothing in return" (Luke 6:35). This is a man of genuine motive freely lending without calculating interest or expecting even the principal back. (7) Agape also jeopardizes social status. If the word got back to the Samaritan's hometown that he was aiding Jews he would most certainly be considered a traitor to the Samaritan cause. He was putting his reputation and social status on the line. He might face ostracism or formal punishment from his own people.

The parable leaves no doubt about it. Agape love is courageous and aggressive. It is more than warm fuzzy feelings and good attitudes toward others. It doesn't stop with a mushy smile. Positive attitudes and sweet smiles are a fine warm-up but they are not the mark of kingdom love. This kind of love is aggressive and costly, both socially and economically. Although the parable sharpens the shape of agape it doesn't answer all the questions. What would have been an agape response if the Samaritan had found the robbers beating the victim? Would he have used force or violence to stop the atrocity? Does agape only apply Band-Aids to the wounded? Or did the Samaritan get to the root of the problem by going back to the caves to find the robbers? And if he found them, what did he do to them?

A One-Legged Law

A brief survey of the Gospels shows that love is the one and only ordinance of the Upside-Down Kingdom. In second place, after the greatest commandment to love God, comes the revolutionary instruction to love the neighbor in the same way that one loves oneself. All three synoptic writers report this as the Christian manifesto (Matthew 22:37-40; Mark 12:28-31; Luke 10:25-27). The simple phrase holds dynamite. First of all it assumes that self-love is appropriate. It's okay to say I'm okay. There's a place for personal respect and dignity. It's all right to aspire for and achieve personal goals. But the revolutionary phrase here calls for caring about our neighbor with the same intensity that we care about ourself. We must work just as hard to help our neighbor achieve his goals as we work for our own. Agape expects us to exert just as much effort and money toward our neighbor's house purchase as we did to our own. With vast numbers of neighbors around us, that seems like an impossible dream. Such a prescription of love elevates the neighbor's need to the same level as our own. This eradicates pride. Arrogance comes when personal achievements are lauded over a neighbor's failures. Concentrating on the neighbor's goal with the same intensity as our own eliminates any preoccupation with selfish achievements.

For Jesus this single norm of love summed up the entire law and the whole message of the prophets (Matthew 7:12). Although agape was the key to Old Testament righteousness, Jesus also called it a new commandment. We are to love as He loved us. Our mutual love will be the sign to others that we are indeed His disciples (John 13:34, 35). Jesus added new dimensions which superseded the Old Testament understanding and the current Jewish teaching. A skeptical Gentile once told a rabbi that he would accept the Jewish faith if the rabbi could summarize the Jewish law while the Gentile stood on one leg. The rabbi replied, "Do not do to another what would be hurtful to you." Jesus pushed beyond the Jewish maxim when He said, "As you wish that men would do to you, do so to them" (Luke 6:31, Matthew 7:12). Jesus turned the negative Jewish rule upside down by making it into a plea for positive action.

Too often agape is characterized as a love which sweetly smiles as the world goes by. Jesus certainly didn't stand by and watch the world grind on. He acted agape by speaking out forcibly on behalf of the poor. He quickly violated civil and religious laws in the face of human need. His words and acts insulted the rich and powerful. They probably didn't think He was very loving. He relentlessly worked on behalf of the downtrodden and oppressed even when His behavior created a fuss. Agape results in an active involvement and identification with the poor and oppressed. It dare not be a condescending and paternalistic benevolence which occasionally tosses a few tithes or fruit baskets over the edge of the table. It means living and thinking in the other person's world so that his problems become our own.

Agape is not only forthright in speaking out and acting on behalf of others, it is also firm in responding to exploiters. Although agape willingly bears suffering and abuse it understands that a firm and gentle "no" can also be an expression of loving care. The young child, the emotionally disturbed, the adolescent with a character disorder, and the irresponsible adult do not always need sweet smiles of affirmation for careless behavior. Kind but firm confrontation of the problem can be the deepest expression of agape. Agape confronts when others selfishly exploit relationships. Saying that agape can be firm and confrontive dare not, however, be used as an excuse for violence or for authoritarian demands.

To say that agape for the neighbor is the single ordinance of the kingdom might sound nice, but it's not a panacea by any means. How does one respond when the needs of three or four different neighbors conflict? Caring for one may harm the interests of others. In an age of aggressive competition how does a Christian enterprise or business live agape among its competitors? Does the term "neighbor" refer to corporate competitors as well as individuals? How does one love his neighbor when the neighbor's goals do not coincide with the values of Christian faith?

Beyond Tit for Tat

The most revolutionary aspect of Jesus' definition of love was the way that it cut through the widespread norm of reciprocity. The norm of reciprocity is one of the most basic and universal rules of social organization in all cultures. This rule of human relations calls for similar exchanges between social actors. If I buy you a cup of coffee, you are obligated to say "thank you" and to return the favor sometime. The exchange does not have to be equal in value or form. For example, a 20-cent bar of candy would probably be an acceptable reciprocation for a 30-cent cup of coffee. The underlying expectation is that favors should be returned. If you are invited to someone's house for dinner, you are expected to return the favor sometime.

The rule specifies that people should help those who have helped them and should not injure those who have helped them. The norm of reciprocity maintains a balance in social exchange and a sense of equilibrium in personal and group relationships. Individuals feel awkward and uncomfortable if they receive gifts from others and are not able to reciprocate them. Gift giving and card exchanges at Christmastime conform to the norm. Gifts need to be of a similar value so that "things don't get out of balance." Giving a $2.00 gift to a person who gives you a $25.00 gift would make you very uncomfortable. We predict who will send us

Christmas cards so that we can be sure to send them one before it's so late that a deliberate exchange is obvious. The rule of equal exchange is not just a seasonal thing. It pervades all aspects of human relations. The little "thank you's" we say and do throughout the day are governed by it. It controls the exchange of labor for wages and fees for services rendered. A moment's reflection reveals that it's the most basic social rule which governs all types of relationships. Polite and proper etiquette means that we follow the rule. Persons who don't return equal exchanges are considered rude and impolite.

Additional assumptions underlying the norm specify that one has a particular obligation to reciprocate and "help out" friends, neighbors, associates, and relatives. One is not obligated to "go out of the way" to do a favor for a stranger or unknown person. Even with friends one does not necessarily have to take the initiative. The crucial thing is to reciprocate if someone else initiates a kind act toward you. A person who initiates a favor can expect and anticipate a return favor from the other person. Finally it is even permissible to manipulate the norm for personal gain by building up an indebtedness with a person. This happens when a salesman "wines and dines" a prospective customer—thereby obligating the prospect to return the favor by making a purchase. Gifts and awards from salesmen perform the same function. When we want to ask someone to do a favor for us we may take them out to lunch first. This makes them indebted to us and puts subtle pressure on them to perform our request.

In a fascinating way Jesus' teaching on love slices through the norm of reciprocity. "If you love those who love you, what credit is that to you? For even sinners love those who love them. . . . And if you lend to those from whom you hope to receive, what credit is that to you? Even sinners lend to sinners, to receive as much again" (Luke 6:32-34). "For if you love those who love you, what reward have you? Do not even the tax collectors do the same? And if you salute only your brethren, what more are you doing than others?" (Matthew 5:46, 47). In other words agape love goes way beyond the norm of reciprocity.

Don't be tricked into thinking that agape love is the same as the norm of reciprocity: returning a smile for a smile or a favor for a favor. Even sinners play by that rule. Pharisees and tax collectors smile back when people smile at them. Pagans return favors to persons who have favored them. Gentiles politely conform to these rules of social etiquette. It's no big deal if you simply follow the convention of reciprocity. That's not a unique display of kingdom love. The way of agape is a norm of excess which goes beyond reciprocity. The foolish father didn't play by the rule of reciprocity when he welcomed home a son contaminated with pig dung. The Samaritan crossbreed didn't follow that convention when he got off his donkey. Your heavenly Father doesn't play by the rule either, for He sends the sun and rain on the unjust as well as the just (Matthew 5:45).

Our Father is the stimulus and model for exceeding the norm of reciprocity. You should be merciful just as He is merciful (Luke 6:36). "You received without pay, give without pay" (Matthew 10:8).

Normally a social transaction has two actors who reciprocate each other to maintain a balance in their relationship. God brings a divine dimension to the tit for tat formula. He doesn't merely ask His children to go beyond the norm of equal exchange, He enters the equation of social relationships Himself. He has taken the initiative in doing us a favor. He loved the world. He cared for us by incarnating Himself. He redeemed and saved us in the work of Jesus Christ. He is the first Actor who starts the chain reaction. Because we have been forgiven and liberated we have a debt to Him. We are under obligation. How do we repay our indebtedness? Not by reciprocating God directly but by taking the initiative of love with our neighbors. In this network of social relations there are three actors. God takes the initiative by declaring unconditional love and forgiveness just like the foolish father. We reciprocate our indebtedness to Him by taking the initiative to love others.

As we love beyond the typical expectations of the norm of reciprocity we are cleaning up our indebtedness to God. Paul spells out this "love debt" succinctly: "Owe no one anything, except to love one another; for he who loves his neighbor has fulfilled the law" (Romans 13:8). Jesus spells it out just as clearly when He says: "Truly, I say to you, as you did it to one of the least of these my brethren, you did it to me" (Matthew 25:40). In this context He is describing acts of love to the most destitute types of persons: hungry, sick, prisoners, thirsty, strangers, and the naked. As you love even the least of these least—the people who aren't even on the bottom rung of the social prestige ladder—you have repaid Me! Now the transaction is complete and a new chain reaction has begun. The least of these who has been loved has felt God's care and can pass on the love to others. The Jubilee refrain rings in our ears once again. As I have liberated you—so liberate others! This is not a cold, calculating poker-face exchange where we frantically seek to "repay" God in some legalistic fashion. It's impossible to ever completely repay Him. This is a joyous response of gratitude to His marvelous grace.

There are three specific ways in which our love for others in response to God's initiative goes beyond the norm of reciprocity. First, the initiative now is on us. Instead of waiting to return a favor, we make the move of favoring because we have been favored. A favor is not only buying someone a cup of coffee. It means giving one's entire life and energy in loving service. Second, agape is irrespective of the type of person it serves. It doesn't love just social equals or friends to whom we are obligated to "be nice." As the act of the Samaritan half-breed indicates, strangers, enemies, and outcasts are cared for just as much as close friends under the reign of agape. In the third place, agape love doesn't expect a return. Since God has taken the initiative, we have already been paid. In typical upside-down fashion, agape tells the neighbor to pass the love on—to reciprocate the favor to someone else rather than returning it.

Jesus articulates this clearly: "When you give a dinner or a banquet, do not invite your friends or your brothers or your kinsmen or rich neighbors, lest they also invite you in return, and you be repaid. But when you give a feast, invite the poor, the maimed, the lame, the blind, and you will be blessed, because they cannot repay you. You will be repaid at the resurrection of the just" (Luke 14:12-14). The disciple of Jesus does not love for personal gain, nor does he expect or calculate a return. After mocking those who pride themselves in politely following the norm of reciprocity, Jesus spells out the vulnerableness and boundless nature of agape: "But love your enemies, and do good, and lend, expecting nothing in return; and your reward will be great, and you will be sons of the Most High; for he is kind to the ungrateful and the selfish" (Luke 6:35). Social deviants violate the norm of reciprocity. Nice people conform to the expectations of reciprocity. The disciples of Jesus engage in upside-down deviance by exceeding all the conventional, normative expectations. They take the initiative without discriminating among recipients and expect no return.

It is difficult for most of us to accept a gift. We don't like the feeling of indebtedness. Our immediate reaction is to think about how we can reciprocate it. Lavishly giving to others makes them feel awkward and threatens their personal dignity. I have discovered in both my giving and receiving that the agape interpretation alleviates that awkwardness. When someone gives to me and says, "I don't want anything back—just pass it on to someone else when you can," it releases me from indebtedness to the giver and still protects my self-dignity since I can reciprocate in due time to someone else. Demanding that someone take a gift destroys dignity. Suggesting that they pass the kindness on to someone else when they can allows them to share in the redeeming process.

Beyond a Cut for a Cut

So far we have only looked at the positive side of the norm of reciprocity—do good to those who do good to you. The negative side of the reciprocal coin specifies that we have a right to harm someone who has harmed us. It is fair and just to retaliate when someone has deliberately hurt us. In fact, it's not just an eye for an eye. Many would agree that it's even proper to take both of the other person's eyes if they intentionally poked out one of your eyes without cause or provocation. This negative norm of reciprocity ranges from sibling pinches to international war. If someone takes advantage of me, I have the right to take advantage of them. If someone files a suit against me, I have the right to file a counter suit. If someone swindles me in an agreement, I have a right to swindle him back. If another nation launches missiles against us, we have a right to send cruise missiles back. This negative side of the norm of reciprocity not only permits self-defense, but also legitimates retaliation which may exceed the amount of original insult so that the aggressor "learns his lesson." We express the negative norm when we say, "He had it coming to him," "He got what he deserved," or "It serves him right."

If Jesus' approach to the positive norm of reciprocity seemed upside down, his rejection of the negative norm can only appear insane. Nevertheless, His words and actions are forthright. There can be no question that He intended to suspend the negative side of the norm as well as the positive. "You have heard that it was said, 'an eye for an eye and a tooth for a tooth.' But I say to you, Do not resist one who is evil. But if any one strikes you on the right cheek, turn to him the other also; and if any one would sue you and take your coat, let him have your cloak as well; and if any one forces you to go one mile, go with him two miles. Give to him who begs from you, and do not refuse him who would borrow from you.

"You have heard that it was said, 'You shall love your neighbor and hate your enemy.' But I say to you, 'Love your enemies and pray for those who persecute you.' " (Matthew 5:43, 44).

In Luke's Gospel Jesus describes the Upside-Down Kingdom way of dealing with seven types of evil aggressors (Luke 6:27-30). It's important to note that Jesus delineates the Christian's response when someone else has taken an evil initiative. What treatment would the old norm of reciprocity prescribe for these aggressors? An item-by-item contrast between the "just" and "fair" response prescribed by the norm of negative reciprocity and the kingdom response is helpful (Luke 6:27-30).

Type of Person	Conventional Response	Kingdom Response
Enemies	Kill	Love
Haters	Hate back	Do good
Cursers	Curse back	Bless
Abusers	Take advantage of	Pray
Strikers	Slug back	Offer the other cheek
Beggars	Avoid	Give
Stealers	Call the police	Do not ask for your goods

Matthew (5:39) tells us to turn the other cheek if someone strikes us on the right cheek. Jeremias reports that a blow on the right cheek had a special significance in Jewish culture. It symbolized the greatest possible contempt and abuse and was punishable by a fine equivalent to over a year's wages.[8] In other words Jesus forbids His disciples to retaliate even in the midst of the most abusive insult.

In calling for enemy love Jesus is bucking the Essenes, Zealots, and Pharisees. The Zealots, as we have seen, eagerly killed enemies. The isolated Essenes, living in the Dead Sea communities, thought it was their righteous duty to hate sinners. The Jewish law said it was not necessary to love an enemy. Jesus overturns all of these typical solutions to evil. Members of the Upside-Down Kingdom don't play by the old kingdom rules. In the new kingdom there is no place for grudges, revenge, and retaliation.

Just as aggressive love supersedes the positive rule of reciprocity, forgiveness negates the transaction of blow for blow exchanges. Forgiveness wipes out retaliation and vengeance. This forgiveness is the startling mark of Jesus' disciples. They are to forgive up to 490 times (70 x 7) in one day (Matthew 18:22; Luke 17:3, 4). This is not a mechanical formula but a hilarious symbol that they are called to perpetual forgiveness. Once again the disciple can forgive because he was so graciously forgiven. If the disciple does not perpetuate the forgiveness, he jeopardizes his own forgiveness. "If you do not forgive men their trespasses, neither will your Father forgive your trespasses" (Matthew 6:15). Forgiveness replaces retaliation as the number one value in this new order.

Jesus models this overwhelming forgiveness when He tells the woman caught in adultery to go and sin no more when she should have been stoned on the spot. The epitome of upside-down forgiveness is Jesus' own words of "forgive them" spoken in excruciating pain from the cross. Forgiveness is certainly not a panacea for success—at least not according to the conventional criteria for success. Jesus urges us to "love one another as I have loved you. Greater love has no man than this, that a man lay down his life for his friends" (John 15:12, 13).

As we have already seen, in the new kingdom even enemies are treated as friends. The kind of love and forgiveness which Jesus demonstrated was vulnerable—so vulnerable that it resulted in death. He invites us to live the same way, forgiving abundantly even at the expense of our own lives. There is no witness, no redemption, no love if we play the game by the old rule of retaliation. The willingness to suffer in the midst of injustice witnesses to a powerful love which overrules the norm of reciprocity. In front of the cross Jesus rejects self-defense. "All who take the sword will perish by the sword" (Matthew 26:52). "If my kingship where of this world, my servants would fight, that I might not be handed over to the Jews" (John 18:36). In the face of violence this is a sweeping rejection, of self-defense, resistance, and retaliation. The agonizing prayer in Gethsemane, "Nevertheless not my will, but thine, be done" (Luke 22:42), was not so much submission to a programmed sequence of events as it was a struggle to continue living the way of forgiving love even in the midst of impending doom. God wills that men live in forgiveness in the middle of hatred. Even Jesus found that a difficult agenda. The centrality of suffering love in the Christian experience protrudes from the witness of the early church in the Book of Acts and in the Epistles.[9]

The message and life of Jesus is clear, blunt, and unequivocal. The use of violence in any form is evil. Violence includes both physical harm and mental or emotional torture. Jesus's suspension of the norm of reciprocity negates every form of violence. In refusing to support the Zealots, Jesus was even rejecting the use of violence to protect others from violence. In Zealot eyes the Romans were clearly out of their place. They had taken the initiative by occupying Palestine. They were doing violence to the people through physical brutality and excessive taxes. In refusing the Zealot temptation which reasserted itself again and again like no other temptation, Jesus was saying no to the use of violence to squelch a Hitler or an Adi Amin. Violence is not the way of God in such circumstances. It is also contrary to the Torah of love to engage in violent self-defense and retaliation as well.

These words of Jesus have defied the logic of humankind down through the centuries. Even the church has been unwilling many times to listen. There are essentially four types of responses Christian people have made to the Prince of Peace. The most blatant prostitution of the gospel uses Jesus-talk to justify religious crusades of violence. This is still alive in subtle forms today in the logic that "the greatest way to serve God is to sacrifice my life in the defense of freedom."[10] Less subtle forms also abound in the slogan from Vietnam war days of "Kill a Commie for Christ."

A second understanding of Jesus' counsel to love enemies is to restrict it to personal enemies. According to this view, Jesus' words only apply to individual and private ethics. Since government is ordained by God, one is obligated to obey the call of conscription and defend the country. This perversion of the gospel elevates national allegiance above kingdom obedience. Romans 13:1-7, which is sandwiched between two ardent pleas by Paul for suffering love, is grossly interpreted out of context and used to negate Jesus' words and example. War is sin. The Christian can have no part in the production, management, and execution of war.

In a third response some churches and individuals have affirmed the way of peace in public statements but they consider it a peripheral appendage to the gospel. Instead of seeing it at the heart of reconciliation and salvation, they see it simply as a higher rung on the Christian maturity ladder. The irony is that such peace advocates would never baptize prostitutes and allow them to continue their profession. Yet they are not troubled by baptizing new converts and allowing them to continue killing. While they say that it's a question of individual conscience as to whether or not a Christian can kill they would never say the same about robbing banks. A take it or leave it peace stance is not the message of Jesus.

A final perversion of the way of Jesus overemphasizes

the "nonresistance" of Jesus to the exclusion of His active and aggressive love. This view sees only a passive and mild Jesus humbly stooping under the cross. This perspective distorts the fact that Jesus' behavior in front of the cross was a short three-day affair in contrast to three years of active ministry. It was precisely because of His assertive love that the cross came about. To act serene in the face of evil does not mean that one is always mild and passive. Jesus did not call us to be passive peace-keepers who maintain the status quo. His blessing is on active peacemakers (Matthew 5:9). As we have already seen in His relation to the religious establishment, Jesus acted forcefully and exerted a great deal of social power. In a later chapter we will look at His understanding of power.

We often think of peace as the absence of violent conflict. Shalom, the Old Testament word for peace is closely connected with the ideas of justice, righteousness, and salvation. It refers to a pervasive sense of well-being in personal, social, economic, and political spheres.[11] There is no peace when greedy systems oppress poor people. There is no peace when the stigmatized find no justice in the courts. The peace which comes from a balance of nuclear warheads is a false peace which could explode any moment. Arrogant selfishness which looks out for number one destroys our peace with God. Shalom comes when there are right relationships among people in every area of life. Peace is God's gift to His people. It is their message to proclaim. Through Jesus Christ we have peace with God and our fellowmen. Shalom is most basic for understanding God's plan and intent for the created order. God is a God of peace. Jesus is the Prince of Peace. The Holy Spirit is the Spirit of peace. The kingdom of God is justice, peace, and joy. The children of God are peacemakers. The gospel is the good news of peace. Shalom is the core (not the peeling) of God's message. To see it as peripheral is a fundamental perversion of the gospel itself.

Talk about lovable enemies is hard to hear in a world haunted by the real possibility of nuclear holocaust. The Stockholm International Peace Research Institute reported that thirty-five countries will be able to construct atomic weapons within eight years.[12] Many sober think tanks and scientists predict that a nuclear doomsday is inevitable before the end of the twentieth century. The mad snowballing of nuclear fire power in many hands can only end in devastating catastrophe. The accessibility of nuclear dynamite to unstable leaders and international terrorist groups is horrifying. The statistics stagger the mind. The United States alone has 9,000 nuclear weapons—enough to kill everyone in the world twelve times. This is equivalent to 615,385 Hiroshima bombs. One nuclear submarine alone carries more fire power than all the bombs dropped in World War II and can destroy 160 cities. The Trident Submarine presently under construction and due for release in 1979 will have the capacity to destroy 408 different cities each with a blast five times greater than the Hiroshima explosion. The Navy wants 30 of these "tools of peace" by 1990. Such overkill capacity boggles the imagination. The international arms market of which the United States controls 50 percent amounts to 20 billion dollars a year. The arms race among world governments amounts to $300 billion annually. The neutron bomb can destroy people, leaving buildings intact—heralding the irony that in military terms buildings are more important than people.

Talk of deterrence, equivalence, and power balance may have had a taint of rationality when only two nations were in the nuclear ball game. But with dozens of nations entering the game, and with terrorist groups at large, such talk is meaningless. Control and rationality are impossible. We are literally sitting on a mammoth powder keg which is no more than the flick of a switch away from igniting. The rampant nuclear proliferation can only bring an international nightmare. This is the final result of the norm of reciprocity aided by sophisticated weaponry.

In the midst of this insanity the Carpenter's words almost sound logical. Kingdom people must shout from the mountaintops that WAR IS SIN. They must insist that madness in the name of peace is death in disguise. The preservation of freedom with violence is slavery to death. It is better to die graciously in the name of life than to serve destruction throughout a lifetime. War is the antithesis of God's shalom. The disciple of Jesus rejects it unconditionally without any ifs, ands, or buts!

Questions for Discussion

1. How would you describe the motive of agape love?
2. What are the implications of saying that everyone is my neighbor?
3. Does the term neighbor refer to business competitors as well as individual persons?
4. Identify instances where persons or organizations have gone beyond the norm of reciprocity.
5. Is it possible to live the way of agape and be successful in a competitive society?
6. Why do you think many churches have been so reluctant to accept the centrality of peace in the gospel?
7. What form should the churches' witness take against the nuclear arms race?

10
INSIDE OUTSIDERS

Birds of a Feather

In the last chapter we explored Jesus' teaching on agape. Now we turn to His translation of that love into active caring in social relationships. What does it mean to be an agape person in social interaction? Before investigating the gospel record on this question, a few words about the nature of social relationships are appropriate.

Somewhere along the human journey a sage observed that, "Birds of a feather flock together." In other words, similar people migrate toward each other. A great deal of social science research confirms a positive correlation between attitude similarity and interpersonal attraction. In other words we tend to like people who think as we do. At least we think that they think as we do. And we begin to think like people whom we like and respect. Oh, but don't opposites also attract? Social-psychological research has revealed that opposites do attract on an emotional level. Aggressive persons tend to marry passive ones. Shy persons move toward gregarious ones. But when it comes to attitudes, beliefs, and convictions, opposites repel and birds of a feather do flock together.

We enjoy people with whom we have things in common.

It's easy to talk with others whose interests are similar to our own. We feel awkward and ill at ease in unfamiliar settings with people from strange backgrounds. As a teacher I know very little about plumbing. I was surprised recently when I heard a plumber talking about male and female pipe fittings. I wasn't sure if he was serious or joking.

Many adhesive factors glue people together. Some of the crucial ones include income, education, occupation, race, religion, politics, lifestyle, family, ethnic background, and national heritage. We migrate toward people who are similar to us in all these areas. We feel most comfortable with persons who have the same amount of education that we do. We can "talk shop" easier with persons in a similar occupation. Attorneys and garbage collectors don't know what to talk about. It feels good to be with someone whose political and religious views are compatible with our own. People with a similar past experience frequently are attracted together. Vietnam veterans still feel a comradeship ten years later. Alumni from the same school enjoy a common solidarity. It is a very normal and typical social process to move toward other persons who have things in common with us.

One of the reasons this happens is because we like our ideas to be reinforced and supported by others. There aren't many objective yardsticks to determine whether our ideas are definitely right or wrong. Ideas are generally confirmed or disapproved in a social context. For most of us it's not a pleasant experience to have our own ideas knocked down. So we seek out people and friendship groups where our ideas will be applauded. There is security and serenity in being with friends who agree with us. Strange ideas and foreign beliefs threaten our own positions. They force us to reevaluate and defend our convictions. We might even need to change! Since change is usually difficult, and especially since agreeable feedback makes us feel good, we snuggle up with others who are similar. It's true that some groups may pride themselves in airing diverse opinions. They may encourage vigorous debate of opposing ideas. But that is precisely their commonality—they all endorse the idea that vigorous debate is an important value.

The "birds of a feather" principle not only works with one-to-one personal relationships but lies at the very heart of informal and formal group interaction. Friendship clusters emerge because persons have certain beliefs and experiences in common. Persons quickly drop out of cliques because "they're just not my kind of people." Networks of friends do not pop up haphazardly or randomly. They consist of persons who have many experiences and beliefs in common. As real estate agents and social scientists know, the same thing happens in the composition of residential neighborhoods. People with similar educational and job characteristics live in the same area. If we know a person lives on "the hill," in "the ward," or on "the lower side" we immediately can predict with a great deal of accuracy their educational level, job prestige, income level, and racial characteristics. Safe predictions about standard of living, political attitudes, and education can also be made if we know that someone lives in "Walnut Hill Estates" or in "Executive Manor." Religious parishes and congregations are also usually made up of people who not only share similar theological beliefs but who also are quite homogeneous in their socioeconomic characteristics. There are, of course, some exceptions to these patterns, but they do not erase the fact that in most places most of the time, mostly similar people merge into groups.

At first we might balk at this idea and argue that our friends are very different and certainly don't agree with us most of the time. That may be true. But when we realize how extremely different our friends would be if they were randomly picked out of the world population, even if they were randomly picked from our own geographical region or town, the differences would be much more serious. In contrast to such a diverse friendship selection, our friends are indeed a homogeneous bunch!

The Social Checkerboard

A checkerboard is a helpful image for visualizing social interaction. Each square on the board can represent a particular category of persons. As friendship groups develop they create their own unique identity. The group establishes informal rules for acceptable behavior. Secret code words, special jokes, and peculiar ways of speaking and acting develop. Group members distinguish between themselves and members of other groups. Boundaries emerge to set groups apart from each other. Members have a clear sense of whether they are "in" or "out" of a group and whether or not they have "made it" in the group. A "we/them" and "ours/theirs" feeling naturally grows.

Social interaction is organized around the boxes and lines on the social checkerboard. We relate primarily to persons in our own square and in nearby squares. We drink coffee, bowl, vacation, dine, travel, and swim with people in our own or neighboring boxes. It's a very rare occasion indeed when we relate intimately with persons living in boxes at the other side of the board. There is a strong expectation to be "friendly and neighborly" to "inbox" members. There is little obligation to go "out of our way" for people in faraway boxes. We invite people to our house from similar boxes. This way we need not worry about dealing with strange, weird, and stupid people living in other squares who do "funny" things.

Groups which occupy a space on the social checkerboard often have special turfs and territories. High schools provide separate bathrooms, lounges, and parking lots for faculty and students. There is an executive dining room and a general cafeteria in many large hospitals, colleges, and businesses. If there is only one dining area, an informal eating sphere is often marked off in the minds of employees assuring that the white collars don't have to eat with the blue collars. There are exquisite private swimming pools which cater to elite groups of wealthy from specific ethnic backgrounds. And there are public pools where the poor splash together. Special institutions like prisons, nursing homes, juvenile detention homes, halfway houses, mental retardation units, and psychiatric hospitals hide stigmatized people from public scrutiny.

The architecture of businesses, homes, and churches conforms to and helps to perpetuate the patterns of interaction on the social checkerboard. Persons in a certain box dare not step on the turf controlled by the members of another square. Guests in a restaurant may not walk into the kitchen or food preparation area. Children may not sit up in the front of a church sanctuary beside the minister during the service. Clients at a gas station should not bolt into the garage bays without asking permission. We feel very uncomfortable if we step on another group's turf without invitation. Some formal and many informal "No trespassing" and "Keep out" signs order our social interaction on the board.

Titles and uniforms also help social actors in various boxes maintain social distance from each other. Labels such as Doctor, Attorney, Reverend, Professor, and Mister are used to maintain a reserved and formal distance from others. Special uniforms for policemen, clerks, dental assistants, doctors, and waitresses continually remind us that this particular person lives in another box and that we should respect their box by not becoming too friendly or intimate with them because "after all, he is a cop." Persons occupying distant boxes often avoid each other completely or interact in a cold and mechanical fashion. Many times groups in separate squares compete with each other for goods, finances, and services. Labor and management hassle each other. Liberals and conservatives battle in the senate. Demonstrators and police brutalize each other. Inmates and guards share mutual distrust. Parents and teenagers bicker over TV programs. These clusterings of persons on squares and the lines of interaction give social life order and predictability.

Individuals as well as groups occupy a box on the board. And it is obvious that most people occupy several boxes. I am a father, husband, teacher, neighbor, and beekeeper. Depending on the social occasion one box is usually more prominent than the others. Right now I'm mostly in the box labeled "writer." Some of our boxes we inherit without choice—race, sex, and nationality, for instance. We put ourselves in other boxes such as occupation, religion, politics, and education. Even many of these are strongly influenced by our family background. Each box has rights, privileges, status, and obligations tacked on the side. The social definition of a box determines to a large extent how the actor inside perceives himself and how he thinks others should respond to him. The label on the box also tells those on the outside how to relate to the actor in the box. Take a policeman's uniform for instance. It is a reminder to the cop himself that he should behave properly since everybody knows who he is. He also expects citizens to relate to him with respect when he's wearing it. When I see a police uniform it reminds me that I need to be careful around cops. The whole purpose of the plainclothes cop is to deceive people into forgetting all these norms. Under those circumstances he's really a cop without a formal box.

Playing Social Checkers

In a real sense each of us carries a social checkerboard around in our mind. As we meet persons we sort them into the boxes or bins which constitute the categories in our mind. It's impossible to collect enough information quickly to make fair and individual judgments about each person. If we have no other information about the person, we simply toss them into a square on the basis of their appearance—white, oriental, sloppy, suave, dirty, smooth, policeman, or trucker. We simply don't have enough mental categories, or at least we don't take the time to make enough, for each individual person. So we sort them on the basis of externally obvious data on our first encounter. In other situations we may have more information about a person and can bin them more accurately as a "fundamentalist," "Jew," "good guy," "born again," "liberal," "politician," "drug addict," or "gay."

In addition to boxing people, we also make generalizations about the kind of behavior which we think is characteristic of most other people in that bin. In other words, we stereotype particular persons by assuming that they behave like we think the other people in their box act. We assume that charismatics try to get people to speak in tongues. Theological liberals, of course, don't believe in the Virgin Birth. Puerto Ricans are lazy. Blacks are on welfare. Fundamentalists have no social concern. Republicans are fiscally conservative. Jews are tight. Wealthy persons are indifferent and callous to need. Salesmen are tricky. Women are emotional. Teenagers are irresponsible and parents are rigid.

Three types of serious errors occur in these mental processes. In the first place, we may have put the person in the wrong box. The generalization about how people in that box act may be mostly myth and far from fact. Second, even if the stereotype is true, this particular person may be an exception to the general pattern of behavior normally found in that box. The most tragic consequence of boxing is that we tend to relate to people on the basis of the label on their box rather than encountering them as authentic persons. It's difficult for us to get around the box and meet the real person. During any interaction we concentrate on the fact that this is the president of the college rather than on the fact that this is Joe Brown. We modify our behavior, body language, vocabulary, and appearance to fit what we think a college president expects. We tailor our response to his questions to please the actor in the presidential box. The same thing happens when we meet other persons. The way we present ourselves to them is based on our stereotype of the label on their box. In some cases we may avoid interaction with them completely because their box is dangerous or immoral (ex-convicts, prostitutes, and homosexuals). The more we interact with persons, the more we tend to slip by their boxes and encounter them as real persons. There's always the tendency to slide back and remind ourselves that "after all, this is the manager and I'd better be careful what I say."

Boxing people is not entirely harmful. It helps to make social life orderly and predictable. The bins are necessary for smooth functioning of organizations. As we look at the ministry of Jesus we find that, although He does not destroy boxes, He quickly penetrates them and deals with the real person. He violates the rules which govern the social checkerboard in Palestine. He shows no reverence for the barricades and walls erected between adversary groups. Wandering all over the social checkerboard of His time, He pays no attention to the "No trespassing" and "Stay out" signs hanging around the necks of many people. He disregards the social norms which specify the who, what, when, and how of social interaction. In fact, when the Herodians and Pharisees tried to trap Jesus on the question of taxes, they prefaced their tricky question with some flattery: "For you do not regard the position of men, but truly teach the way of God" (Mark 12:14). In other words, Jesus paid no attention to a person's box. His eyes and words penetrated through their labels.

Purebred Pedigrees

One of the boxes that Jesus shattered was the national purity box. Racial purity was a big deal in Palestinian culture.[1] Careful genealogical histories were kept so that each person knew whether or not his blood was tainted. The thoroughbreds included the priests, Levites, and other Jews who could prove that they had pure ancestral connections. Persons were careful not to contaminate the blood of their children by marrying someone with bad blood. Maintaining these holy pedigrees wasn't just a hobby—it determined one's civil rights in Hebrew culture. A clean pedigree was required to participate in a legal court and in public offices of any type. In short, a pure family tree was a necessary ticket to any position of power and influence.

People weren't only divided into purebred and bad blood boxes. After the thoroughbreds came Jews with a slight racial blemish such as illegitimate descendents of priests and proselytes. Third, there was a box labeled "grave racial blemish" which contained bastards, temple slaves, eunuchs, and persons without known fathers. Then came Gentile slaves who were in a box all by themselves. They were circumcised but were not an integral part of the Jewish community. Finally on the far lower side of the Jewish checkerboard were Samaritans and Gentiles. Jews treated Gentiles with the same contempt and animosity as they did the Samaritans. In the Jewish mind there were two major boxes, Jew and Gentile. The Gentiles were unclean outsiders—pagans who contaminated the purity of Hebrew ceremonial ritual. Jews could not have intimate relationships with Gentiles and had to be very careful not to be tainted by them in mundane transactions. Gentiles were often referred to as "wild dogs" who roamed the streets.

The Gentile Box

The Old Testament envisions Abraham's blessing benefiting all the nations. In the early pages of the book of Moses the Gentiles are included as recipients of the divine blessing. By the time of Jesus only a few devout Jews retained this vision. To the average layman and scribe, the Gentile was a pagan dog who polluted Jewish purity. Our modern word "ethnic" comes from the Greek word which is translated "Gentile" in the New Testament. Ethnic refers to a group of people with a common national, religious, and racial background. In the New Testament the Greek term "ethnic" is translated into English in two ways. When it is used to mean all peoples, including Jews, it is translated "nations." When it refers to other people in contrast to Jews, the term "Gentile" is used. Thus to the Jew, anyone who didn't have Jewish blood and faith was a Gentile.

In an earlier chapter we left a riddle dangling. Why did the mood of the Nazareth synagogue crowd change so abruptly from applause to hatred? Why the quick shift from red carpet to machine gun? After his speech "all spoke well of him, and wondered at the gracious words which proceeded out of his mouth" (Luke 4:22). A few sentences later, "All in the synagogue were filled with wrath. And they rose up and put him out of the city, and led him to the brow of the hill on which their city was built, that they might throw him down headlong" (Luke 4:28-29). What was the dynamite in those few sentences which exploded the crowd? How did Jesus turn them off so quickly? He reminded them that a prophet is not acceptable in His own country and then He told two stories. He prefaced the first story by saying there were many widows in Israel in the days of Elijah. But in the time of famine Elijah wasn't sent to any pure-blooded Jewish widow. He was sent to a Gentile widow in the land of Sidon for help. The second story has the same opening and punch line. There were many lepers in Israel at the time of Elisha the prophet. But it was Naaman, a Gentile Syrian, who was cleansed.

The message cuts clear. Belonging to Israel doesn't give persons a special right to be healed. Neither does coming from Jesus' hometown or having a pure pedigree give anyone a special right to the gospel. This Jubilee news is good for all. The synagogue audience had hearing ears. In two swift strokes Jesus cut through their ethnicity. He shattered all their tribal pride. Jews would have no exlusive membership cards in the Upside-Down Kingdom. The Old Testament Jubilee applied only to Hebrews. Gentile slaves and debts were not released in the seventh year. Hebrews could charge Gentiles interest on loans. In one split second Jesus elevated the Gentile community up on equal par with the Hebrews.

In Luke's Gospel Jesus never returns to Nazareth. This is the beginning of the road that leads to Jerusalem and to Gentile lands of Rome and Greece. God's favorable year, His announcement of salvation, applies to all peoples. No more favorite Hebrew pets! These battle words shredded the arrogant nationalistic hopes of the synagogue audience. They cut deeply—so deeply that they put Jesus out of the city hoping to break His neck in a shove over the cliff.[2]

Between the lines Jesus spoke clearly. The Gentiles were on board. On another occasion, this time in Mark's Gospel, Jesus spoke between the lines again but the punch line was the same. Lying between Mark 6:30 and 8:30 are fascinating symbolic signs of Gentile inclusion in the kingdom.[3] I can only sketch the rough skeleton here. The sequence begins when Jesus feeds the five thousand. Then Mark reports that Jesus walks on the water at night and announces, "It is I." Mark says the disciples are astonished at His water-walking because they didn't understand the meaning of the huge picnic. Mark implies that if they had understood the meaning of the loaves they wouldn't be startled to see Him walking on the water. This is followed by a controversy with the Pharisees over Jesus' rude refusal to wash before eating. Next Jesus enters Gentile territory and is rebutted by a widow when He refuses to heal her child. In her rebuttal she calls Him Lord. He is amazed and casts the demon out of her child. Then He goes to another Gentile region on the east side of Lake Galilee and heals a deaf mute. Now a new sequence begins. There's another feeding of 4,000 persons, another controversy with the Pharisees over a sign, and another discussion with the disciples about bread. Jesus asks the disciples if they understand the significance of the numbers. A blind man receives sight. It takes two touches for Him to see clearly. This is followed by Peter's declaration that indeed Jesus was the Christ! The incidents in these three chapters come in twos. Two feedings. Two sides of the lake. Two boat rides. Two discussions of bread. Two controversies with the Pharisees. Two healings. Two touches to the blind man's eyes. Two sets of numbers are associated with the bread feedings. Do you understand? Do you perceive the meaning of the numbers? Do they make sense? Do you hear? Do you see the two boxes?

The first feeding is to five thousand with five loaves. There are twelve baskets left over. It is on the western Jewish side of the lake. There are five books of Moses in the Law. There are twelve tribes of Israel. This is the Jewish feeding. This is mundane bread broken for the hungry five thousand. Yet it's more—it's prophetic bread—the Messiah's own life is breaking for the life of His own Jewish people. It's after this that Jesus announced on the water, "It is I" (Mark 6:50). This is the same utterance that we find in Exodus 3:14 when God declares his identity as, "I AM WHO I AM." According to Mark, Jesus is informing the disciples that Almighty God is here. The Messiah is among them! If they had understood the symbolic feeding, they would not be shocked to see the Messiah walking on the water. Because they missed the symbols they were utterly astounded.

Next the Pharisees quarrel with Jesus over washing before He eats bread. They reject this non-washer who mocks their ceremonial traditions. They have no place for Him in their scheme of things. So Jesus moves on to Gentile turf in the land of Tyre and Sidon (Mark 7:24-30; Matthew 15:21-28). He tries to evade the public eye but a courageous woman begs him to exorcise a demon from her daughter. She pleads with Jesus to heal her child. He stalls and turns away. She persists and finally Jesus defends His hesitancy with a Jewish proverb, "It is not right to take the children's bread and throw it to the dogs." As we have already seen, the term dogs was often used to refer to Gentiles. Jesus tells her that it's unwise to share the Jewish Messiah with Gentiles. But she courageously uses His own proverb to argue back: "Yes, Lord; yet even the dogs under the table eat the children's crumbs" (Mark 7:28). Jesus sees beyond her box and heals the child. The upside-down moment arrives, filled with irony and paradox.

In the feeding of the five thousand Jesus symbolically announces his messianic mission. The disciples are blind and deaf. The Pharisees are blind and deaf. They are incensed because He forgets to wash. Now on Gentile turf, when He tries to decoy his identity, the pagan woman perceives. She sees and she hears! Jesus returns to the area around the Sea of Galilee but then he pushes east toward another Gentile area known as the Decapolis—a circle of ten cities outside of Jewish jurisdiction. Here a deaf mute is healed, perhaps as a sign of Gentile hearing. This miracle leads to the second bread feeding.

There's a second set of numbers. This time it's seven loaves, seven basketfuls of leftovers, and four thousand people. Is it just another feeding? In contrast to the five thousand, this luncheon is on the eastern Gentile side of the lake. Seven is the biblical symbol for wholeness, completeness, and perfection. It completes the Jubilee cycle. The symbolism of the number four points us to the four corners of the earth—signifying the time when men will come from east, west, north, and south to eat at the salvation banquet. Here the messianic bread is broken for all humankind. The inclusion of the Gentiles makes it a complete and perfect messianic meal.

Irony visits again. The Pharisees immediately come asking for a sign—for a symbol. In the midst of all these symbols, they don't see; neither do they hear! After Jesus breaks the Jewish bread, they hassle Him about not washing before eating bread. And now, after a Gentile feeding loaded with symbols, they come asking for a sign! The disciples are in the same boat. They don't hear or see the symbolic meaning of the numbers either (Mark 8:17-21).

Jesus tries again. A blind man cries out for healing. Jesus touches Him and asks, "Do you see anything?" He replies, "I see men; but they look like trees, walking" (Mark 8:24). So Jesus touches Him again and this time He sees everything clearly. Two touches: one foggy and one transparent. The Pharisees and the disciples had foggy eyes and plugged ears. They were not hearing and seeing the messianic announcement. But everything was transparent to the Gentile woman even before the second feeding. Suddenly Peter begins to hear and see. The numbers start to click, the fog clears. "You"—he stammers in amazement—"You are the Christ" (Mark 8:29).

In the rich symbolism of these passages Mark points us to Jesus' embrace of the Gentiles. Parts of the message rise from Jesus' own words and bits of it flow from Mark's editorial work. But the message is plain. The boxes are shattered. Jews and Gentiles now stand arm-in-arm together.

In another instance a Roman centurion—commander of 100 men—asks Jesus to heal his servant (Matthew 8:5-13, Luke 7:1-10). The centurion doesn't even speak to Jesus directly in Luke's account. The army officer makes it clear that he believes Jesus can heal his assistant without even seeing him. Jesus is startled by this kind of faith. He doesn't even go to the man's home. The subordinate is cured and Jesus exclaims, "Truly, I say to you, not even in Israel have I found such faith" (Matthew 8:10). This is upside down indeed! A Gentile army officer has more faith than the religious leaders of Israel. At the end of the incident Matthew reports Jesus saying: "I tell you, many will come from east and west and sit at table with Abraham, Isaac, and Jacob in the kingdom of heaven, while the sons of the kingdom will be thrown into the outer darkness; there men will weep and gnash their teeth" (Matthew 8:11, 12). In the Upside-Down Kingdom Gentiles come from the four corners of the earth while some of the sons of Abraham are locked out of the banquet.

Jesus had another Gentile contact in the country of the Gerasenes, some non-Jewish territory east of the Sea of Galilee. This was the chain-snapping demoniac. Mark says that he worshiped Jesus and called him "Jesus, Son of the Most High God." After the demons are exorcised, Jesus tells the man, "Go home to your friends, and tell them how much the Lord has done for you" (Mark 5:19). This is in sharp contrast to Jewish healings where Jesus strictly warns the healed to hush up and tell no one! And so we see Jesus ministering to three Gentiles: the Syrophoenician woman, the Roman centurion, and the Gerasene demoniac. Not only were they Gentiles; they were also stigmatized by sex, politics, and mental illness. We hear two of them—the woman and demoniac—confessing Jesus as the Messiah. The centurion receives the "Great Faith" award and Jesus urges the demoniac to spread the good news. None of this had occurred yet in Jewish territory. The kingdom was breaking in among the Gentiles.

The Gentile vision flashes through the gospels in other places. Seventy missionaries are sent out by Jesus symbolizing the wholeness and completeness of His mission (Luke 10:1). The disciples are instructed to be light and salt, not just to Judaism but to the world (Matthew 5:13-14). The money changers are chased out of the Gentile Court of the temple so that it might be a house of prayer for all people (Mark 11:17). Jesus' earthly sojourn began and ended in "Galilee of the Gentiles" where His disciples received a final mandate to go and make disciples of all nations (Matthew 28:19).

There are other witnesses to this multi-ethnic vision of the kingdom. Matthew sees Jesus' ministry fulfilling the words of Isaiah: "I will put my Spirit upon him, and he shall proclaim justice to the Gentiles. . . . And in his name will the Gentiles hope" (Matthew 12:18, 21).[4] Devout Simeon seeing the Babe in the temple understood that this salvation had been "prepared in the presence of all peoples, a light for revelation to the Gentiles" (Luke 2:31, 32). John the Baptist prepared the way in the wilderness so that "all flesh shall see the salvation of God" (Luke 3:6). There can be no doubt, no question, that the kingdom is breaking out of the Jewish box. This is clearly enunciated in the Acts of the Apostles. Paul's concept of justification focused on the social reconciliation of Jews and Gentiles in the community of faith.[5] The socioreligious barricades which boxed off Jew and Gentile crumbled in the activity of Jesus, in the witness of the Gospel editors, and in the life of the early church.

The Samaritan Box

We have already seen that an ethnic barrier separated Jew and Samaritan. Jesus also shattered this ethnic wall. It was the Samaritan mongrel which Jesus held up as the supreme example of agape love. A Samaritan, whom Jesus called a foreigner, was the only one of ten lepers to return and give thanks. This thankful half-breed was the sole recipient of Jesus' blessing (Luke 17:16-19). Jesus refuses to comply with the disciples' wish to dynamite Samaritan villages (Luke 9:55). The disciples' anger boils out because some Samaritans refuse Jesus' request to lodge in their village.

The last place the typical Jewish rabbi wanted to be found was in a Samaritan village. This upside-down rabbi however took the initiative to move into the Samaritan box. The box-conscious Samaritans couldn't stand having a Jew in their village who was headed for the rival temple in

Jerusalem. So they kicked Him out. In the most daring irreverence for social boxes, Jesus strikes up a private conversation with a promiscuous Samaritan woman in a public place (John 4:7). The record is clear. Jesus doesn't pussyfoot around Samaritans just because of their name tags. He encounters them. He boldly walks on their turf because He loves them.

The Female Box

Even with modern talk of male chauvinism, it's almost impossible for us to grasp the extremely inferior status of women in Hebrew culture. Male and female boxes were as different as day and night in Jesus' time.[6] One of the six major divisions of the Mishnah—the oral law—was devoted entirely to rules relating to women. None of the divisions, of course, deal exclusively with men. The Mishnah section on uncleanness has seventy-nine legal paragraphs on the problems of ritual contamination caused by menstruation!

Women were excluded from public life. When they walked outside the house, they covered themselves with two head veils to conceal their identity. A chief priest in Jerusalem didn't even recognize his own mother when he accused her of adultery. Some strict women covered themselves at home so the rafters wouldn't see a hair of their head! A woman in a public place was to remain unseen. Social custom prohibited men from being alone with women. They could not look at a married woman or even greet one in the street. A women could be divorced for talking to someone on the street. In short, women were to stay inside. Public life was the exclusive domain of men.

Young girls were engaged around twelve years of age and married a year later. A father could sell his daughter into slavery if she was under twelve years of age. He could also force her to marry anyone of his choice before she was twelve. After this age she could not be married against her will. The father of the bride received a considerable gift in money from his new son-in-law. Because of this paternal power, daughters were considered a source of cheap labor and profit.

In the house, the woman was confined to domestic chores. In addition, she was a slave to her husband, washing his face, hands, and feet. A wife was considered the same as a Gentile slave. She was obligated to obey her husband as she would a master. In case of threat of death, the husband's life must be saved first. The husband alone had the right to divorce his wife.

The most important function of the wife was to make male babies. The absence of children was considered a divine punishment. There was joy in a home at the birth of a boy. Sorrow greeted a baby girl. The most precious gift a wife could give her husband was a baby boy. A daily prayer repeated by the males said, "Blessed be God that hath not made me a woman."[7] A woman was subject to almost all of the taboos in the Torah, but she didn't need to participate in some of the positive ordinances such as the annual pilgrimages to Jerusalem and other pious duties. Girls were not permitted to study the Holy Law—the Torah. Women could not go beyond the court of the Gentiles and the court of women in the temple area. During their monthly period of purification from menstruation they were not allowed into the temple area at all. Women were forbidden to teach and were not allowed to pronounce a benediction after a meal. Only in exceptional cases could a woman appear as a witness in court since she was generally considered a liar. Women, Gentile slaves, and children were all in the same box.

The extremely low opinion of women excluded them from public life, valued them chiefly as male producers, declared them servants to fathers and husbands, and viewed them as religiously inferior. The Hebrew adjectives for "pious," "just," and "holy" interestingly do not have a feminine form in the Old Testament. Even the linguistic structure reflected the low status of females. Jeremias remarks that in light of this background, Jesus knowingly overturned social custom when he allowed women to follow Him in public.[8] Jesus doesn't merely elevate them socially; He views them as equal with men before God. This is evident when He declares that female harlots will enter the kingdom of God before the righteous Jewish males (Matthew 21:31). The prominence of women in the Gospels and Jesus' own relationships with them confirm His irreverence for sexual boxes. He didn't hesitate to violate social norms to elevate women to a new dignity and status.

We turn now to a few examples of Jesus' revolutionary attitude toward women. The best known and most powerful is His talk with the Samaritan woman at Jacob's well (John 4:1-42). Samaria was sandwiched between Galilee in the north and Judea in the south. Jews moving between these two Jewish areas often detoured around Samaria since Jewish travelers who intruded on Samaritan territory were frequently attacked. In this instance Jesus is northbound and takes the shortcut right through Samaritan country. He waits alone at the well while the disciples attempt to buy food in a nearby village. A person approaches with three naughty tags hanging around her neck. She is a woman, a Samaritan, and a flirt. Jesus asks her for a drink. In a mini-second He shattered a complex of social norms designed to prohibit precisely this kind of behavior. Jesus wasn't merely being nice and sweet to a woman. His brief request sliced through five social rules which should have isolated Him from her.

In the first place, Jesus is violating turf rules. He has no business being here. This land is outside the Jewish box. He is aligned with a rival religion. Jesus has wandered into enemy territory. In the second place she was a women. Men were not to even look at married women in public, let alone talk with them. The rabbis said, "A man should hold no conversation with a woman in the street, not even with his own wife, still less with any other woman, lest men should gossip."[9] Jesus disregards the fact that she is a woman and addresses her. He is very vulnerable. Anyone might walk around the corner and have jeopardizing evidence to hurt His reputation. He doesn't care about that. This is a person. He cares for her.

Third, this is not just another woman. This one is going to bed with her sixth man. She's a promiscuous flirt. Everybody in town knows her number. She's the swinger of this Samaritan village. Rabbis and holy men run away from such profane persons. Jesus doesn't run. He takes a risk and puts His career on the line by asking for her help. Fourth, she is more than a promiscuous woman. She's a Samaritan. The Jewish rabbis said that Samaritan women were menstraunts from the cradle—perpetually unclean. Jews are forbidden to talk with Samaritans. These half-breeds run a perverted temple which competes with the Jerusalem holy of holies. The social norm says to look the other way. Avoid her. Act as though you don't see her. His words pierce through the social custom and address her.

Finally, and worst of all, he deliberately defiles Himself. As a cradle menstruant she was very unclean. Anything that she touched became unclean. A whole Jewish village was declared unclean if a Samaritan woman entered it. By asking for water which she had touched, Jesus was intentionally polluting Himself. The religious rule said to stay as far away as possible from unclean things. In his brief request He mocked the norms of purity. Jesus was completely out of place doing the wrong thing to the wrong person in the wrong place. In the four-word sentence, "Give me a drink," he shattered the five social norms which imprisoned this woman in a tight box.

Such unprecedented and radical behavior blew the minds of the woman and the disciples when they returned. In her words, "How is it that you, a Jew, ask a drink of me, a woman of Samaria?" The disciples "marveled that he was talking with a woman" (John 4:9, 27). The conversation disregards all the social trappings which separate and keep people in boxes. It began with water—the one element of existence which all humans need regardless of their box. When it came to water they were on an equal basis. Jews and Samaritans, males and females, flirts and straights all need it. As the living water, Jesus provided life for all. On top of all this unconventional behavior, this is the one and only person in His entire ministry to whom He privately announced His messianic identity. This promiscuous half-breed brought up the subject of the Messiah. And Jesus reponded tersely, "I who speak to you am he."

How upside down! An unclean scum from a rival religion is the one and only person in all the Gospels who receives the honor of hearing the Messiah identify Himself in first person. Jesus not only cuts through five norms of social red tape to ask for a drink. He lifts this enemy woman up to the privileged holy of holies and whispers, "It is I." Truly a flip-flop. The despised, the outlaws, the no-goods are pulled out of their boxes and elevated to authentic personhood. They have an equal dignity with everyone else in this very unusual kingdom. The miracle of this encounter is that the Samaritan villagers beg Jesus to stay with them. They are moved by His authentic love and truth-telling. The unheard of thing happens. Enemies are fellowshiping and eating together. Many believed. They switched temples not from Mt. Gerizim to Jerusalem but from Mt. Gerizim to the temple of spirit and truth. Here was one of the first churches composed of Samaritan half-breeds declaring "this is indeed the Savior of the world" (John 4:42). Not the Savior of the Jews but the Savior of all boxes!

In another dramatic encounter with a female, we again find things upside down. The story of the prostitute anointing Jesus at a Pharisee luncheon merits only a few words here since we looked at it in more detail in a previous chapter. The term "Messiah" means "The Anointed One." Jesus is anointed only one time throughout His ministry. At the baptism and transfiguration the heavenly voice says, "This is my beloved son." But the single anointing is done by a woman. This prostitute who was forgiven by Jesus is so overwhelmed by His love that she takes the tainted perfume of her trade—worth a year's wages—and anoints Jesus. Perfume was used to prepare bodies for burial. In a split second this outcast female anoints the Messiah and signals his death. A woman has the honor of anointing the Messiah! The Jewish religious boxes have been blasted to pieces!

On another occasion Jesus was touched by a woman with a twelve year hemorrhage (Mark 5:25-34). Such a person was considered filthy and ceremonially unclean. The Old Testament purity laws viewed her as a perpetual menstruant (Leviticus 15:26, 27). Anyone touching the things which she touched polluted themselves. This woman also suffered medical abuse in addition to her social ostracism. Mark reports she had suffered under many physicians, had spent all her money, and was getting worse. She touched the edge of His coat and was healed. By touching other persons she made them unclean. They would have to go through ceremonial washing to disinfect themselves. It took daring audacity on her part to deliberately make a religious leader unclean. Apparently she perceived a different attitude in Jesus and took the risk. The typical rabbi would have cursed the filthy woman and ran for his ceremonial cleansing. Jesus invites her to come forward not for a rebuke but for a blessing; "Daughter, your faith has made you well; go in peace, and be healed of your disease" (Mark 5:34). He understood her agony. He knew the social castigation she felt. He loved her as a person regardless of her social and sexual stigma.

Luke reports Jesus' act of compassion for a widow. He came upon a funeral procession. The dead man was the only son of a widow. When a man died, his property went to the eldest son, not the wife. If there were no sons, the youngest brother of the dead husband often married the widow; but he had the right to refuse. In that case the widow became an object of charity since she had no means of support. Jesus understood that the death of this widow's only son meant a very uncertain financial future for her—possibly poverty. He was moved with compassion and raised her son from death.

Luke, who seems to have a special interest in Jesus' relationship with women, tells another story. He's about to dine with Martha and Mary. Martha, like a good Jewish domestic, is engulfed with kitchen duties. Women were seen as household servants. They were not to study the Torah or enter into discourse with rabbis. Mary was acting out of her culturally prescribed role. She forgot the kitchen. She enjoyed Jesus' teaching. Naturally Martha was peeved. She wasn't only offended by Mary's impropriety, she was also angry because she ended up with a double load of work in the kitchen. In a few words, Jesus redefined the role of a Jewish woman. He chides Martha for fretting about Mary's deviance. Mary has chosen the good portion. As a human she is entitled to think and engage in intellectual discourse. The message was clear; women belonged in the box labeled human. They were more than domestic servants. (See Luke 10:38-42.)

Apparently many women followed Jesus as disciples. As He went preaching the good news of the kingdom of God the twelve were with him and some women—Mary Magdalene, Joanna, Susanna, and *many* others. These women disciples used their financial resources to help support the disciple group (Luke 8:1-3). The Greek here suggests that they served as deaconesses. By permitting women to travel in public places and to listen to His teaching, Jesus was overturning a number of social norms.

Women were only to walk in public places if they were on a domestic errand. They were not supposed to be wandering around the countryside. They had no business studying and talking about religious matters. Finally, to travel in a mixed group made them sexually suspect. The other great rabbis would never permit women to follow them or listen to their teaching. One teacher even said that it was better to burn the law than to let a woman study it. By permitting women disciples to join His company as they headed for Jerusalem, Jesus outrageously violated social and religious protocol. Female boxes constructed in a male-dominated Hebrew culture crumbled before the mushrooming kingdom.

The fascinating thing is that the women are also the most loyal disciples. Tough Peter, who swore he'd never chicken out, denies his association with Jesus as the rooster crows. The other male disciples also scamper when the crunch comes in Gethsemane (Mark 14:50). But not the women. They hang on to the bitter end. All four Gospels report that the same women who followed from Galilee watched the bloody crucifixion (Matthew 27:55; Mark 15:40; Luke 23:49; John 19:25). They don't run in the moment of crisis. They have their reward. The announcement of the resurrection is made to them. Mary Magdalene is honored as the first person to see Jesus after the crucifixion (John 20:11-18). When the eleven males heard the females report that Jesus arose, "These words seemed to them an idle tale, and they did not believe them" (Luke 24:11). The upside-down moment visits again. We already noted that women were not used as witnesses in Jewish courts because they were considered liars. These inferior liars are now chosen as the witnesses of the triumphant news of the resurrection. They are given the distinctive honor of announcing the victory. Second-rate gossips have been turned into heralds of Upside-Down Kingdom news. This is a gross insult to the eleven males. They were so insulted that they refused to believe at first.

Beyond His specific encounters with women, Jesus also referred to them in His teaching. In an earlier chapter we saw Jesus highlight a widow as a model giver. He uses female imagery to describe His compassion for Jerusalem. "How often would I have gathered your children together as a hen gathers her brood under her wings, and you would not!" (Matthew 23:37). In another instance Jesus compares God to a woman looking for a coin (Luke 15:8-10). Male interpreters have overemphasized the lostness of the coin. But there's another side to this coin. God is like a woman who diligently searches—who doesn't give up looking until she finds it. In His acts and in His teaching Jesus debunks the female Jewish box. His teaching and especially His behavior penetrate sexual boxes. Women confess Him as Lord (Matthew 15:22-28). He reveals His messianic identity to one person—a woman (John 4:26). A woman is the only one to anoint Him as Messiah (Luke 7:38). And women are chosen as the first witnesses to the resurrection. In a male controlled Jewish culture these were powerful signs of the new status of women in the Upside-Down Kingdom.

Other Outsiders

One of the most fascinating instances of unboxing is found in the calling of the twelve apostles. In this motley crew we find Matthew—the former tax collector. It is obvious by now that Jewish tax collectors working for the Romans were considered outright traitors—especially by the Zealots. Another disciple was Simon the Zealot (Luke 6:15). It's possible that other disciples were former Zealots or at least had Zealot sympathies. James and John, "Sons of Thunder," Judas Iscariot, and Simon Peter are possible candidates. In any event, Simon the Zealot definitely was a cutthroat.

Some have argued that Jesus was a Zealot because at least one of the disciples was a Zealot. Matthew, however, didn't continue collecting taxes as he wandered after Jesus. He left all (Luke 5:28). Joining the disciple group required repentance and a change of loyalties. Matthew and Simon were not the best of friends. They came from polar opposite sides of the political checkerboard. Simon may have killed his share of tax collectors. Here were political opponents walking and sleeping together; unheard of and unbelievable! What we have here is not evidence that Jesus was a Zealot but a mighty witness to the unboxing that occurs when Jesus is Lord. Old labels and tags are ripped off. Former enemies now stand together in Jesus.

Another place where Jesus brings political adversaries together is at the cross. The lawbreaker and the law keeper find themselves face-to-face with Jesus between them. One of the criminals assigned to the cross beside Jesus is moved by his suffering and forgiving love. This insurrectionist believes and asks Jesus to remember him. Jesus assures him of paradise that very day (Luke 23:43). The Roman centurion—exterminator of Jewish rebels—is overwhelmed by the crucifixion. He sees the truth, praises God, and confesses: "Truly this was the Son of God!" (Matthew 27:54).

Occupation, power, and wealth boxes often coincide with each other. Jesus moves around the Palestinian checkerboard with little care for the labels on persons. He's with Nicodemus, a ruler of the Pharisees. Rich Joseph of Arimathea, a silent sympathizer, donates his tomb. Jarius, the ruler of the synagogue, has a daughter healed. The Roman centurion's request is honored. Zacchaeus has a surprise guest. Doctors of the law debate with Him. The rich young ruler converses with Jesus. Foreign kings visit the manger. Jesus interacts with these men of wealth, prestige, and influence. Many of them seek Him out. They apparently perceive an unusual openness and acceptance. They know that they won't be rejected just because of the nameplate on their box.

Across the tracks Jesus also confronts the lowly. Shepherds as well as kings visit the manger. The irony here is that being a herdsman was a despised occupation. Most of the time shepherds watched over flocks owned by wealthy persons living in Jerusalem. They were distrusted and considered dishonest because they often led their flocks on other people's land. They sold milk and young animals on the sly and pocketed the money. It was forbidden to buy wool, milk, and kids from them because they often embezzled the money. Some rabbis said that there was no more disreputable occupation than that of a shepherd.[10] The upside-down moment strikes again. The incarnation is announced not to the chief priests in the Jerusalem temple but to dishonest shepherds in a Bethlehem field.

From the beginning to end, from start to finish, the thread of inversion and irony is woven throughout the gospel. Despised shepherds are the first to hear incarnation news and untrustworthy women are the first resurrection witnesses. In parabolic form Jesus compared God to a shepherd who goes through all kinds of obstructions to find a lost sheep. Jesus Himself is the Good Shepherd. Stigmatized occupations are flipped over and sanitized in the Upside-Down Kingdom. Jesus accompanies fishermen who enjoy a moderate prestige status. He pounds nails Himself as a respected carpenter. He spends most of His time with masses of poor and sick who follow to see miracles. Although Jesus related to people in all sorts of boxes, the Gospels show an unequivocal commitment to those in boxes branded with the word "stigma." Jesus went out of His way to minister to stigmatized persons. This hated label was slapped on them for various reasons: social, political, religious, emotional, and physical. We've already met some of the people who lived in boxes marked stigma—demoniacs, blind, deaf, prostitutes, tax collectors, sinners, adulterers, widows, lame, lepers, diseased, paralyzed, Samaritans, women, and Gentiles.

While it is true that Jesus moved all around the Hebrew checkerboard, He clearly focused most of His energy on these social cast outs. Such unproductive liabilities were usually spit and trampled on by the powerful and strong. They were an embarrassment to the healthy and prominent. Many like the lepers were literally quarantined out of the cities. They sat and begged on the edge of the village limits. Jesus touched the untouchables, loved the unlovables, and accepted the stigmatized.

In addition to His acts, His words maintained a similar commitment. Again and again the same catalogue of people are mentioned: the poor, the blind, the lame, the oppressed. They pop up in the Nazareth inaugural sermon. Jesus lists them in His reply to John the Baptist's disciples who inquire about his messianic identity. They are the ones welcomed at the banquet when the invited guests refuse to come. We are instructed to invite the stigmatized to meals instead of friends. In the final judgment scene the list appears again. People are rewarded or damned on the basis of how they responded to the hungry, thirsty, naked, strangers, prisoners, and sick (Matthew 25:31-46). This is not an exhaustive list.

In the East these are images of the dead.[11] People without hope. Men who find life too miserable to call it life. Jesus enters such boxes and brings life to those who are as good as dead. Now there is healing, walking, talking, sanity, purity, and freedom. Those who were dead live. These images of transformation signal the age of salvation. The Messiah is here. Restoration is complete. Now is the favorable year of the Lord.

The eyes of Jesus penetrate through shielded boxes. The barricades of suspicion, mistrust, stigma, and hate crumble in His presence. He calls us to see persons behind social labels. His kingdom transcends racial, ethnic, political, sexual, occupational, economic, and pious boundaries. He welcomes persons from all turfs. His love aggressively disregards the norms and customs which box people in. The social barricades which divide, separate, and isolate stand in severe judgment before Him. Jesus' insistence on slicing the social norms which roped people off and His interest in all sorts of persons is at the heart of the gospel itself. This was not a peripheral sidelight of His ministry. If He had stayed in Nazareth and only talked with His own family and townspeople there would be no cross—no gospel. Reconciliation is at the heart of the gospel, not only man to God in a mystical way, but man to man in concrete social forms. The agape of Jesus reached out and hugged boxed up people. It was a sign of God's love which washed away their stigma and integrated them back into the social community.

The Dog and the Checkerboard Tail

Once again we are faced with a dog and tail question. How does the dog of faith relate to the tail of social organization? Do our faith and theology make a difference in our social relationships? Or do conventional social relationships wag our theology? To say it in another way, does our commitment to Christ push us into boxes marked with "Keep out" and "Stigma"? Or do we play social checkers like everybody else—simply interacting with people who are like us and politely obeying all the "No trespassing" signs tacked on the boxes which are different from our own? We may even mouth pious slogans to keep us from others—slogans such as, "To each his own" or "Never trust a stranger." When this happens, the tail of social custom wags the dog of faith.

Does our faith in Christ alter and modify our social life or does it simply mean that now we are in the "Jesus box" and life goes on as usual. God has created us as social beings. Boxing and binning are natural social processes. But they also need redemption. Labeling persons can become a vicious process which dehumanizes others. At the same time it is a needful and necessary aspect of social organization. We need to allow the Holy Spirit to redeem our attitudes about the people behind the labels and we need His power to transform our pattern of social interaction. This does not mean that we will no longer live in boxes, but it does mean that we will never allow the tag on a bin or any social norm to prevent us from caring for and loving persons. Living the incarnation means that we need a conversion of our social thinking. Such regeneration will lead us to sit down for lunch and coffee with those in other boxes. And it will take us to strange residential and occupational turfs.

Church Boxes

A significant question to ask is, "How do the people of God relate to each other?" Are their social relations transformed or do they categorize people like everybody else? Are there holy turfs and stigmatized labels in the church? Unfortunately many of the labels which persons acquire outside the church follow them inside. Internal patterns of social relationships are often based on the external boxes which tag along inside the church. Too often we relate to other members of the body of Christ as doctors, bank presidents, salesmen, Republicans, or females rather than as brothers and sisters in the Lord. These external labels are more important to us than our sibling status in the family of God. Plumbers relate to other craftsmen. Professionals get together. Clusters and subgroups of people emerge.

These informal networks are often oriented around common occupational, educational, and theological interests. The charismatics cling to each other. Members of the local country club huddle and chat after the service. The college crowd sticks together. The elderly sit together. The snowmobilers and waterskiers flock together. The "committed" who are involved in the committee work of the church interact primarily with each other. The number and type of subgroups vary by parish and denomination. A careful observer can detect them in virtually every religious setting. These informal groups tend to sit together in the worship service. They talk together after the service, participate in the same church activities, and eat together at fellowship meals.

Is this all bad? No. This is simply an expression of the natural "birds of a feather" social law. All of us migrate toward people and settings where we feel comfortable, accepted, and understood. But these subgroupings in the congregation also need redemption and transformation. They have the potential to become devisive and antagonistic power groups in congregational life. They can become ghettos of gossip and exclusive cliques which throw derogatory barbs at the members of other clusters. They can foster vicious power struggles in the decision-making process of church life dealing with pastoral leadership, buildings, theology, educational curriculum, and the like.

Four steps can hasten their redemption and prevent them from becoming arrogant cliques. In the first place subgroups need to be recognized and talked about. To look the other way and pretend they are not there is foolish. Subgroup formation is as natural as breathing and it will occur in every social and religious setting. The quicker we recognize this reality the sooner we can experience redemption. Second, the teaching and preaching ministry must continually call people to a common faith in Jesus Christ which transcends social ties. Is our common bond of unity in Christ stronger than the social glue which adheres us together?

This is precisely the genius of the gospel—utterly diverse people from all sorts of boxes are reconciled together in a common faith in Jesus Christ. This doesn't mean that people jump out of their boxes. But now the boxes synchronize together in the complementary way. Suddenly fellow Christians realize that they need each other. The intellectuals need the charismatics. The evangelicals need the social activists. The young need the old. The complementary nature of the boxes builds up the whole so that the entire body matures in Jesus Christ. Paul's analogy of the body applies just as much to subgroups as to individuals.

Third, individuals need to take the initiative to disrupt

boxing patterns. We need to be conscious of when we are in our own group's box and deliberately move out of it at times. Sit in different pews in the worship service. Invite people from other boxes to your home. Participate in activities even when your own group doesn't. Intentionally go to people in other boxes, slip by their label, and love them.

Finally, the organizational structure of the congregation can be modified to redeem our boxedness. Sitting on a pew for an hour each week doesn't help transcend boxes. Time for social interaction is absolutely necessary to get behind tags and labels. Weekend or week-long congregational retreats in a camp setting are an excellent way to discover each other. More unboxing can happen in a three-day retreat than in fifty-two Sundays of bench sitting. In an age of specialization the church has rightly developed very specific curriculums, classes, and retreats for special people: the elderly, teens, adoptive parents, singles, handicapped, professionals, and the like.

We also need to create specific times when the peach basket is upset and everyone rolls together. One congregation worked at this in their Sunday school. In one quarter of each year the Sunday school classes were formed around common birthdays. All the December babies went together for twelve Sundays. In this fashion young and old, male and female, conservative and liberal studied together. The rest of the year they returned to their boxes. Church leaders need to incarnate the reconciliation of boxes carefully into the very structure and organization of church life.

One of the most unfortunate and serious forms of boxing which the church has perpetuated is the subordinate status of women. This is obvious in our liturgy, language, and theology. It can also be seen in the way women have been denied power, influence, and leadership within the body of Christ. Such subordination cannot be justified on the basis of the gospel. Although some changes in the status of women have come in the last ten years, the irony is that they have been thrust on the church by secular forces from outside. This is a clear case of the social checkerboard wagging the dog of faith. If the dog of faith had been wagging the checkerboard as it should have, the church would have been far ahead of the rest of society in ascribing males and females equal status. In the body of Christ the distribution and use of gifts dare not be thwarted by racial, national, or sexual factors.

Although we must deliberately work at unboxing in church life we also need boxes for our psychological and emotional health. We need a warm place where we can hang out our frustrations, doubts, and hassles. We usually find this kind of acceptance among people who are most like us. They understand and care best because they identify closely with our kind of problem. Even though Jesus hopped all over the social checkerboard it is also true that He related more intimately with an inner circle of three. Peter, James, and John witnessed the transfiguration and huddled closely with Jesus in Gethsemane. We need the close fellowship of similar others but the way of Jesus also uses our special gift for ministry to the whole body and calls us frequently to visit other boxes. A healthy tension needs to be maintained between our natural tendency to snuggle up to other similar birds and Jesus' mandate to invade other boxes.

Boxing is not only an issue within church life, it's also of crucial importance in the church's commission to evangelize. Churches as well as people and subgroups within churches carry labels. Denominations carve out a unique historical identity. They reiterate their historical founding to their children. The leading architects of the denomination's beginning are highlighted and esteemed. Songs, books, and creeds articulate the denomination's history and its unique contribution to the history of the larger church. In some denominations there are museums and tours to places of historical significance. Denominational schools, publications, and annual conferences sharpen the consciousness of a people. Eventually in the minds of members a particular image emerges of "Methodists," "Lutherans," "Pentecostals," or "Mennonites." Catholics act so and so. A good Presbyterian should think so and so.

Specialized words develop in each denomination which often have secret meanings known only to the members of that church. "Confirmation," "second work of grace," "neo-evangelicalism," and "discipleship" are some examples. These words stir the passions of the insiders who can uncode their secret meanings but they leave outsiders cold. It's normal and natural for congregations and denominations to cultivate this sense of common solidarity and identity. It sharpens the participants' sense of belonging. They know who they are, where they come from, and where they are going. Members feel a part of the stream of church history. They have a place, a group—a people. This religious ethnicity, as sociologists call it, also presents some problems. It can subtly become idolatrous, demanding more deference and respect than the Scriptures themselves. It can distract from the centrality of Jesus Christ. The biblical Jesus can easily become a denominational Jesus—a Presbyterian or Baptist Messiah. In addition, denominational glue can clog the free exchange of love and cooperation among denominations.

Most seriously, denominational boxing can barricade others out of the kingdom. We've already looked at the indictment which Jesus leveled on the Pharisees. Too much denominational glue frightens others away. Strange words, implausible religious rites, and rigid traditions are social barriers which effectively keep outsiders out. Churches composed of cliques where a few family names predominate scare away strangers. Although a common theological solidarity is necessary to do church, ethnicity dare not undermine evangelism. It's always easier to glory in our own denomination's history than to integrate outsiders into the fellowship. Newcomers often question and doubt the validity of ancient traditions. By exalting our own box we can enjoy its smugness and at the same time evade reassessing our traditional ways.

One of the problems in church growth and evangelism is that birds of a feather do flock together. Lower-class folk feel more at home in a congregation made up of other lower-class persons. Congregations in upper-socioeconomic strata attract individuals from similar upper-class backgrounds. Latino's feel most at home in services which express Latin culture. Professionals migrate toward congregations which endorse heady intellectual discussions. As we have already seen, this is a natural social phenomena.

Some church growth strategists suggest that congregations should focus their evangelism efforts on homogeneous neighborhood units which are already similar to the congregation's profile of racial, social, and economic characteristics. This certainly is a sound strategy if one's only goal is to raise the attendance record as quickly as possible. While it is helpful to take advantage of psychosocial insights in church growth, it is also imperative that the gospel's message of box reconciliation is not jeopardized. Simply getting the same kind of people together is no great feat—it's a normal social process which occurs in all types of organizations and clubs. If the gospel transforms social relationships—if the church is more than just another Rotary Club—spiritual and social reconciliation need to be at the forefront of its ministry.

The genius of the gospel is that when persons declare Jesus as Lord they experience a new unity which transcends their social boxes. True church growth uses the best insights from social science but also calls different kinds of people together under a new Lord. A gospel which only calls people with the same socioeconomic characteristics together is a perversion of the good news which bonds together Jew and Gentile, male and female, black and white. This does not mean that these social characteristics are taken lightly or considered irrelevant. Just the opposite. They are taken seriously as very real determinants of social life. Church leaders need to encourage their uniqueness and emergence and a tension between homogeneity and heterogeneity needs to be maintained. The natural tendency is to seek only homogeneity—groups where everyone is homogenized together. The good news of Jesus Christ welcomes newcomers to small homogeneous units—small groups or house fellowships of similar persons, but it also integrates them into a larger body of siblings from very different backgrounds.

Questions for Discussion

1. Discuss how the "birds of a feather" principle operates in your own life.

2. Reflect for a few minutes on the persons you've invited to your house or have joined you for fun and recreation during the pass six months. How many of these came from boxes which were very different from your own?

3. Identify some of the stigmatized boxes in your community. How is your church penetrating the barricades around those boxes?

4. What kind of boxes and bins exist inside your church fellowship? What can be done to minimize them?

5. What type of social etiquette rules might Upside-Down Kingdom people violate if they take social boxes less seriously?

6. Share experiences when you have distinctly felt close to very different people because of your common faith in Jesus Christ.

11
LOW IS HIGH

The Social Ladder

In the last chapter we viewed human interaction as a checkerboard. Actually the board isn't flat. We can think of the checkerboard standing on edge with the boxes or squares stacked upon each other like mailboxes in a post office lobby. In other words, some boxes are considerably higher than others in their importance and prestige. Another helpful symbol is a ladder. Sometimes we jokingly refer to the pecking order. In reality, it's no joke.

All of these word pictures accurately reflect the fact that society is not flat. People are not equal. We don't all live on the same social level. Some persons are much more important and distinguished than others. Stratification is the technical term for this social ranking process. It comes from geology where stratification refers to the various strata or layers of rock which are stacked up on each other. In this chapter we want to explore Christian perspectives on power and stratification.

Now some people are repulsed by the suggestion that we rank other persons on a ladder in our minds. They want to smile sweetly and think that, after all, everybody is equal. A little thinking should convince anyone that stratification is a very real and hard fact of social life. In all societies everywhere, people are ranked on various kinds of socially important ladders. A father with a son who graduates from law school bubbles over with pride when he talks with friends about his son's achievement. The same father is embarrassed to report that another one of his sons is a garbage collector. Social scientists discovered that on a scale of 1 to 90 a supreme court justice ranks number one and a shoe shiner falls into the ninetieth rung in the minds of most people.[1]

Stratification doesn't apply only to occupations. Within a family, parents usually have more power and influence than their children. In a factory, the general manager is above the line foreman who is above the assembly worker. The chairman of a committee has more prestige and power than rank and file members. Episcopalians are higher on the social prestige ladder of denominations than Pentecostals. Jews as an ethnic group wield much more political influence in American politics than Chicanos. The United States is near the top of the pile in terms of international power and influence. Nations, churches, ethnic groups, occupations, and persons are ranked and layered in our minds. Social pecking orders emerge universally in all societies. It's the nature of social man to assign unequal status to his fellow humans.

Social stratification is not just "out there" in the larger society in the form of social classes and occupational ladders. It stares most of us in the face at work each day. Increasing population density, technology, and occupational specialization contribute to the mushrooming of bureaucracies. Our modern life is more and more made up of many overlapping and complex organizations. The one thing that most large organizations have in common is a rigid ladder of social hierarchy. By nature, bureaucracies consist of specialists organized in a structure of clearly specified positions of authority. The army, of course, is the epitome of an autocratic hierarchy. The organization flow chart and managerial grid of hospitals and factories reminds us of the presence of hierarchy in our daily lives.

In colleges and universities the stacking and ranking of persons is especially obvious and rigid. At the top is the president or chancellor, followed by academic deans. Frequently there are division heads such as the chairman of the humanities. Then come departmental chairmen and three kinds of professors: full professors, associate professors, and assistant professors. Next are instructors, paraprofessionals, secretaries, maintenance personnel, and housekeepers. Students come somewhere near the bottom—a bit above housekeepers.

Social scientists believe that stratification develops for a number of reasons.[2] There are different jobs to do both in a society and in a department store. Persons with appropriate skills plug into the jobs that need to be done. In brief, a division of labor emerges. The various job functions need to be coordinated together. Some of the jobs are viewed by members of the society as more crucial than others. Performing surgery in a hospital is thought to be much more significant than sweeping the hospital floors. The more important jobs often require more training than the less significant ones. The financial rewards are much greater for the more highly valued roles which require longer training. The sizable prestige and paychecks attached to the top jobs entice individuals to push upward. Inequality sets in. Persons occupying the upper positions not only enjoy the applause and financial benefits of the top spots but they also control the rewards and obligations of those below them. Persons in positions of power are able to protect their own privilege and rewards and at the same time prevent others from sharing in the goodies. Although it is conceivable theoretically, it is indeed rare for power, prestige, and privilege to be equally distributed among the members of an organization.[3]

One of the unfortunate results of stratification is that

persons are valued not as persons per se but as performers of functions. Individuals performing important jobs like presidents, doctors, and managers are considered more valuable than those who work as shoe shiners, repairmen, and typists. In other words, people are not just people. Some are very valuable and others aren't worth much. The cold fact that underscores this truth is the weekly paycheck. Persons are paid according to their socially determined value. The paycheck is a weekly reminder of how much we are worth. Although it would be nice, it's very difficult in fact to sort out the difference between a person's "personal" worth and "financial" worth. We can tell persons that they are very important and valuable but when we turn around and pay them half as much as others, they know good and well that they're really only worth half as much as the others. The paycheck is an important determinant of our self-esteem and our perception of self-worth.

Our position on the societal ladder of stratification also makes an immense difference on our life chances. Being born into a Kennedy family or into a poor slum family makes a world of difference in whether or not we will experience malnutrition, infant mortality, college, prison, and mental illness. The quality of our medical care, education, work, and house are also dependent on where we happen to be born on the societal ladder.

Social Muscle

Power is a much used and abused term. It is thrown around so freely that its meaning is endangered. A few definitions may help to clean up fuzzy conceptions. In a broad sense, power is the ability to affect social life.[4] It's the capacity to make things happen. In order to "make things happen" we need resources such as knowledge, money, and position. The people who own and control the resources are the ones who make things happen. An important distinction can be made between individual and institutional power—in other words between John Doe's and General Motor's ability to make things happen.

There are four major types of power based on the resources that an individual or organization has access to: (1) *Financial power* emerges when an individual or organization controls economic resources. Money does speak. It makes things happen. It is one of the most important sources of power. (2) *Expert power* is derived from knowledge or special information that one has. Doctors and lawyers exercise expert power over us because they control special knowledge in medicine and law. (3) *Organizational power* results from a person's position within an organization. An executive vice-president has more power than a typist because of their different positions within the organizational flow chart. (4) *Personal power* is based on an individual's appearance and personality traits. We are attracted to certain persons because of their pleasant interpersonal style and manner. They express a charismatic aura which appeals to us. Now if one individual or institution has access to all four types of power they are indeed very powerful. To be president, personable, wealthy, and smart is to be exceedingly powerful!

There are not only different types of power but also various ways of using power. These modes of expressing power range across a continuum from *control* to *influence.* On the control side of the continuum, the one wielding power can always determine the outcome of the power relationship in advance. In other words, the powerful person can force a subordinate to obey him. The force or coercion is real because the powerful actor controls the rewards and punishments which the weaker person receives. The boss can raise an employee's salary or fire him. In the extreme use of force the powerful person can make the underling obey because he controls the instruments of torture or death.

Influence is on the opposite side of the power expression

continuum. In this situation the outcome of a power attempt can not be predetermined. Here persuasion and appeal are used to convince another person to do something. But the appealer can not force the other person to comply with his wishes. Influence can be very subtle. Advertising is one type of influence. When it manipulates symbols in a way that unconsciously makes someone buy a product, it moves toward the control end of the continuum. Asking a friend to go along swimming is an example of a pure influence attempt if the friend is certain that there will be no subtle punishment for refusing to go.

Another frequently used term related to power is authority. This refers to a person's or institution's right to use power. A policeman has power because he can make things happen. The presence of his car along the side of the road slows down traffic. But a policeman also has authority because he has a legal "right" to exercise power. Authority or the right to use power arises from three sources. Tradition establishes certain patterns of authority. A father or bishop has the right to exercise power because of customs and beliefs associated with his position. Authority also comes from legal understandings. The policeman or corporate officer can freely use power because of formal or legal agreements known to the members of the society or organization. Charismatic authority emerges when a person is believed to have very special personal or magical powers.

Power is not necessarily bad or evil. All of us exercise some of it every day. It is a natural part of social life but it can easily be abused. Christians need to grapple with questions of how power is used and disbursed. To what extent should it be centralized? What are proper and improper uses of it from a Christian perspective?

Before investigating Jesus' perspective on stratification and power we need to sharpen three other terms. Power doesn't live alone. *Privilege, prestige,* and *status* accompany it. *Status* refers to one's position within a social structure in relation to other positions. The status of mother is higher than the status of child in the family. The status of choir director is lower than the status of pastor in church life. Status refers to the relative ranking of positions on a ladder of stratification. *Prestige* is the amount of favorable evaluation received from others. A prestigious position or job is one that people look up to and respect. In other words, prestige refers to the desirability and acclaim which people place on a particular role. Finally, *privilege* refers to the goods, rights, and services which are granted to a person in a particular status.

Power, status, prestige, and privilege rise and fall together. The chief executive of a bank is obviously in a high status position—above all the other positions in the bank. He or she also has more power than any other employee. They can make things happen and the buck stops at their desk. It is also a prestigious position. It's an honor to be selected for it. Other employees dream about moving up to the job some day. Finally, the position carries a great deal of privilege with it such as a private washroom, travel allowance, company car, a large desk, and advance information on interest rate changes which assist in "playing the market" more profitably.

Joe Down and Doc Up

An illustration from the academic world sharpens the inequalities produced by social stratification. We'll compare Dr. Up, a full professor on a college campus and Joe Down, a janitor who cleans the floors and offices in the building where Dr. Up's office is located. Let's contrast the two persons on the four dimensions of status, power, privilege, and prestige. Joe and Doc are at the opposite ends of the status hierarchy on campus. Doc is near the top of the "professional" community. Joe is part of the lowly esteemed maintenance crew.

The status difference is present in their titles. Dr. Up is called "prof," "doctor," and sometimes just "Mr. Up" by a few disrespectful students. Dr. Up also has a nameplate bearing his name and title outside his office. Since Joe doesn't have a title he is simply called "Joe." Their clothing confirms their status difference. Joe wears old jeans, T-shirts, and tattered sneakers. Dr. Up wears a tie and coat, chews Certs, and keeps his hair well groomed.

Joe and Doc also part ways when it comes to power. Doc asks Joe to do work for him in the office like hanging pictures, rearranging furniture, and dusting cobwebs. If the air conditioner is turned up too high, Doc yells for Joe to turn it down. If Doc forgets the key to his door, he calls for Joe to open it with the master key. Joe even makes the coffee for Dr. Up and his colleagues. If Joe doesn't comply with Dr. Up's requests the doctor sends a memo to Joe's supervisor and bingo, that's the end of any raise for Joe. If things are too bad it could even be the end of Joe's job. In sharp contrast Joe really doesn't have any control power over Doc. He might ask Doc for a favor but he has no real power over Doc. He certainly can't reward or punish him. Doc knows the college president and dean personally and often asks them to make special exceptions for him. Joe's sure that the president doesn't even know his name and would never go out of his way for a request from "some old janitor."

In terms of prestige there's also a whopping difference. When Doc comes striding down the hall students reverently greet him with smiles and choruses of "Hello, Doc." They politely step out of his way if he's in a hurry. The president always shakes Doc's hand and smiles warmly. When students bring friends or parents on campus they generally bring them over to Doc's office for introductions. Doc is very pleased to tell others that he's a college prof, because he knows that it's a very respectable and esteemed job. When Joe comes down the hall, the most he gets is a nod or a "Hi, Joe," from professors who know him. He's not normally entitled to warm smiles from the president or introductions to parents. And he really doesn't like to tell people what he does—after all, it's the kind of thing that any old Tom, Dick, or Harry could do.

When it comes to privilege, things are really different. The salary is the most obvious advantage that Doc has. He makes nearly $20,000 a year for about eight months of work. Joe on the other hand gets one week of vacation, plus three personal days and makes around $7,000. Doc has firm control of his schedule. He arrives in the morning when he feels like it and leaves when he needs to. Everything's fine as long as he doesn't miss his twelve hours of classroom time each week. If something important turns up, Doc can even cancel his classes for that day with an "out of town" note. As long as he doesn't miss classes, Doc can take off for the dentist or for a snack with an out-of-state friend without telling anyone. He goes off campus for coffee breaks to a good shop downtown. Doc also has a desk and a private office all of his own which he can lock when he needs to tuck in his shirttail. Doc's fringe benefits are more lucrative than Joe's. His life and health insurance benefits are much higher since many of them are based on a percentage of his salary and matched halfway by the college.

For Joe things are quite different. There's a time clock to be punched morning and evening. Vacation days need to be scheduled at least two months in advance. Coffee breaks must be on campus since Joe must be ready to work at any moment. About the only privilege Joe has is the opportunity to read anyone's junk mail as he pours out the wastebaskets.

Mark Hatfield, U.S. Senator from Oregon, provides an excellent description of the prestige and privilege which accompanies the status of senator:

> My every move through the Senate perpetuates this ego

> massage. When I leave my office to go to the Senate floor, an elevator comes immediately at senatorial command, reversing its direction if necessary and bypassing the floors of the other bewildered passengers aboard in order to get me to the basement. As I walk down the corridor, a policeman notices me coming and rings for a subway car to wait for my arrival and take me to the Capitol Building. The elevator operator, the Capitol policeman, and the subway drivers all deferentially greet me. On the subway car I may take the front seat, which is reserved for Senators who may ride there alone; tourists already seated there are removed by a policeman unless I insist otherwise. At the Capitol another elevator marked FOR SENATORS ONLY takes me to the Senate floor. There at the raising of an eyebrow a page comes to give me a glass of water, deliver a message, or get whatever I need. Aides scurry about telling me when votes will occur on which bills, although no one bothers me with all the details unless I ask."[5]

Says Who?

Stratification isn't unique to the modern world. The gospels are peppered with stratification language. Jesus Himself was very aware of the realities of social ranking. The angel told Mary that Jesus would be called the Son of the *Most* High and that the power of the *Most* High would overshadow her (Luke 1:32, 35). Zechariah prophesied that his son John would be a prophet of the *Most* High (Luke 1:76). Jesus promised that we will be sons of the *Most* High if we love our enemies, do good, and lend, expecting nothing in return (Luke 6:35). A demoniac called Jesus the Son of the "*Most* High God" (Mark 5:7). Most High is used as another name for God. This is a fascinating notion. God's on top of the highest ladder. No other persons or powers rank higher than God.

The term "authority" is frequently on the lips of Jesus. Luke's account of Jesus' life begins by showing Him rejecting the "authority" and the "glory" of the kingdoms of the world (Luke 4:6). Later in the same chapter, after Jesus expels a demon, the people are all amazed and say to one another,

"What is this word? For with authority and power he commands the unclean spirits, and they come out" (Luke 4:36). Jesus has chosen between two diametrically different types of authority. He turned His back on the legal right to rule by political authority. But He by no means rejected authority. His right to rule comes not from coercive political force but from the Most High. He doesn't command armies, but He does command demons. Although His authority doesn't come from white horses, great chariots, and military victories the people recognize it as a bona fide and genuine authority. "And when Jesus finished these sayings, the crowds were astonished at his teaching, for he taught them as one who had authority, and not as their scribes (Matthew 7:28, 29; Mark 1:22).

Ironically, Jesus comes to the people without the traditional legitimation needed to establish His authority. He doesn't have any political clout nor has He gone through the prescribed training to be ordained as a scribe. After another teaching session, "The Jews marveled at it, saying, 'How is it that this man has learning, when he has never studied?' " (John 7:15). Without a scribe's license He was not only teaching but teaching in a way that superseded the scribes. His words earned their own authority. The audience certified His authority, not a board of theological experts in Jerusalem.

The Jewish crowds weren't the only ones who ratified His authority. When the centurion approached Jesus to request healing for his servant, Jesus began walking toward his home. The centurion hedged, saying he wasn't worthy to have Jesus enter his house. "Only say the word, and my servant will be healed. For I am a man under authority, with soldiers under me; and I say to one, 'Go,' and he goes, and to another, 'Come,' and he comes, and to my slave, 'Do this,' and he does it" (Matthew 8:8, 9). When Jesus heard this He marveled and healed the servant. Here was a powerful military man. He obeyed the orders of a regional commander. The soldiers and slaves under him jumped at his words.

Why is Jesus so impressed when the officer describes his powerful position? Is he threatening Jesus to heal his servant or else? Far from it! What he really is doing is comparing Jesus' authority with his own. This Gentile centurion understands that Jesus, like himself, is also a man of authority. He perceives that Jesus has been given the authority by Someone above Him. And he knows that Jesus can also execute His power. This is a Gentile confession of faith, not a military threat. He acknowledges that Jesus has the power to heal his servant even from a distance. Jesus marvels that this Gentile has such a full understanding of Jesus' authority and power.

Another upside-down fact was that the religiously ignorant crowds and this Gentile understood the nature of Jesus' authority. But the religious authorities themselves were perplexed by His authority. One day the chief priests and elders interrupted His teaching and asked, "By what authority are you doing these things, and who gave you this authority?" (Matthew 21:23 and Mark 11:28). In other words, who said so? Who gave Him the right to teach? Who signed His ordination papers? Jesus answered by asking them a question. Where did John's baptism come from? The heavyweights were in a jam. If they said John's authority came from heaven, then why had they refused to listen to John? If they said that his authority merely came from his personal powers of persuasion, the crowd would be angry because they thought John was a prophet. Jesus didn't answer their question because they couldn't answer His. In asking the question about the Baptist he parallels Himself with John. The questions and answers about the authority of John's ministry also fit His own ministry. The Pharisees earlier had said that Jesus' authority came from Beelzebub. Now the chief priests had two options. Either Jesus had the endorsement of the Most High or else He was a skillful crowd psychologist.

In John's Gospel Jesus answers the question of His authority.

> I can do nothing on my own authority . . . I seek not my own will but the will of him who sent me. John 5:30.
>
> The Father . . . has granted the Son . . . authority to execute judgment. John 5:26, 27.
>
> My teaching is not mine, but his who sent me. John 7:16.
>
> I do nothing on my own authority but speak thus as the Father taught me. John 8:28.
>
> For I have not spoken on my own authority; the Father who sent me has himself given me commandment what to say and what to speak. John 12:49.

Again and again Jesus emphatically underscores the source of His authority. It is not His own. He is a steward of the Father's authority. The Father has conferred on Him the power of attorney. He acts on behalf of the Father. The Father has given Him the "right" to speak about the kingdom. This is a most fundamental issue. The one who speaks on behalf of another points people to the other. The self-appointed spokesman who speaks on his own authority points others to himself. Jesus understood this well when he said, "He who speaks on his own authority seeks his own glory" (John 7:18). After Jesus healed the paralytic, the crowds "were afraid, and they glorified God, who had given such authority to men" (Matthew 9:8). Jesus uses His authority in a way that clearly points to God. He is not a self-acclaimed puppet prophet who relishes the crowd's applause.

In summary a few things stand out in Jesus' understanding and use of authority. (1) There is no question that He saw Himself as a steward of God's power. It was God who gave Him the right to speak. (2) He was careful to use His authority in a way that didn't bring Himself personal prestige. His word and act always reflected the Father. (3) He used His authority to serve and assist others. The needs of others were the recipients of his power. (4) Although His preaching license wasn't certified through the proper channels, the crowds perceived the authenticity of His message and gave it grass roots accreditation.

Stop Climbing

Jesus sharply rebukes the ladder climbing Pharisees in all three synoptic Gospels. He pinpoints three tools of stratifica-ion which the religious leaders used to remind the people of their eminent rungs on the Jewish ladder. Their first instrument of prestige was ostentatious clothing. In the words of Jesus they made their robes long, their phylacteries broad, and added long fringes to their robes (Matthew 23:5; Mark 12:38; Luke 20:46). The extravagant clothing of the Pharisees reminded people that they occupied a superior rung in the Hebrew stratification system. They didn't think of themselves as regular people. They were important religious dignitaries who deserved the applause and respect of the common people. Their unnecessary and elaborate clothing only served to highlight their socioreligious position.

Second, the leaders understood that the architectural pattern of buildings also conforms to the shape of social stratification. In the synagogue a special place was provided for prominent people. The scribes sat on the seat of Moses at the front of the room facing the people. This way everyone could see them and admire their special seat. Jesus derides them for seeking out these prestigious seats in the house of worship (Matthew 23:6; Mark 12:39; Luke 20:46). Not only did they scramble for the upper rung seats in the synagogue, the same thing happened at feasts. They rushed for the distinguished positions on the right-hand side of the host. Jesus made it clear that such maneuvering for prestigious chairs in public meetings is not part of the kingdom way.

Third, language is another mechanism for maintaining set patterns of stratification. The scribes utilized its full potential. They insisted on being called rabbi (Matthew 23:8). Since a greeting represented a communication of peace, there were strict ceremonial rules governing to whom and how a greeting was given.[6] Jesus perceived that titles are simply another reinforcement of social stratification. They continually call our attention to status differences. They perpetually remind us that everyone isn't equal after all. Jesus unequivocally wipes out titles. "But you are not to be called rabbi, for you have one teacher, and you are all brethren. And call no man your father on earth, for you have one Father, who is in heaven. Neither be called masters, for you have one master, the Christ" (Matthew 23:8-10). Tagging each other with titles has no place in the Upside-Down Kingdom. The instruments of stratification are more numerous than language, architecture, and dress. In His critique of the prestige hungry scribes and Pharisees Jesus categorically debunked the status-seeking which infiltrates all realms of social life.

Growing Down

The pecking order was not only a Pharisee problem. The disciples were snared by it also. As they walked along the way one day, the motley crew began arguing about which one of them was the greatest (Mark 9:33, 34). Peter felt he should be number one since he was the first to realize that Jesus was the Messiah. James and John thought they should be in on it because they witnessed the transfiguration. In fact one day James and John were so uptight about it that they pulled Jesus aside and demanded, "Do for us whatever we ask of you" (Mark 10:35). They wanted to sit on the right-and left-hand side of Jesus in His Kingdom. They were eyeballing the best seats at the top of the ladder.

Matthew reports that their mother made the demand (Matthew 20:20, 21). In any event, we find the old autocratic spirit of "do this and do that" right smack in the middle of the disciple group. The bossing mentality is accompanied by the social comparison process which ranks people from greatest to least. Jesus rebuked their clamoring for status and power by taking a child in His arms. "Whoever receives one such child in my name receives me; and whoever receives me, receives not me but him who sent me" (Mark 9:37).

A few days later as the disciples were screening incoming visitors, they pushed aside mothers with children who simply wanted to touch Jesus. He was indignant and furious when He saw this power play (Mark 10:13, 14). As far as the disciples were concerned, these children were social nobodies. They didn't hold any prominent positions. They wouldn't be able to help advance the cause. There were certainly more important people that Jesus should spend His time with. These children were deflecting Jesus from His mission. The disciples still hadn't caught on to the upside-down logic. As far as Jesus was concerned the children were just as important as the adults. Jesus not only spent time with these small fry, He actually held them up as model kingdom citizens. "For to such belongs the kingdom of God. Truly, I say to you, whoever does not receive the kingdom of God like a child shall not enter it" (Mark 10:14, 15).

In these two occasions, as the disciples competed for the number one position and as they pushed children away from a busy Jesus, He pointed to a child as the symbol of kingdom living. Normally we tell people to grow up and "act their age." Here Jesus tells us to grow down and regress to childlike behavior. Why is this? What is it about the nature of a child that's instructive for kingdom learners? Why does Jesus go to the very bottom of the ladder for His example? Why doesn't He select devout Simeon or some other saint for His lesson?

In virtually all societies children are at the bottom of the social status ladder. They have no power in the society. They are totally dependent on other members. They are an economic liability. Children do not make social distinctions among people. They don't place people into boxes. One child when asked what the president of the United States does quickly replied, "He goes to the bathroom." They don't play by the normal social rules. They are friendly to strangers. They learn racist and ethnic slurs from their parents. Color, nationality, title, and social position mean nothing to the very young child. They have no sense of bureaucratic structures and hierarchies. The infant has no possessions and is totally dependent on others for care and survival.

The use and manipulation of power is foreign to the baby, although its cry certainly does "make things happen" (Mommy comes running). This, however, is a response to biological needs. It is not the cunning power which maneuvers people and situations to its own advantage. The child learns the tactics and strategies of power broking as he grows up. A trusting confidence characterizes the manner of a child almost to the point of naivete even in the presence of danger. The child of the good mother trusts her completely.

Jesus calls kingdom citizens to babyhood in all these areas. Instead of pursuing the number one spot, He prods us to flatten our hierarchies and forget them as children do. And as infants we are to be blind to status differences, seeing all others as equally significant regardless of their social position and function. The disciple of Jesus relates to people as a child. In the child's eyes the garbage collector and president of the country are equals. As children of the kingdom we are to see people and structures on a flat perspective without ups and downs. Instead of hankering over power, the follower of Jesus lives powerlessly as a child. We also welcome interdependence. Rather than claiming self-sufficient independence, we acknowledge our need for community and dependence on others. And in childlike faith we call our heavenly Father, "Daddy." Even the *Most High* is not addressed with prestigious titles but with the intimate and warm word, "Daddy."

As children of the heavenly Father we are to live as children in social relationships, for the kingdom is made up of such spiritual infants.

Bottom Up

The disciples still didn't understand, even after Jesus taught them with the example of a child. In fact as they sit around the table during the last supper an argument about greatness breaks out. After all the teaching on babyhood and and in the middle of this sacred event they dispute again about who is the greatest. They are quite normal. They are preoccupied with their internal hierarchy. How do they stack up with each other? In response to their status bickering, Jesus tries again. He completely revamps the meaning of "greatness." "The kings of the Gentiles exercise lordship over them; and those in authority over them are called benefactors. But not so with you; rather let the greatest among you become as the youngest, and the leader as one who serves. For which is the greater, one who sits at table, or one who serves? Is it not the one who sits at table? But I am among you as one who serves" (Luke 22:25-27). Matthew and Mark report Jesus saying that "the rulers of the Gentiles lord it over them, and their great men exercise authority over them. It shall not be so among you; but whoever would be great among you must be your servant, and whoever would be first among you must be your slave; even as the Son of man came not to be served but to serve, and to give his life as a ransom for many" (Matthew 20:25-28, Mark 10:42-45).

Jesus has just turned our social worlds upside down. He has reversed our assumptions and expectations. He has utterly redefined greatness. This is no sweet proverb about social relationships. These words strike at the root problem of domination found in all social organizations. The sequence of thoughts that naturally flow together in our minds fit the following equation:

Greatness = Top, powerful, master, first, ruler, adult.

Jesus radically inverts the equation to read:

Greatness = Bottom, servant, slave, last, child, youngest.

There can be no misunderstanding here. Jesus totally inverts the conventional definition of greatness among the people of God. The pagans lord it over their subjects. They are the ones who develop hierarchies of power. "Not so among you," thunders Jesus. In the Upside-Down Kingdom greatness is not measured by how much power one has over others. Upside-down prestige isn't calculated by how high one is on the social ladder. In this inverted kingdom, greatness is determined by one's willingness to serve—one's willingness to be a slave.

Then Jesus poses the profound question of who is greater, the chairman of Exxon who sits at the table in the executive dining hall or the waitress who serves him? The president of the country flying in the first-class section or the stewardess who serves him? The answer is obvious—of course the chairman of the board and president of the country are more important. There's no doubt about this. Waitresses are a dime a dozen. Any common person can be a waitress. The chairman of the board has years of special training and experience. Any nitwit can tell you that he's more important than a waitress. Not so, says Jesus. I am among you as a waiter. I am not here as a ruler or boss; I'm among you as a slave, a servant, a waiter. Instead of giving orders and directives down the hierarchy, I'm looking up the hierarchy asking what can I do for you. This is an utterly upside-down perspective. Instead of a "down from the top" posture, the Jesus way is "up from the bottom".

Servanthood sounds nice. But we must be careful not to throw it around glibly as "professional service," "human service," or "service is our first and last word." Such slogans and words are tossed around to create a pleasant service image. We need to distinguish between pseudo service and the way of Jesus. Much of modern service rhetoric falls short of the way of Jesus. Many times it does not truly seek to meet the needs of others but it used to manipulate persons into buying additional products or "services" which they really don't need. When this happens, the so-called servant is not a servant at all but an artful manipulator or adman using the language of service to his own ends. Many of the "professional service" people are quite high on the social status ladder and look at their clients from a top down perspective. They will "serve" their clients as long as it pays well for them both in dollars and prestige. But when the needs of their clients run counter to the "servant's" own financial and status interests, the "service" abruptly ends. Such self-serving "service" is not Christian service.

In sharp contrast, the servanthood of Jesus ended on the cross. He was willing to serve the needs of the sick on the Sabbath even when it meant jeopardizing His very life. He announced forgiveness of sins even when such blasphemous words were sure to trigger His death. The Jesus style of service brought neither personal financial gain nor social prestige. In fact, quite the opposite. His service was rewarded by outrage from the authorities and a violent death. For Jesus, serving did not mean catering to the well-to-do who could make substantial financial repayment. Rather, His instruction is to serve the "*least of these,*" those at the very bottom—the least of the least who certainly will not be able to pay back. In fact, serving such social throwouts will undoubtedly tarnish the "professional reputation" of the professional community. After all, only incompetent lawyers, doctors, and teachers will serve the stigmatized as a last resort if they can't develop a profitable practice among the respectable. The disciples of Jesus give a cup of cold water in His name to the little ones who have no political clout or social prestige (Matthew 10:42).

We have heard Jesus redefine greatness. What does He really mean when He says the least among us is the greatest in the kingdom? He clearly understands that social greatness is highly correlated with access to power. Usually those who boss and lord it over others are seen as the great persons. The president, the chief executive officer, the head of the department, these persons who control power and manage people receive prestigious applause not necessarily by their subordinates but by society at large. Does Jesus intend to suggest that persons who are at the bottom of the typical social hierarchies—the janitors, females, weak, and stigmatized—are automatically at the top of the kingdom ladder? Is He calling for a complete inversion where the top rungers in this world exchange places with the bottom rungers in the kingdom of God and vice versa? I think not. Instead of turning the hierarchy upside down and making a new one, Jesus is questioning the need for hierarchy and declaring it unconstitutional for His people. He also proposes new criteria for evaluating greatness.

Describing John the Baptist, Jesus says, "I tell you, among those born of women none is greater than John; yet he who is least in the kingdom of God is greater than he" (Luke 7:28). What does Jesus mean by these baffling words? He is comparing two orders of stratification. Among persons born in the flesh there is none greater than John. He is the greatest and last of the prophets. But in the kingdom order among those born of the Spirit, even the least is greater than John. If the least of the kingdom citizens is greater than John, the rest of them are obviously also greater. Jesus is not debunking John's significance. He is merely saying that everyone in the kingdom born of the Spirit is just as great as the greatest of the prophets. His eye twinkles as He says this. The point is that in the Upside-Down Kingdom everyone is the greatest!

As Francis Schaeffer has said, there are no little people in this kingdom. Everyone is on the same level and everyone is a great person.

Jesus is actually poking fun and spoofing the language of "greatest and least." That kind of talk has no place in kingdom conversations. Kingdom people don't think in those terms. Rather than exchanging a new hierarchy for an old one, Jesus levels all hierarchies. He understands that all hierarchies soon begin to function as deities. Men bow down and worship them. They obey them. Paul Minear is correct when he says "that wherever a man or a group yields to any authority as ultimate—there a particular deity stands revealed."[7] Jesus once and for all is disarming the authority of hierarchies to act like gods. He calls us to participate in a flat kingdom where everyone is the greatest. In this kingdom the values of service and compassion replace dominance and command. In this flat family, the greatest are those who teach and do the commandments of God (Matthew 5:19). They love God and others as much as themselves.

Looking Down

Arrogance is a corollary of power and prestige. Those who make it to the top sometimes pride themselves in "their great accomplishments." A "look at what I've done" attitude oozes from their interpersonal relationships. Jesus understands that such haughtiness is a by-product of the hierarchical ladder. He tells the story of a man at a feast who carefully checks out the prestige value of all the seats at the table. He picks a distinguished one to display his prominence. The seats fill up. A very eminent guest arrives a few minutes late after the top seats are all taken. The toastmaster unfortunately needs to ask the earlier guest to take a lowly seat far from the head table. It is better, Jesus says, to select the bottom seat unless the master of ceremonies motions you to another seat. Inversion visits again. "For every one who exalts himself will be humbled, and he who humbles himself will be exalted" (Luke 14:11). We find this same rule of thumb pronounced by Jesus after the parable of the breast-beating tax collector and haughty Pharisee (Luke 18:14) and after he rebuked the Pharisees for their status-seeking with clothing and titles (Matthew 23:12).

What is the meaning of the humble and exalted riddle? As parables go it is not intended merely to teach dining etiquette. Although the meaning may certainly affect dining protocol, it goes beyond that. The normal tendency is to chase after the positions of honor and prestige. We all enjoy the oh's and ah's of other people. We take it for granted that upward is better. Rather than endorsing such upward mobility, Jesus calls us to downward mobility—to the seats at the bottom. His disciples defer to others. They happily yield up the good seats. In fact, they are so busy waiting on tables that they don't have time to sit. Serving is their occupation, not seat picking. The adage that the exalted will be humbled and vice versa is not a tidbit of proverbial wisdom such as, "Pride cometh before a fall." Rather it suggests that those who exalt themselves over others have no place in the kingdom. Self-glorifying status hunters have no need for God and no place in His kingdom. Those who confess their sinful ladder climbing and go about serving others in quiet meekness are exalted in the Upside-Down Kingdom. Ego trips end at the kingdom's door. Kingdom people look down instead of up. They willingly move downward.

Contrary to kingdom thinking it is typical for people to look down the ladder and mutter, "If I did it they can do it too. If they'd just work a little and be responsible they could pull themselves up by their bootstraps, too."

Some proud top rungers tend to assume that their own hard work and motivation is the only reason they are at the top. This "if Abe did it I can" mentality naively assumes that anyone can make it to the White House if he tries hard enough. There are at least seven factors which contribute to where we stand on the ladder of social stratification. (1) Personal motivation is certainly an important aspect. The amount of hard work and energy we exert minimizes or maximizes the influence of the other six factors. (2) Biological givens also determine our place in life. Physical and intellectual abilities are for the most part inherited and beyond our personal control.The retarded child obviously does not choose to be stigmatized. (3) Cultural values also condition our experience. In some cultures children are taught to work hard and to enjoy it. In others, hard work is not an important value. Top rungers who work hard dare not thank themselves if they happened to be born into a culture which taught them to enjoy hard work. (4) Community assets also make a difference. The child born into an upper-class community with topnotch jobs, libraries, schools, and hospitals has overwhelming advantages over a child born into a community with deficient social institutions. No matter how hard he works, the average child in the poor high school may never get to college. (5) The emotional security of the family makes a grave impact on the child's own emotional makeup. Children growing up in emotionally disturbed homes may have nagging insecurities the rest of their lives which hinder their best performance. (6) Inheritance is a major factor determining a child's socioeconomic position in life. Inheriting the family business, fortune, or political name puts many people into powerful positions who never would have made it on their own. (7) Chance also affects our niche in life. Some make it rich because real estate prices triple overnight. Others lose everything through a social or financial catastrophe.

The point of all of this is that it is arrogant for persons to assume that they "made it" just because they worked hard. The cult of haughty individualism takes personal credit for a person's social achievements. It should be obvious that we don't choose our mothers, communities, or cultures. Many factors shaping our place in life are simply beyond our control. This doesn't mean that we are only robots or puppets yanked up and down the ladder of stratification by mysterious forces. Personal motivation does make a difference in how we respond to the tugs of the six other factors. Hard work is an important factor in our place on the ladder. But contrary to the cult of individualism, it is not the only factor. It is only one of many. The tragedy of such individualism is that it breeds unfounded pride in one's "personal" achievements and bitter contempt for others who stand on lower rungs.

The Jesus people are moved to caring compassion when they look down the ladder, for they understand that it is only by the grace of God that they stand where they do. They also understand that most of those below them are not there because of irresponsible laziness. They know that many of the lower ones stand where they do because of social, economic, and biological factors beyond their control. This realistic understanding of why people are at different places on the ladder wipes out any haughty individualism and propels the people of God toward downward mobility. This in no way derides the value of hard work and initiative but merely recognizes that it is one of many factors which place us on the social ladder. Thus the disciple humbles himself in the face of these realities and looks for a lower seat beside those who beg for care and compassion.

Jesus Power

Jesus is not a typical king who barks orders to his generals and threatens his subjects. He had no niche in the religious, economic, or political power structure of His day. As far as the formal organizational charts were concerned, He was powerless. Instead of pointing to warriors, generals, and kings as examples of power models he holds up the younger, the last, the least, the child, the servant, and the slave as ideal kingdom citizens. He describes Himself as gentle and lowly in heart and says that His yoke is easy and His burden is light (Matthew 11:29, 30). His truth is revealed to babes rather than to wise eggheads (Matthew 11:25). Should we conclude from all of this that Jesus carried no stick? Was he a flimsy, wishy-washy weakling?

The answer is a definite no. Although it is true that He had no formal positions of power, it is not true that He was powerless. In fact He was so powerful—He could make things happen so fast—that He was killed. His power threatened the religious and political structures so much that they couldn't stand to have Him around. He did not run from power. He exercised a great deal of power. If He had stayed in the desert and quietly taught His disciples in a serene hideaway He would have been no threat at all to the ruling religious and political powers.

The threat came from the fact that His very life and message eroded the base of the prevailing power structures. Social scientists have discovered that in virtually all forms of social organizations, from friendship groups to nations, a small self-perpetuating group grabs most of the power sooner or later.[8] This tendency for power to concentrate in the hands of a few persons is known as the law of oligarchy. Jesus boldly condemns oligarchy in social, economic, political, and religious spheres of life. Designating Himself as a waiter and criticizing the scribes' drive for prestige touches the social area. In earlier chapters we heard His hard words about economic stratification where the rich dominate the poor. The comment that His disciples should not be like the kings of the Gentiles who lord it over their subordinates strikes at oligarchy in the political sphere. Jesus' harsh words and acts against the oral law and the temple demonstrate His rejection of oligarchy in religious institutions.

The inbreaking reign of God in the life of Jesus undercut the authority of all the other reigning power structures. His whole life directly challenged the legitimacy of the power structures of his day.[9] He was killed because the challenge was so relevant to the fundamental issue of domination in human organization. His power base was so strong, in fact, that the authorities had to be very careful how they dealt with Him. He not only had a small band of devoted followers but He allowed large masses to follow Him. His power over the masses was so strong that the authorities feared a revolution. They had to be very careful how they treated Jesus or they would have a revolt on their hands (Luke 22:2). Their nighttime seizure of Jesus was under the cover of darkness to prevent a tumult.

Although Jesus had great power over the crowd, He did not exploit it. Perhaps one of the reasons that He kept His messianic identity a secret was to prevent the crowd from declaring Him king. The one time that He thought they might make Him king by force He ran to the hills to escape (John 6:15). Furthermore, His power over the crowd was not mandated because of His position in a formal social structure. They voluntarily chose to follow Him because of His genuine authority. His authority was authenticated by His willingness to reject status and power, and to serve.

In general terms we can say that Jesus exhibited both expert and personal power. His knowledge of the law and His sharp and penetrating insights were the base of His expert power. He controlled the secrets of the kingdom. His personal power came not from physical charm but from His obvious care and compassion for all, including the sick and outcast. He had no financial power or organizational power. His expression of power was primarily through influence—never coercion and control. Hengel points out that the teaching style of Jesus, in particular His parables and sayings, was not that of an irrational demagogue. Even here, Jesus sought to gain the assent of men through rational influence, not through emotional manipulation.[10] He had access to no soldiers or pay raises by which He could control the outcome of His influence attempts. He simply spoke the truth and allowed individuals to make free will decisions. He describes Himself as the Good Shepherd. He doesn't chase or drive His sheep. He calls them. Those that recognize His voice follow (John 10:4).

Alongside His powerful words stood mighty acts. His activity was powerful because it was relevant deviance. Deliberately breaking social norms—healing on the Sabbath, eating with sinners, talking with women, affirming Gentiles and Samaritans, and cleaning the temple—all of these were powerful acts of deviance. They were not done just for the sake of creating trouble. Jesus didn't enjoy antagonizing people nor was He crazy. Here was a Man with the wisdom of a prophet who didn't hesitate to violate social custom when it obviously functioned to dominate and subordinate certain persons. The power of Jesus' acts was not found in coercive rewards or punishments which He parceled out but in the fact that He was willing to risk His very life for the sake of these injustices. He cared so much that He was willing to be vulnerable to the instruments of violence controlled by the authorities.

Another aspect of His upside-down power was His willingness to reject what was rightfully His. Instead of acting like a typical messiah—ruling, demanding, and dominating from the top—Jesus worked from the bottom up. Rather than demanding service, He served. He knelt down and washed the disciples' feet. He worked at the bottom as a servant, waiter, and janitor. He served the needs of the social outcasts scattered below the bottom rung—the lepers, blind, sick, and poor. Precisely because He willingly gave up what was rightfully His and went to the bottom, risking His life to save and heal others, He was taken up to the authorities at the top of the power structure. They punished His unorthodox power with their kind of power—violence.

Thus we cannot conclude that Jesus was powerless. He was extremely powerful. But it is clear that Jesus categorically rejects domination and hierarchy as acceptable forms of social governance. Three factors characterize His use of power: (1) Influence, not control, is His primary expression of power. He beckons individuals to follow Him. His word and act create a crisis. We are forced to make a choice. But it is a voluntary decision. (2) The focus of His power is on the needs of others. He mobilizes His resources to serve the needs of the hurting and stigmatized. (3) The power is not used for self-gain or glory. He willingly suspends His own rights and serves at the bottom of the ladder. It does not fit typical social custom. He redefines "rights" and "expectations" and engages in social deviance for the sake of others.

From There to Here

I will summarize some of the basic issues and assumptions regarding a Christian perspective on power which emerges from our study before looking at details:

(1) *Power should be used to help others become powerful.*[11] This is the opposite of what normally happens. Power usually snowballs. Powerful persons and institutions tend to use their power to become more powerful at the expense of others. The exercise of power often perpetuates and increases power inequities. The end result is that the powerful become more powerful and the less powerful lose power. The upside-down perspective seeks to use power to equalize power.

(2) *Power should be distributed as widely as possible among individuals and organizations.* Power tends to concentrate in the hands of a few people. Those in the center of an organization have great clout while those on the sidelines usually have little say. There will always be power differentials. As Christians we should work to diffuse and decentralize power whenever possible.

(3) *Hierarchy in social governance should be reduced to a*

minimum. Once again the tendency is to increase the rungs on the ladder. Ladders should be flattened out. As this happens coordination replaces domination. Flattening ladders is another way of diffusing power.

(4) *Authority for leadership should be freely given by the led*. Leadership should not be imposed on a group by an outside agency. Nor should leadership be self-appointed. Leadership is only worthy of allegiance when it is freely given by the led to the leader in response to the leader's servant posture.[12]

(5) *The Christian perspective looks down the ladder*. Our normal tendency is to scramble up ladders as fast as possible. The disciple of Jesus works to serve the powerless at the bottom. This may be in the form of personal ministry or through changing the structure of the ladder itself. The Christian is more concerned about the plight of those at the bottom than about advancing his own position on the ladder.

Unfortunately, the Christian church historically has been the perpetuator of some of the most rigid systems of hierarchy and stratification. In the context of church life, rigid chains of command and domination are often sanctified with pious language. It is difficult to peel away the religious jargon to see the utter incongruence between the sacred hierarchies and the way of Jesus. Let us be clear on one thing. This is not a call for anarchy, disorder, or confusion. The Spirit of God brings orderliness to the life of His people. This does not mean, however, that the church should blindly adopt secular bureaucratic procedures and structures. The form and shape of corporate life in the church patterned on the principles of Jesus will be radically different from the typical bureaucratic pattern.

Consensus will be used in decision-making to insure maximum participation and ownership by members. All members will have access to the decision-making process rather than a small group of elites. Servant leaders do not dictate the goals and strategies of the group. Instead they facilitate the fellowship in articulating and achieving its common goals. Rather than intimidating the led with "I think this and I think that," servant leaders ask, "Where do we want to go?" "What are we saying?" and "How do we feel about this?" The servant leader uses his power to help the believers discern the Spirit's will for the group. Size is the friend of bureaucracy and hierarchy. Decision-making involving all members is best facilitated in groups of less than 100 persons. Rather than snowballing bureaucratic structures as size increases, congregations can multiply into small units of less than 100 persons which permit fuller participation in charting the corporate life.

There will be a division of labor in church life. The Holy Spirit endows each person with unique gifts and abilities. These gifts will be used in various ways to build up and minister to the total body. Each contribution, each function whether it's preaching, washing windows, or setting up chairs will be equally esteemed. Each job is considered just as important as every other regardless of its place within the structure of the body. If persons are considered equal and the jobs are considered equivalent, it only follows that the same rate of pay will be given across the board when remuneration is necessary. To pay the minister and janitor on different scales declares that their functions and their persons are fundamentally unequal. To be sure, they are not identical. But they are of equal significance and prestige in the body of Christ and should be paid accordingly.

Titles also are foreign to the body of Christ. Doctor, Reverend, Mister, and Sister perpetuate status differences which are not in harmony with the way of Christ. The most respectful title we can use is a person's first name. Calling each other by titles pays tribute to the position, degree, or status rather than the person. Members of flat kingdoms call each other by the first name.

These are only a few of the particulars which flow from Jesus' view of power and stratification. They are relevant for local congregations of believers as well as denominational agencies such as publishing houses, mission boards, and schools. They also pave the way for a servant posture in the larger society. Christians involved in business, education, and public life will use their influence to nudge organizations and institutions in the flat direction. Two considerations govern how the Christian lives an Upside-Down Kingdom agenda in the larger society. The Christian in a "top" spot in management or professional life seeks to express power through servanthood rather than domination. One's own job should not be considered more significant than jobs at the bottom of the organizational chart. We should be willing to work at the "top" job for the same salary and privilege as those near the bottom if we truly believe that our work is no more important than theirs.

The bottom-up perspective does not mean that teachers will become janitors and lawyers will become shoe shiners. There is nothing wrong with pursuing a vocation which brings personal fulfillment and which meets legitimate needs of others. The critical question, however, is how one employs a particular vocation or interest. A medical doctor can practice in a plush suburban area with an excess of doctors and receive a lucrative income. Or he or she can defy the typical upward mobility patterns and practice in a poor community and receive a bare-bone salary. A truck driver can take a good paying cross-country run which tears his family apart or he can accept a local run which keeps the family intact and the salary down. Likewise, a businessman can expand a subsidiary into a community with a dependable labor supply which already has a low employment rate or he can place the new plant in an area which desperately needs new jobs. The disciple of Jesus must ask whether his gifts and training are being used to perpetuate inequality and self-advancement or whether they are truly being utilized to serve others who really hurt even though that may terminate an illustrious professional career.

Questions for Discussion

1. What stratification ladders or dimensions are important in your community? In your congregation?

2. What are some of the consequences of allowing paychecks to determine the importance of persons?

3. Discuss the kinds of power which are prominent in the life of your congregation?

4. Are there any situations where it would be proper for a Christian to use "control"?

5. In what ways is Jesus' understanding of power and authority relevant to us today?

6. In what specific ways does your congregation embody flat kingdom ideals in contrast to other secular organizations?

7. How have the seven factors of stratification influenced your own position on the social status ladder?

8. Identify specific ways to work at the flat kingdom agenda in your work and community.

12
SUCCESSFUL FAILURES

The Politics of the Basin

We have seen that Jesus did not identify Himself with the existing religious parties and power structures in Palestine. He did not endorse the "realistic" Sadducees who cooperated extensively with the Roman occupation to preserve the sacred functions of the temple and their economic interests. There can be no question that He rejected the formal establishment of proper religion represented by the progressive Pharisees. He was not lured by a serene life in the desert in an Essene commune. He gave an emphatic and definitive NO to the righteous revolutionary violence of the Zealots. He rejected the symbols of these four strategies for dealing with Rome's domination. The temple, oral law, wilderness, and sword find little prominence in his kingdom. Although Jesus did not participate in any of these feasible political options, He did stay right in the middle of things. His in-the-middle-of-things involvement was unusually upside down.

Every kingdom has a flag. This symbol represents the collective meanings of the kingdom and serves as a rallying point for loyalty and action. The symbols of the Upside-Down Kingdom are indeed upside down! They are certainly not the typical symbols which accompany a right-side-up king. The flags of this kingdom are a manger, stable, desert, donkey, thorns, basin, cross, and tomb. These are not the signs of successful kings. Such rulers are born in V.I.P. suites of prominent hospitals; they ride armored limousines, wear golden crowns, and receive international applause. But don't be mistaken. This Jesus is a King. He doesn't walk into Jerusalem on His feet. He rides in kingly fashion. His beast, however, is not the white stallion of a commander-in-chief; it's the poor man's donkey. He is a King but not a conventional one by any means.

The cross has become the symbol par excellence of the Christian church. It represents both the atoning sacrifice of God's beloved Son for the sins of humankind and the nonresistant way of Jesus. A preoccupation with the cross, however, can detract from the very reason that the cross came about in the first place. There are three upside-down symbols which must be seen flowing together in telling the gospel story: the basin, the cross, and the tomb. In a real sense the basin is truly the Christian symbol par excellence because it is this symbol that Jesus Himself voluntarily selected and used. The cross was the Roman symbol. It was used by them to crucify criminals. The cross was forced on Jesus by the ruling powers. It was the sign of evil men reacting to the way of the basin. The empty tomb is God's final word that He is triumphant over even the most vicious forces of evil.

In the context of the Last Supper as His earthly ministry was about to conclude, Jesus hoisted the flag of His Upside-Down Kingdom:

> [Jesus] laid aside his garments, and girded himself with a towel. Then he poured water into a basin, and began to wash the disciples' feet, and to wipe them with the towel with which he was girded. John 13:4, 5.

The towel and basin are the tools of the slave.[1] This Upside-Down King uses the instruments of the servant. Instead of the typical powerful kingly symbols of sword, chariot, and white stallion Jesus reaches for the tools of service found at the bottom of the ladder. In Palestinian culture it was customary for a household slave to wash the feet of the guests while they ate their meal reclining on couches. In typical fashion loaded with rich symbolism, Jesus turns things upside down. As the Master of these disciples it is He who has the traditional right to expect and demand that they wash His feet. This is merely the normal honor which goes with His position. Jesus categorically forfeits these customary privileges. Instead of demanding service He serves and now symbolically moves the disciple up to the position of master. As Jesus kneels down to wash, the disciple sits in the upper role as master. Foot washing is not the most pleasant task. It means bending over and looking down to the bottom of the person. The bending over symbolizes humble and obedient service, so foreign to the arrogant "I'll serve you if you pay me well" attitude. The servant looks at the dirty part of the body. He touches the repulsive feet covered with filth and mud. This is not clean and prissy service—this is dirty work. Normally a master washes his own hands and face but not his crusty feet—that's the slave's dirty work. The foot washer concentrates on the feet of the other, not on his own hunger. Jesus voluntarily bends over and washes. He's not ordered or forced to do it. He chooses to serve and is willing to take orders. These are His symbols. The towel that He uses is flexible. It gives personal care by adjusting to the size of the other's foot.

Walter Brueggemann has called the towel and the basin the tools and agents of shalom.[2] They are not only symbols. They are the means by which something is actually done. The tools define our trade. We can only do the kind of thing for which we have tools. The towel and basin are slave tools which do the work no professional or competent master would do. These tools place us in the lower position, serve the other, and raise the other to the superior position. In this act Jesus is now turning the old social hierarchy upside down and exchanging it for a new one. For as the disciples all become servants and take turns washing each other's feet the whole distinction between master and servant fades. As all become servants to each other they are all simultaneously the greatest in the kingdom.

This is not the first time this King has gone down to the bottom. This King has been washing feet all His life. The towel and basin are the fundamental symbols which represent what Jesus was all about. Jesus had been using the basin for three years, not like Pilate did to absolve himself of responsibility, not like the Pharisees did to exclude others. His basin was one of assertive love which took responsibility for others and included them in the flat kingdom. It was His basin work, in fact, which set the stage for the cross.

We must understand that the cross did not miraculously drop out of the sky. It wasn't something which Jesus couldn't avoid. The cross was the natural social response of evil men to the presence of the basin. It was the violent tool of the powerful trying to crush His basin ministry. Without the basin there would be no cross. The true cross comes after the basin. In other words, we must be sure to distinguish between the cross and what led up to the cross.[3]

We have already seen the shape of the basin ministry. Jesus spoke out forcefully against the rich who callously perpetuated their economic dominance of the poor. He healed and shelled grain on the Sabbath. He ate with sinners and tax collectors. He committed blasphemy by calling God His Father and by forgiving sins. He violated and condemned the oral law. He allowed a prostitute to touch and anoint Him. He traveled with women in public. He told parables which stung the religious leaders. He talked freely with Samaritans and Gentiles. He healed the sick. He blessed the helpless. He touched lepers. He entered the homes of pagans. He purged the sacred temple. He stirred up large crowds.

In almost every instance He was breaking informal and formal social rules created by the powerful religious authorities. He didn't make a fuss just for the sake of making a fuss. He actively and aggressively used the basin and towel to serve the poor and helpless regardless of the conventional social customs. He was quite aware that His deviant behavior would trigger His death. He knew full well that death was the prescribed punishment for some of His behavior. But the harassment from the authorities and the threat of death didn't stop His acts of love. Although He was not a violent revolutionary, His behavior was a political threat to the entrenched powers. The chief priests and Pharisees said, "If we let him go on thus, every one will believe in him, and the Romans will come and destroy both our holy place and our nation" (John 11:48). Many of the charges at His trial were false. But there can be no question that in the minds of the Jewish leaders His new teaching and acting threatened the false sense of peace in Palestine. The Romans considered any source of instability a political threat to their control of Palestine. So they executed Him as a political insurrectionist and hung the tag "King of the Jews" on His cross.

At the end of the foot washing in the upper room Jesus instructed His disciples to do likewise: "If I then, your Lord and Teacher, have washed your feet, you also ought to wash one another's feet. For I have given you an example, that you also should do as I have done to you" (John 13:14, 15). This is an invitation to enter the basin ministry with Jesus. He certainly is suggesting more than a twice-a-year ceremonial ritual. His example was a life of service. He extends an invitation to enter the basin trade full time. The Gospels make it clear that the disciple is called to follow the Master by doing the work of the kingdom. This is not a kingdom of saints on rocking chairs pondering the mystery of God's salvation. This is a kingdom of basin people. The word and event become one in Jesus Christ. The Word became flesh and lived among us. The disciple incarnates the Word by acting in the name of Christ. Words without acts are empty. Acts are powerful authenticators of the word.

The greatest disciples in the kingdom are the ones who *do* and teach the commandments (Matthew 5:19). "Not everyone who says, 'Lord, Lord,' shall enter the kingdom of heaven, but he who *does* the will of my Father" (Matthew 7:21). The sheep and goats are separated at the judgment on the basis of their acts of clothing, feeding, visiting, and welcoming (Matthew 25:31-46). The family of God is made up of the ones who *do* His will (Mark 3:35). The one who hears and *does* the words of Jesus is compared to a wise man "Why do you call me 'Lord, Lord,' and not *do* what I tell you?" (Luke 6:46). The lawyer is told that he will live if he *does* the Great Commandment (Luke 10:28). After the Good Samaritan story we are instructed to go and *do* likewise (Luke 10:37). In parabolic form Jesus tells us that the servant who knows his master's will, but doesn't *do* it, will receive a severe beating (Luke 12:47). This call to an active basin ministry permeates the Gospels. We are asked to sell, give, love, forgive, lend, teach, serve, and go. There is only one caution. An aggressive basin ministry will likely result in a cross.

If

"If any man would come after me, let him deny himself and take up his cross daily and follow me. For whoever would save his life will lose it; and whoever loses his life for my sake, he will save it. For what does it profit a man if he gains the whole world and loses or forfeits himself? For whoever is ashamed of me and of my words, of him will the Son of man be ashamed when he comes in his glory and the glory of the Father and of the holy angels" (Luke 9:23-26).

For many years I had the impression that the cross was symbolic of suffering. Thus, any kind of personal suffering which I endured was a personal cross which I needed to bear as Jesus did. In other words, I thought of a tragedy, misfortune, accident, or physical disease as a cross. It was something that I couldn't avoid, something which in His divine providence God allowed to happen to me. As a disciple of Jesus, bearing my cross meant accepting the suffering without complaint and bitterness. This is a gross misunderstanding of the meaning of the cross.[4]

A cross is never something which God puts on us. It is not an accident or tragedy beyond our control. A cross is something that we deliberately choose. We determine if we want to accept a cross. We make the voluntary decision of embracing the cross. Jesus' use of the words, "If any man," implies a free, deliberate choice. The cross for Jesus was not something which God forced on him. The cross was the natural, legal, and political consequence of His basin ministry. Long before Gethsemane, He was aware that a cross was the inevitable outcome of His aggressive love for others which frequently violated social norms. He repeatedly warned His disciples that He would eventually suffer and die. Even in Gethsemane the struggle to "take this cup from me" was not so much a struggle with a predetermined plan as it was a struggle to be willing to continue to live the way of love even in the midst of physical violence. It was the struggle to run, fight, and retaliate in the face of the ugly cross. To view the cross as less than a voluntary choice makes a farce out of the authenticity of Jesus' temptation in the wilderness.

We can define a cross as an expensive decision. It has costly social consequences. We might paraphrase Jesus by saying, "Take up your basin with the full awareness that it may bring suffering, rejection, punishment, and apparent failure." There are three ways in which Jesus makes the social consequences of cross-bearing clear. First of all, we must be willing to deny personal ambition before we can pick up a cross. Personal ambition is defined by the values which our society considers successful. Personal ambition means attempting to conform to the "success" image of whatever society we live in. Denying ourself does not mean belittling or demeaning ourself. It means refusing to allow our ambition to be molded by the secular values of our cultural environment.

Second, Jesus indicates that if we follow in His way it will probably look like we have "lost" our life in this world. In other words, we may appear like a social failure if we engage in a significant basin ministry. Since the tools of our trade are the tools of a slave and since a slave is not generally considered the most successful person in most social systems, we can expect to be thought of as having "lost" our life by the standards of this world. These words of Jesus articulate the most fundamental inversion of the Upside-Down Kingdom. He seems to be saying that if we pick up our basin and cross for His sake we will appear like social failures in this world. On the other hand, if we play by the rules of this world's game and make it to the top of the success ladder we may have "lost" our life in the kingdom of God. Such a direct inversion between the values of the kingdom and this world is a hard saying indeed. But a fair exegesis can hardly yield a different meaning.

Jesus hints at the third social consequence of the cross when He talks about shame. Shame is a social concept. He is fully aware that we may be socially ashamed to engage in a basin ministry which runs counter to the prevailing social values. We may plunge into upside-down basin activities but when ridicule and social flak come we will be tempted to give it up and play by the old rules. And so He says if we are ashamed of Him and His words, so will the Father be ashamed of us (Luke 9:26). "Whoever denies me before men, I also will deny before my Father who is in heaven" (Matthew 10:33). These three clues point to the fact that Jesus was not talking about some inner spiritualized or mystical cross.

Nor was He talking about accidents. He was describing actual decisions which entail real social consequences just as His own decision to move toward Jerusalem and cleanse the temple had the real social consequence of violent death.

Cost Analysis

The life of discipleship for Jesus was no Mickey Mouse thing. It was a serious commitment which ruptured all other loyalties and ties. "So therefore, whoever of you does not renounce all that he has cannot be my disciple" (Luke 14:33). He understood that the basin/cross way was very costly and He was concerned that enthusiastic joiners might misinterpret the expensive nature of following Him. One day as a huge multitude of enthusiasts were surging after Him, He told two parables to remind them of the cost (Luke 14:25-33).

A farmer building a tall tower in his vineyard to watch for robbers needs to sit down and calculate the cost of the materials before he starts building. If he has to stop after the foundation because of insufficient funds and materials the neighbors will mock and ridicule his stupidity. So the disciple who doesn't carefully evaluate the social cost of following Jesus will end up looking like a fool if he doesn't follow through on His commitment.

In the second story, a king going to war with another king sits down first and calculates the strength of both forces to see whether or not he has a reasonable chance of winning. If he doesn't take the time to check out the strength of the other side, and enters the battle with only half as many soldiers as the opposing force, his army will be disastrously crushed. So the disciples should also calculate the cost of following Jesus to prevent a disaster.

On another occasion two bright-eyed enthusiasts ran up to Jesus and wanted to join the disciple crowd. Jesus reminded the first one that a disciple's life brings insecurity and social ostracism. "The Son of man has nowhere to lay his head" (Luke 9:58). Another potential follower wanted to go home first to say farewell. But Jesus informed him, "No one who puts his hand to the plow and looks back is fit for the kingdom of God" (Luke 9:62). One hand guides the light Palestinian plow.[5] The other hand, usually the right, carries a six-foot stick with a spike on the end to prod the oxen. The left hand regulates the depth of the plow, lifts it over the rocks, and keeps it upright. The plowman continually looks between the hind legs of the oxen to keep the furrow in sight. Any plowman who doesn't totally concentrate on the job ends up meandering in circles on the field. Such confusion awaits the disciple who is not fully engrossed in the basin ministry.

In another instance when Jesus asks someone to follow Him, the prospect wants to go home first for the six-day mourning ceremony for his dead father. Jesus tells him to come immediately and proclaim the kingdom and let the dead bury the dead (Luke 9:60).

In all of these instances Jesus is saying two things. Following Him will be socially expensive. When the disciples decided to follow Jesus they "left all" (Luke 5:11, 28). Second, he expects prospective disciples to sit down and coldly calculate the cost of following Him before they decide. They should only follow after they have deliberately and rationally performed a cost analysis. Otherwise they will end up in ridicule, disaster, and confusion.

There is no hocus-pocus involved here. The disciple follows in the Jesus way with the full awareness that He might be fired or lose a promotion. The disciple deliberately loves and serves even when it brings ridicule and social harassment from the power-holders who oppress others. Picking up the cross means that the disciple engages in an active basin ministry fully aware that the cross might come in the form of social ostracism and abuse. The nature of the cross will vary depending on the social and political setting. The same act of love in one political setting may bring frowns and gossip, while in another political milieu it might result in imprisonment, torture, or death. Regardless of the shape or form of the cross, the disciple does not engage in retaliation or revenge even for self-defense when the cross appears.

Cross-bearing is not a once and done teenage decision. It is a daily assessment of our willingness to make expensive decisions for the sake of Christ. This is the one and only area where we are called to be like Jesus.[6] "Whoever does not bear his own cross and come after me, cannot be my disciple" (Luke 14:27). "He who does not take his cross and follow me is not worthy of me" (Matthew 10:38). Following in the way of Jesus does not mean going barefoot, remaining celibate, or living in rural areas. The one and only way in which we are to imitate Him is in our willingness to embrace the basin and the cross with their most concrete social meanings.

A Cold Prickly

Too often the Christian church has perverted the meaning of the cross. We've made it into a nice "warm fuzzy" devoid of any social content. Too often we are taught to believe in the cross and expect everything to turn out fine. The test of whether or not we do believe in the cross is found in whether we are willing to be obedient to the way of the cross. The cold prickly cross that we find in the Gospels is contrary to much modern evangelism that worships the God of success. Just follow Jesus, we are told, and we will be successful in almost everything. Just give our hearts to Him and we will rise to the top of the ladder. Be "born again" and we will win more beauty contests, hit more home runs, make more sales, and receive more awards. This kind of theology simply pours pious syrup over the old success ladder. This plastic Jesus doesn't flatten the ladder—He actually helps us to climb it as long as we are sure to "give Him all the honor and glory." This perverted approach gives us the old worldly success syndrome with a religious halo on top of it.

The Jesus of the New Testament calls us to costly discipleship. Following Jesus means not only a turning around in some personal habits and attitudes, but most fundamentally it means a completely new way of thinking—a new logic. The logic of the Upside-Down Kingdom is difficult to grasp because it runs counter to most of the logic that we've learned since childhood. To be converted to the Jesus way means a fundamental overturning of the conventional logic that we take so much for granted. Simply to baptize the old logic with a new language is not the meaning of conversion. To follow Jesus—to be converted—means a complete upsetting of the assumptions, logic, values, and presuppositions of the dominant culture.

This is evident when Jesus tells us that His followers will look like they have lost their life in this world. The temptation for most of us is to try to make it in both systems. We want to save our life in this world and in the community of God's people. We want to appear successful by secular standards and at the same time we hope to appear successful in the church. But to make it in both kingdoms involves serious accommodation and compromise on the part of the people of God. We quickly water down the scandalous nature of the gospel so that it meshes smoothly with the success symbols of modern culture. If the gospel today, as in Jesus' time, threatens the bastions of political, social, and economic power, His disciples will not be a very popular crowd around town—much less will they be considered successful. Jesus appears to be drawing a hard inverted line when He says that the ones who truly save their life according to the values of the Upside-Down Kingdom will have already lost it in the value system of this world.

The cross is not the last word. It is only the middle word in the basin-cross-tomb sequence. The cross is not the symbol of failure and defeat as it first appears. The empty tomb is

God's final word. The cross exposes the power of evil men in all its brutality and violence. The resurrection symbolizes God's final and ultimate victory over the principalities and powers of darkness. Now the Christian can live in hope since God has declared the triumph over sin. Basins which bring crosses are now picked up with hope. There is light at the end of the tunnel. The followers of Jesus can suffer in the face of evil because they know the victory has already been won in the empty tomb.

The Upside-Down Community

The citizens of the Upside-Down Kingdom do not run about doing their own thing. The fundamental definition of the kingdom involves doing God's thing together. Jesus would have been much less of a threat if He had not gathered a community of followers around Him. A wandering vagabond isn't much of a threat to the established order. Jesus' kingdom words on riches, power, love, and compassion assume that His people share a corporate life together. He calls us to repent and join a disciple group characterized by interdependence in spiritual, emotional, and economic spheres. Leaving their own ambitions behind, kingdom citizens use their gifts to build up the body of Christ. The character of this new community of interdependence erupted in the early church at the time of Pentecost.

Today church is often no more than periodic attendance at a Sunday worship and occasional participation in other meetings. Professional commitment and participation in occupational or leisure organizations takes first priority. Church attendance is nice if we have time and is occasionally necessary for window dressing our social status. Jesus calls us to participate in a corporate life of His people which takes absolute allegiance over any other involvements. In fact, our other involvements flow out of the context of this discerning community. The shape and pattern of life in this community will vary from complete communal experiences to more traditional models. In any event the church will not be a caboose to the rest of life. It will be the locomotive which affects the totality of our life.

This task of rebuilding the church is the most urgent and paramount agenda for kingdom citizens.[7] Creating a new style of corporate life is more critical than having all the right answers to the question of political and economic involvement.[8] In a real sense the creation of bona fide Christian community is a political act since it represents a distinct social reality. John Yoder flatly declares, "This is the original revolution; the creation of a distinct community with its own deviant set of values."[9] This is not a situation where a few devout Christians occasionally come together to worship. This is the creation of a countercommunity with a distinct social environment. As the disciples of Jesus come together, their agenda and corporate structure will appear upside down in contrast to conventional social organizations, including many churches.

When it is faithful to its mission to be in the world, but not of it, the church is a prophetic minority or deviant subculture. Jesus had no illusions of a Christian society. He didn't expect His movement eventually to baptize the entire society. Jeremias points out that fourteen times Jesus describes the spirit of His age with the words, "this generation."[10] In all but one case "this generation" is described with words of extreme rebuke. It is evil, unfaithful, entrenched in unbelief, adulterous, and peevish. Jesus describes the larger society as the broad way which leads to destruction. His followers walk the narrow way which leads to life. But the narrow way is not separated physically from the broad one. The narrow way is in the world. As salt, light, and leaven the community of disciples penetrates the world.

These images which Jesus uses are symbols of a distinctive subculture which functions as an alternative social reality. The community of God doesn't deliberately stand off against the prevailing cultural values just for the sake of being deviant. Jesus made it clear that repenting and accepting God's upside-down way would often conflict with the dominant society ruled by the prince of evil. Deviant subcultures are not appreciated by the rulers of any age who want everyone to conform. Jesus expected His disciples to experience persecution. "Blessed are you when men hate you, and when they exclude you and revile you, and cast out your name as evil, on account of the Son of man!" (Luke 6:22).

The people of God are continually tempted to accommodate and assimilate the values of their surrounding cultural environment. It's easy to temper the scandalous nature of the gospel by making it palatable and acceptable to the majority. Before they know it the people of God borrow the ideology, logic, and bureaucratic structures from their worldly neighbors. They put a little religious coating on top, but underneath the mentality and procedures are often foreign to the way of Jesus. The structures of the Christian church must always be functional and relevant to their cultural context, but they dare not be determined by the culture. The moment this happens the church is in and of the world. The light is dimmed. The salt is tasteless. The leaven is gone.

The necessity of Christian community is obvious beyond the fact that this is God's design for social life. Individuals trying to live the Upside-Down Kingdom agenda alone will soon burn out emotionally. It is not psychologically healthy to be the only oddball around. Embracing a deviant lifestyle requires a community of others who can provide the needed emotional support and affirmation. Christian community is also important for economic sharing. This doesn't need to be a full-blown communalism where everyone dumps everything into the same pot. It must, however, involve a firm commitment to be totally liable for each other's economic needs. One can only live the Jubilee in the context of this kind of community.

The community is essential as a corporate witness to God's love and grace. Without the community context, the upside-down Christian is seen as "just another good guy" or "some nice guy." It's not unusual for a "nice guy" to come along occasionally. It is unusual, however, for people to live together intimately as nice guys. The witness of corporate love and caring is overwhelming in a ruthless dog-eat-dog society. The Christian community is a profound witness to how God wills people to live and do business together. It's a demonstration of a new society of redeemed people.

The community is also necessary to discern the real issues in modern life. An individual can easily be overwhelmed by the media blitz. The consumer demons of today come sugarcoated. The individual cannot always detect the depravity behind much of the rhetoric in modern life. The Holy Spirit in the community of faith helps God's people truly discern the times in which they live. Out of the corporate life the Spirit shapes the strategies for the involvement of Christ's disciples in the world. As the times and gifts are discerned, God's people are mobilized for significant ministries. Accenting the primacy of Christian community does not, in any way, signal political irresponsibility or social withdrawal. Jim Wallis has said it well. "Authentic political existence requires an authentic personal and communal existence."[11] Any political involvement which is not supported by a bona fide experience in Christian community is superficial at best since it cannot point to a living demonstration of how God desires for His people to live. True worship and praise erupts into service for others. God's faithful people engage in a rhythm-dialogue of worship and service.

The strategies of kingdom people will vary. The kingdom agenda is more critical than the particular strategy one selects. If we have learned anything from this study, it should be that kingdom people will not blindly jump on the bandwagon and support programs and institutional structures without question. This does not mean that they will withdraw to Dead Sea monasteries as the Essenes did. Like their Lord, they also will embrace a basin ministry in the middle of things. But they will have a keen awareness that upside-down basin ministries often result in crosses. The empty tomb provides hope to pick up the basin. Regardless of the strategy, there will be crosses to bear.

In some cases the Christian community itself may develop and operate ministries under its own auspices. Other kingdom people will be involved in providing social and legal services to the needy. Still others will engage in forms of social action designed to modify unjust social structures. Kingdom people will also be directly involved in political and industrial organizations as long as they can be faithful to the Upside-Down Kingdom agenda. In other cases Christian siblings will openly dissent against militarism, economic oppression, racism, authoritarianism, and other forms of sin and evil. However, they will be more concerned about doing justice than demanding justice. In all of these cases the critical issue is not whether we are pursuing a holy strategy; the issue is whether or not we are willing to be obedient to the way of the basin even if we are fired, demoted, or lose an election. Also more important than the strategy is the need for it to flow out of a vital experience of worship and prayer in the Christian community.

Most Christians have this turned around. They scamper all over the country trying to locate a job and then they try to find a church. The upside-down way establishes Christian community first and then asks how the gifts and skills of each member can be used in the ministry of the body of Christ.

Finally, all of the expressions of ministry and service which flow out of the life of the people of God need to be done in the name of Jesus. Our lives of service should not point others to our self or only to the body, but ultimately to Jesus, our Savior and Lord.

The Marks of Kingdom People

The corporate life of the people of God will be visible, external, and political. These are the people who discern the demonic tendencies of economic, political, and religious institutions to perpetuate injustice. These are the people who conspicuously share instead of consuming. They practice Jubilee rather than accumulate wealth. Their faith wags their pocketbooks. They give without expecting a return. They forgive liberally as they were forgiven. They love without regard to label or obligation. They penetrate boxes marked "Stigma." They express an unequivocal concern for the poor and destitute. They look and move down the ladder. They don't take their own religious structures too seriously. They acknowledge Jesus as Lord of even religious organizations. They serve instead of dominate. They prefer invitation to force.

Love replaces hate among these folk. Even enemies are loved. Basins replace swords in this society. These people share power, love aggressively, and make peace. They flatten hierarchies and behave like children. Compassion replaces ambition among them. Equality supersedes competition and achievement. Obedience to Jesus blots out worldy success. Among these people, servant structures replace bureaucracies. They call each other by first name, for they have one Master and one Lord, Jesus Christ. They join together in a common life for worship and mutual support. Here they discern the times and the Holy Spirit's direction for their individual and corporate ministries.

The future is already present among these people. They are citizens of a future kingdom which is already here. These are the people who turn the world upside down because they know there is another King named Jesus. These children of the Most High welcome the reign of God each day with the words, "Thy kingdom come, thy will be done on earth as it is in heaven."

Questions for Discussion

1. Does it make any difference to see the cross as a result of the basin?
2. Identify some crosses which you are presently facing.
3. In your own words, what does Jesus mean by "saving" and "losing" your life?
4. Discuss the implications of the church as a counterculture.
5. Evaluate the various strategies for Christian service and ministry.
6. Discuss your own involvement in an upside-down community.

NOTES

Chapter One: Down Is Up

1. Joachim Jeremias, *New Testament Theology* (New York: Charles Scribners Sons, 1971), p. 97 points out that the terms "kingdom of God" and "kingdom of heaven" have an identical meaning.

2. Jeremias, *Theology,* pp. 32-34.

3. This is essentially the position taken and more fully developed by John Howard Yoder in *The Politics of Jesus* (Grand Rapids: Eerdmans, 1972), p. 23.

4. Jeremias, *Theology,* p. 98.

5. Discussions of the debate over the timing of the kingdom have been reviewed by numerous scholars. George E. Ladd, *A Theology of the New Testament* (Grand Rapids: Eerdmans, 1974) and *The Presence of the Future* (Eerdmans, 1974); Norman Perrin, *The Kingdom of God in the Teaching of Jesus* (Philadelphia: Westminster, 1963) and *Jesus and the Language of the Kingdom* (Philadelphia: Fortress, 1976); Wolfhart Pannenberg, *Theology and the Kingdom of God* (Philadelphia: Westminster, 1969); Richard H. Hiers, *The Kingdom in the Synoptic Tradition* (Gainesville, Florida: University of Florida Press, 1970), and *The Historical Jesus and the Kingdom of God* (Gainesville, Florida: University of Florida Press, 1973).

6. Two recent advocates of Schweitzer's exclusively apocalyptic analysis of Jesus' teachings are Hiers, *Synoptic Tradition* and *Historical Jesus,* and Jack T. Sanders, *Ethics in the New Testament* (Philadelphia: Fortress, 1975).

7. Ladd, *Presence,* p. 3. See also C. Norman Kraus, *The Community of the Spirit* (Grand Rapids: Eerdmans, 1974), p. 32 and John Bright, *The Kingdom of God* (Nashville: Abingdon, 1953), pp. 216-217.

8. Ladd, *Presence,* p. 123.

9. Perrin, *Language,* pp. 29-35. In the interest of simplicity I have la-

beled Perrin's steno symbol "specific" and his tensive symbol "general."

10. Sanders, *Ethics,* p. 31.

11. Ladd, *Presence,* p. 303.

12. Sanders, *Ethics,* p. 29.

13. Ladd, *Presence,* p. 302 and Bruce C. Birch and Larry L. Rasmussen, *Bible and Ethics in the Christian Life* (Minneapolis: Augsburg, 1976).

Chapter Two: Mountain Politics

1. Martin Hengel in *Christ and Power* (Philadelphia: Fortress, 1977), pp. 17-21 suggests that Jesus took a critical stance against all the political powers of His day. Hengel, however, does not relate this critical posture to the temptation.

2. A number of studies are helpful in reconstructing the political and social history of Israel from the time of the captivity up to the demise of Israel in AD 132. Eduard Lohse, *The New Testament Environment* (Nashville: Abingdon, 1976); F. F. Bruce, *New Testament History,* (New York: Doubleday, 1971), Bruce Metzger, *The New Testament: Its Background, Growth, and Content* (Nashville: Abingdon, 1965); Norton Scott Enslin, *Christian Beginnings I and II* (New York: Harper, 1956); Charles Guignebert, *The Jewish World in the Time of Jesus* (New York: University Books, 1959); Ralph Martin, *New Testament Foundations* (Grand Rapids: Eerdmans, 1975).

3. Enslin, *Beginnings,* p. 8.

4. Lohse, *Environment,* p. 25.

5. Enslin, *Beginnings,* pp. 13-14.

6. Joachim Jeremias, *Jerusalem in the Time of Jesus* (Philadelphia: Fortress, 1975), p. 124.

7. Enslin, *Beginnings,* p. 60.

8. Metzger, *Background,* p. 24.

9. Martin Hengel, *Victory over Violence* (Philadelphia: Fortress, 1973), p. 29.

10. Hengel, *Violence,* p. 32

11. Martin Hengel, *Was Jesus a Revolutionist* (Philadelphia: Fortress, 1971), p. 10.

12. Lohse, *Environment,* p. 42.

13. Werner H. Kelber, *The Kingdom in Mark* (Fortress: Philadelphia, 1974), p. 78, points out the symbolic significance of the mountain in Mark's Gospel.

14. The most important study is S. G. F. Brandon, *Jesus and the Zealots* (New York: Scribners, 1968).

15. Marvin Harris, *Cows, Pigs, Wars, and Witches* (New York: Random House, 1975), pp. 179-203.

16. Oscar Cullmann in *Jesus and the Revolutionaries* (New York: Harper, 1970) outlines the issues in chapter one.

17. Cullmann in *Revolutionaries,* and Hengel in *Violence* and in *Revolutionist,* both provide excellent refutations of the thesis that Jesus was a Zealot.

Chapter Three: Temple Piety

1. Jeremias, *Jerusalem,* p. 25.
2. Martin, *Foundations,* p. 78.
3. Jeremias, *Jerusalem,* pp. 200-205, provides an excellent summary of the temple operation.
4. Lohse, *Environment,* p. 157.
5. Jeremias, *Jerusalem,* p. 83.
6. Metzger, *Background,* p. 55.
7. Jeremias, *Jerusalem,* p. 75.
8. *The Interpreter's Dictionary of the Bible* (Nashville: Abingdon, 1962), Vol. 4, p. 216.
9. Jeremias, *Jerusalem,* pp. 160-212.
10. My discussion of the Torah is based primarily on Guignebert *World,* pp. 62-67.
11. Jeremias, *Jerusalem,* Chapter X is the basic reference for this section on the scribes.
12. Jeremias, *Jerusalem,* p. 243.
13. Jeremias, *Jerusalem,* pp. 246-267.
14. Martin, *Foundations,* pp. 109-116.

Chapter Four: Wilderness Bread

1. Yoder in *Politics,* p. 31 suggests this reading of the bread temptation.
2. Jeremias, *Jerusalem,* pp. 92-99, and Louis Finkelstein in *The Pharisees* (Philadelphia: Jewish Publication Society, 1962), pp. 11-16, describe the affluence of the Jerusalem aristocrats.
3. Salo Wittmayer Baron, *A Social and Religious History of the Jews,* Vol. I (New York: Columbia University Press, 1952), p. 275.
4. Enslin, *Beginnings,* p. 127.
5. F. C. Grant, *The Economic Background of the Gospels* (London, 1926).
6. Harold Hoehner, *Herod Antipas* (Cambridge: The University Press, 1972), p. 70.
7. André Trocmé, *Jesus and the Nonviolent Revolution* (Scottdale, Pa.: Herald Press, 1973), pp. 87-88.
8. Baron, *History,* p. 279.
9. Guignebert, *World,* p. 39.
10. Jeremias, *Theology,* p. 110.
11. Jacob Neusner, *First Century Judaism in Crisis* (Nashville: Abingdon, 1975), p. 29.
12. Hoehner, *Herod Antipas,* p. 73.

13. Martin Hengel, *Property and Riches in the Early Church* (Philadelphia: Fortress, 1974), p. 27.

14. Richard Batelу, *Jesus and the Poor* (New York: Harper and Row, 1972), pp. 5-9.

15. Jeremias, in *Theology,* p. 221, and Batey in *Poor,* pp. 5-9, argue that Jesus was of the poor class. Hengel in *Riches,* p. 27, contends that because of His occupation, Jesus came from a Galilee middle class of skilled workers.

Chapter Five: Free Slaves

1. Trocmé, *Nonviolent Revolution,* especially chapters 2 and 3.

2. Roland de Vaux, *Ancient Israel: Social Institutions,* Vol. I (New York: McGraw Hill, 1965), p. 176. He does not think that Isaiah 61:1, 2 refers to the Jubilee. George Edwards in "Biblical Interpretation and The Politics of Jesus" (unpublished manuscript) also rejects the hypothesis that Jesus was explicitly restoring the Jubilee program in Nazareth. John H. Yoder, *Politics,* follows Trocmé's interpretation of the Jubilee. Metropolitan Paul Gregorios, "To proclaim Liberation" in *To Set at Liberty the Oppressed* (Geneva World Council of Churches, 1975), also makes a clear case for a Jubilean interpretation of Luke 4:18, 19. Don Blosser provides the most extensive study of the Jubilee theme in Luke 4 in his PhD dissertation, "Jesus and the Jubilee: A study of the Social and Economic Teachings of Jesus Based on the Nazareth Sermon in Luke 4:16-30" (Scotland: University of St. Andrews, 1978). Even if Jesus was not explicitly referring to the Jubilee in the Nazareth event, Jubilee nevertheless is a most useful symbol for interpreting the economic principles found in the Gospels.

3. Robert North, SJ, *Sociology of the Biblical Jubilee* (Rome: Pontificio Instituto Biblico, 1954), p. 129. North suggests that the same year was in a certain sense the fiftieth and also the forty-ninth. The forty-ninth year may have loosely been referred to as the "fiftieth."

4. *Interpreter's Dictionary of the Bible, Supplementary Volume* (Nashville: Abingdon, 1976), "Jubilee," p. 496.

5. Jacob Neusner, *From Politics to Piety: The Emergence of Pharisaic Judaism* (Englewood Cliffs, N.J.: Prentice Hall, 1973), pp. 14-18.

6. Trocmé, *Nonviolent Revolution,* p. 39, determines chronologically that Jesus preached in Nazareth in a sabbatical year.

7. August Strobel in *Jesus in Nazareth* (Berlin: Walter de Gruyter, 1972), argues that it was not only a sabbatical year—but was actually the Jubilee year itself when Jesus appeared in the Nazareth synagogue. I am indebted to Walton Z. Moyer for translating Strobel's article for me from the German.

8. Gregorios, *Proclaim Liberation,* p. 187.

9. Jeremias, *Theology,* p. 104.

10. Trocmé, *Nonviolent Revolution,* p. 42.

Chapter Six: Luxurious Poverty

1. Jeremias, *Theology,* p. 236.
2. Yoder, *Politics,* pp. 65-66.
3. Archibald M. Hunter, *The Parables Then and Now* (Philadelphia: Westminster, 1971), p. 28.
4. Joachim Jeremias, *The Parables of Jesus* (New York: Charles Scribner's Sons, 1972), Second Edition, p. 183.
5. Clarence Jordan and Bill Lane Doulos, *Cotton Patch Parables of Liberation* (Scottdale, Pa.: Herald Press, 1976), pp. 65-66.
6. Jeremias, *Parables,* p. 184.
7. John Stanley Glen, *The Parables of Conflict in Luke* (Philadelphia: Westminster, 1962), p. 69.
8. J. Duncan M. Derrett, *Law in the New Testament* (London: Darton, Longman, and Todd, 1970). His discussion of the parable of the unjust steward, pp. 48-85, gives a detailed picture of the economic norms in Palestine and provides the foundation for my discussion. Dan Otto Via, Jr., *The Parables* (Philadelphia: Fortress, 1967), p. 158, agrees with Derrett's interpretation.
9. Derrett, *Law,* p. 62.
10. *Interpreter's Dictionary of the Bible,* Vol. 3, p. 234.
11. Jeremias, *Parables,* p. 165.
12. *Interpreter's Dictionary of the Bible,* Vol. 3, p. 843.
13. Jeremias, *Theology,* pp. 108-113.
14. Jeremias, *Theology,* p. 112, suggests that the Lucan version is surely the original. Matthew's gospel was formulated in a church fighting the temptation of Pharisaic self-righteousness. The "poor in spirit" emphasis was a needed corrective.
15. Jeremias, *Theology,* p. 109.
16. *Interpreter's Dictionary of the Bible,* Vol. 3, p. 531.
17. Baron, *History,* p. 252.
18. Jeremias, *Jerusalem,* pp. 311-312.

Chapter Seven: Right-Side-Up Detours

1. Clarence Jordan, *Parables,* p. 118.
2. Birch and Rasmussen, *Ethics,* pp. 179-182, cite the misinterpretation of this statement as a classic example of the misuse of Scripture of social ethics.
3. Derrett, *Law,* pp. 266-278.
4. Ronald J. Sider, *Rich Christians in an Age of Hunger* (Downers Grove, Ill.: Inter-Varsity Press, 1977), pp. 175-178.
5. Hengel, *Riches,* p. 29.
6. *Newsweek,* August 2, 1976, "The Richest Men in America," p.56-58.
7. Leonard Sloane, New York Time News Service, "Salaries of Top Executives Pale with Those of Stars," *Lancaster Intelligencer Journal,* April 26, 1976.

8. Sider, *Hunger,* pp. 32-37.
9. *Time,* August 29, 1977, p. 15.
10. Sider, *Hunger,* pp. 40-42.

Chapter Eight: Impious Piety

1. Morris Adler, *The World of the Talmud,* Second Edition (New York: Schocken Books, 1963), pp. 40-41.
2. Herbert Danby, translator, *The Mishnah* (London: Oxford University Press, 1933).
3. Hermann L. Strack, *Introduction to the Talmud and Mishnah* (New York: Atheneum, 1969), pp. 26-28.
4. W. D. Davies, *Introduction to Pharisaism* (Philadelphia: Fortress, 1967).
5. Jeremias, *Theology,* pp. 204-211, has a helpful discussion of Jesus' attitude toward the written law and the oral law.
6. Danby, *Mishnah,* p. 106.
7. Danby, *Mishnah,* p. 110.
8. Danby, *Mishnah,* pp. 123-127.
9. Jeremias, *Theology,* p. 144.
10. Jeremias, *Theology,* pp. 115-116.
11. Kelber, *Kingdom,* pp. 97-102, expands the traditional interpretation that the temple cleansing was done primarily to open up the outer court to the Gentiles. He also suggests that the prohibition to carry vessels had more religious significance than stopping people who were taking a shortcut through the temple.
12. Kelber, *Kingdom,* p. 101, makes a convincing case that the purge was intended to shut down the temple operation at least in a symbolic if not final sense.
13. Jeremias, *Jerusalem,* pp. 253-255, points out that Matthew put scribes and Pharisees into the same category. Jesus denounced the Pharisees primarily for their emphasis on tithes and ritual washing while the scribes or lawyers were criticized for their attention to social status. See Luke 11:37-52.
14. Jeremias, *Parables,* pp. 139-144, provides helpful insight for understanding this story.
15. Jeremias, *Parables,* p. 132.
16. Ladd, *Theology,* pp. 105-119.
17. Bright, *Kingdom,* see Chapter VIII, "Between Two Worlds: The Kingdom and the Church."
18. Kraus, *Community,* pp. 30-31.
19. Kraus, *Community,* p. 34.
20. Kraus, *Community,* p. 38.
21. Howard Snyder, *The Problem of Wine Skins* (Downers Grove, Ill.: Inter-Varsity Press, 1975), pp. 160-164.
22. The Anabaptists in the sixteenth-century radical reformation

declared a moratorium on sacred objects and times, etc. See Walter Klaassen, *Anabaptism: Neither Protestant Nor Catholic* (Waterloo, Ont.: Conrad Press, 1975), especially Chapter Two.

23. Howard Snyder, *Wine Skins,* pp. 69-73.

Chapter Nine: Lovable Enemies

1. Jeremias, *Parables,* pp. 128-132, provides helpful cultural background to this parable.

2. Jeremias, *Theology,* pp. 214-217.

3. John Bowman, *The Samaritan Problem* (Pittsburgh: Pickwick Press, 1975), p. 57.

4. Jeremias, *Jerusalem,* p. 352.

5. Jeremias, *Jerusalem,* p. 357.

6. Jeremias, *Jerusalem,* p. 358.

7. John Dominic Crossan, *In Parables* (New York: Harper and Row, 1973), p. 65.

8. Jeremias, *Theology,* p. 239.

9. Yoder, *Politics,* see especially Chapters 7 and 9.

10. In *Our Star-Spangled Faith* (Scottdale, Pa.: Herald Press, 1976), I describe in Chapter 8 this perverted religion which justifies militarism.

11. See Walter Brueggemann, *Living Toward a Vision* (Philadelphia: United Church Press, 1976), for a thorough exegesis of the biblical meaning of shalom, also Chapter four in Kraus, *Community.*

12. A special issue of *Sojourners,* February 1977, was devoted to the nuclear arms buildup. Most of the statistics which I cite come from that issue.

Chapter Ten: Inside Outsiders

1. Jeremias in *Jerusalem* devotes six chapters (12-17) to the maintenance of racial purity in the Hebrew community. My discussion is indebted to his careful research.

2. For an elaboration see Robert C. Tannehill, "The Mission of Jesus According to Luke," in *Jesus in Nazareth,* Walther Eltester, editor (Berlin: Walter de Gruyter, 1972).

3. I am indebted to Willard M. Swartley, my former instructor, for solving the riddle of the symbols in these three chapters. A comprehensive treatment can be found in his PhD dissertation, "A Study in Markan Structure: The Influence of Israel's Holy History Upon the Structure of the Gospel of Mark," Princeton Theological Seminary, May 1973.

4. Matthew generally takes a more negative view toward Gentiles than Mark or Luke. Perhaps because he is writing to a Jewish audience, Matthew often depicts Jesus with the typical Jewish attitude. Matthew is the only writer who reports Jesus saying that He is sent only to the lost sheep of the house of Israel (Matthew 10:6; 15:24). He warns His followers not to pray like the Gentiles who heap up empty phrases (Matthew 6:7). In

a derogatory manner He lumps tax collectors and Gentiles together as negative models for His disciples (Matthew 5:47, 18:17). The Gentiles seek anxiously after things (Matthew 6:32). And the Gentiles have hierarchies of authority (Matthew 20:25). The disciples are warned in these verses not to be like the Gentiles. The disciples can expect to be dragged before Gentiles (Matthew 10:18). Jesus Himself expects to be mocked before Gentiles (Matthew 20:19). In all of these instances the Gentiles are castigated in a negative manner.

5. J. H. Yoder in *Politics,* devotes Chapter eleven to Paul's concept of justification as it relates to the reconciliation of Jew and Greek.

6. Jeremias' excellent discussion of the role of women in Hebrew culture (*Jerusalem,* Chapter 18) is the basic historical source for this section.

7. Jeremias, *Jerusalem,* p. 375.

8. Jeremias, *Jerusalem,* p. 376.

9. Rachel Conrad Wahlberg, *Jesus According to a Woman* (New York: Paulist Press, 1975), p. 94.

10. Jeremias, *Jerusalem,* pp. 305, 311.

11. Jeremias, *Theology,* p. 104.

Chapter Eleven: Low Is High

1. Paul B. Horton and Chester Hunt, *Sociology* (New York: McGraw Hill Co., Fourth Edition, 1976), p. 240.

2. Marvin Olsen, *The Process of Social Organization* (New York: Holt, Rinehart, and Winston, 1968), pp. 200-207.

3. Olsen, *Process,* p. 201.

4. Olsen, *Process,* p. 172.

5. Mark Hatfield, *Between a Rock and a Hard Place* (Waco, Texas: Word Books, 1976), p. 17.

6. Jeremias, *Theology,* p. 219.

7. Paul S. Minear, *To Heal and to Reveal* (New York: Seabury Press, 1976), p. 21. Chapter one is an especially helpful discussion of Jesus' approach to authority and hierarchy.

8. Olsen, *Process,* p. 310.

9. Minear, *Heal,* p. 21 and Hengel, *Power,* pp. 18-20.

10. Hengel, *Power,* p. 21.

11. Calvin Redekop suggests this thesis in "Institutions, Power, and the Gospel," in *Kingdom, Cross, and Community,* ed. by Redekop and J. R. Burkholder (Scottdale, Pa.: Herald Press, 1976), p. 147.

12. Robert K. Greenleaf, *The Servant as Leader,* Center for Applied Studies, Cambridge, Massachusetts, 1970, p. 4. This is a useful pamphlet on servanthood leadership.

Chapter Twelve: Successful Failures

1. Brueggemann (*Vision,* p. 134-135) has an excellent essay on the tools and trade of the Christian's basin ministry, to which I am indebted.

2. Brueggemann, *Vision,* p. 134.

3. Lawrence Burkholder, "Nonresistance, Nonviolent Resistance, and Power" in *Kingdom, Cross, and Community,* Ed. by J. R. Burkholder and Calvin Redekop (Scottdale, Pa.: Herald Press, 1976), p. 134.

4. See Yoder, *Politics,* p. 132-134, for a critique of the way the term "cross" is typically used in Protestant pastoral care.

5. Jeremias, *Parables,* p. 195.

6. Yoder, *Politics,* p. 134.

7. Jim Wallis provides an excellent argument for the urgency of rebuilding the church in Chapter 5 of *Agenda for Biblical People* (New York: Harper & Row, 1976).

8. Jacques Ellul, *The Presence of the Kingdom* (New York: Seabury Press, 1967), p. 145.

9. John H. Yoder, *The Original Revolution* (Scottdale, Pa.: Herald Press, 1971), p. 28.

10. Jeremias, *Theology,* p. 135.

11. Jim Wallis, Editorial in *Sojourners,* July 1977, Vol. 6, No. 8, p. 4.

INDEX OF SCRIPTURE CITED

GENERAL INDEX

Donald B. Kraybill studied sociology at Temple University in Philadelphia and presently teaches sociology at Elizabethtown College.

Before teaching, he worked as an associate director of Mennonite Voluntary Service and served as a pastor.

He is the author of *Our Star-Spangled Faith,* also published by Herald Press.

Kraybill is actively involved in a house church and in ministries to ex-offenders.